Isaiah Berlin

To RDA, MG and LO: incommensurables

Isaiah Berlin

Liberty and Pluralism

George Crowder

polity

First published in 2004 by Polity Press

Polity Press
65 Bridge Street
Cambridge CB2 1UR, UK

Polity Press
350 Main Street
Malden, MA 02148, USA

ISBN: 0-7456-2476-6
ISBN: 0-7456-2477-4 (paperback)

A catalogue record for this book is available from the British Library and has been applied for from the Library of Congress.

Extracts from the following works:
Reproduced with permission of Curtis Brown Group Ltd, London on behalf of the Isaiah Berlin Literary Trust
Introduction to 'Five Essays on Liberty' © Isaiah Berlin 1969
'Political Ideas in the Twentieth Century' copyright Isaiah Berlin 1950, © Isaiah Berlin 1969
'Historical Inevitability' copyright Isaiah Berlin 1954, © Isaiah Berlin 1969, 1997
'Two Concepts of Liberty' © Isaiah Berlin 1958, 1969, 1997
'John Stuart Mill and the Ends of Life' © Isaiah Berlin 1959, 1969
Letter to George Kennan © The Isaiah Berlin Literary Trust 2002

Typeset in 10.5 on 12 pt Palatino
by SNP Best-set Typesetter Ltd., Hong Kong
Printed and bound in Great Britain by MPG Books Ltd, Bodmin, Cornwall

For further information on Polity, visit our website: www.polity.co.uk

Key Contemporary Thinkers

Published

Philip Manning, *Erving Goffman and Modern Sociology*
Michael Moriarty, *Roland Barthes*
Harold W. Noonan, *Frege: A Critical Introduction*
William Outhwaite, *Habermas: A Critical Introduction*
Kari Palonen, *Quentin Skinner: History, Politics, Rhetoric*
John Preston, *Feyerabend: Philosophy, Science and Society*
Chris Rojek, *Stuart Hall*
Susan Sellers, *Hélène Cixous: Authorship, Autobiography and Love*
Wes Sharrock and Rupert Read, *Kuhn: Philosopher of Scientific Revolution*
David Silverman, *Harvey Sacks: Social Science and Conversation Analysis*
Dennis Smith, *Zygmunt Bauman: Prophet of Postmodernity*
Nicholas H. Smith, *Charles Taylor: Meaning, Morals and Modernity*
Geoffrey Stokes, *Popper: Philosophy, Politics and Scientific Method*
Georgia Warnke, *Gadamer: Hermeneutics, Tradition and Reason*
James Williams, *Lyotard: Towards a Postmodern Philosophy*
Jonathan Wolff, *Robert Nozick: Property, Justice and the Minimal State*

Forthcoming

Maria Baghramian, *Hilary Putnam*
Sara Beardsworth, *Kristeva*
James Carey, *Innis and McLuhan*
Thomas D'Andrea, *Alasdair MacIntyre*
Reidar Andreas Due, *Deleuze*
Eric Dunning, *Norbert Elias*
Paul Kelly, *Ronald Dworkin*
Carl Levy, *Antonio Gramsci*
Moya Lloyd, *Judith Butler*
Nigel Mapp, *Paul de Man*
Dermot Moran, *Edmund Husserl*
James O'Shea, *Wilfrid Sellars*
Nicholas Walker, *Heidegger*

Contents

Preface

This book has two principal goals. First, I intend to provide an accessible introduction to the thought of Isaiah Berlin, in particular his political thought, and to the critical literature that his thought has provoked. Secondly, I mean to defend a particular interpretation of Berlin's work, a particular evaluation of the strengths and weaknesses of that work, and a particular account of how Berlin's work should be developed and applied to current concerns.

Because of the book's dual purpose, readers may notice something of a change of gear as I pass from exposition, I hope tolerably impartial, to engaged critical argument. Indeed, I hope they do notice these shifts, because another of my goals is to avoid what I regard as a problem with some previous critical work on Berlin, namely a failure adequately to separate his thought from the critic's own. Throughout the writing of this book I have been conscious of a point neatly put to me by Henry Hardy: that one should be wary of discrepancies between what Berlin says, what he means, and what he ought to say. Accordingly, I have tried to let Berlin speak for himself wherever possible, to interpret where necessary, and to depart from or build on his views where the issues they raise warrant arguments opposed or additional to those that Berlin actually offers. I hope it will be evident which of these tasks I am engaged on at any one time. In particular, in those places where I go beyond Berlin (especially in chapters 7 and 8), I try to make it clear where Berlin ends and further argument begins, and to keep any such further argument within the spirit of Berlin's general position.

To Henry Hardy I owe much more than the advice reported above. Indeed, anyone who studies the work of Berlin owes a special debt to Henry, who is Berlin's editor and one of his literary trustees. Berlin was modest about publishing his work, and much of it would still be available only in scattered locations, if at all, without Henry's energetic intervention. Henry is also responsible for the second most useful tool for research on Berlin after the texts themselves, namely the website called *The Isaiah Berlin Virtual Library*. This contains a comprehensive bibliography of writings by and about Berlin, and much else besides. In addition, I must record a great personal debt to Henry, who has encouraged me in my work over many years and who generously read and commented on the entire typescript of this book, saving me from many mistakes.

The whole typescript was also read by David Miller and by an anonymous reader for Polity, both of whom offered a number of helpful suggestions. Colleagues and friends who read and advised on parts of the text include Rick De Angelis, Martin Griffiths, Anthony Langlois, Lionel Orchard, Norman Wintrop and Peter Woolcock. Jerry Cohen, Michael Freeden, Mark Philp and Alan Ryan gave me useful information and insights in conversation. My thanks also to John Thompson, Reitha Pattison and Elizabeth Molinari at Polity, and to Helen Gray and Jean van Altena for editing. The basic research for the book was assisted by Flinders University through its Outside Studies programme and Small Grants scheme. My largest debt of all is, as always, to my partner, Sue Thiele.

Parts of the text first appeared in 'Hedgehog and Fox', *Australian Journal of Political Science* 38 (2003), 333–9, and I am grateful to the publishers for permission to reuse that material. I also acknowledge, with thanks, the permission of Curtis Brown Group Ltd on behalf of the Isaiah Berlin Literary Trust to quote extensively from Berlin's *Liberty*.

Abbreviations

Books by Berlin

AC	*Against the Current* (1979)
CC	*Concepts and Categories* (1978)
CTH	*The Crooked Timber of Humanity* (1990)
FIB	*Freedom and its Betrayal* (2002)
KM	*Karl Marx*, 1st edn (1939)
L	*Liberty* (2002)
PI	*Personal Impressions*, 2nd edn (1998)
POI	*The Power of Ideas* (2000)
PSM	*The Proper Study of Mankind* (1997)
RR	*The Roots of Romanticism* (1999)
RT	*Russian Thinkers* (1978)
SM	*The Soviet Mind* (2004)
SR	*The Sense of Reality* (1996)
TCE	*Three Critics of the Enlightenment* (2000)

Interviews

Conv.	*Conversations with Isaiah Berlin* (with Ramin Jahanbegloo) (1992)
Sal.	*Salmagundi* interview (with Steven Lukes) (1998)
TCN	'Two Concepts of Nationalism' (with Nathan Gardels) (1991)

Biography

Life	Michael Ignatieff, *Isaiah Berlin: A Life* (1998)

1

Hedgehog and Fox

In one of his most famous essays, Isaiah Berlin quotes a fragment from the Greek poet Archilochus: 'The fox knows many things, but the hedgehog knows one big thing' (*RT*, 22). For Berlin, these words suggest a profound distinction between two kinds of artist or thinker. On the one hand there are those who, like the hedgehog, 'relate everything to a single central vision, one system less or more coherent or articulate, in terms of which they understand, think and feel'. On the other hand there are the foxes, 'those who pursue many ends, often unrelated and even contradictory', who think 'on many levels, seizing upon the essence of a vast variety of experiences and objects for what they are in themselves, without, consciously or unconsciously, seeking to fit them into, or exclude them from, any one unchanging, all-embracing, sometimes self-contradictory and incomplete, at times fanatical, inner vision' (*RT*, 22). The hedgehogs, in Berlin's judgement, include Dante, Plato, Lucretius, Pascal, Hegel and others, while Shakespeare, Herodotus, Aristotle and Montaigne are foxes.

Is Berlin himself a hedgehog or a fox? His reference to the way in which the unitary vision of the hedgehog can become 'fanatical' hints at what may be said to be Berlin's official line: it is safer to follow the fox; beware the hedgehog. The contrast between hedgehog and fox is a metaphor for the crucial distinction at the heart of Berlin's thought, between monism and pluralism in moral and political philosophy: between, that is, the monist view that there is a single right way of answering any moral or political question, and the pluralist view that basic human goods are multiple, conflicting and incommensurable. Monism, Berlin believes, harbours dangers that pluralism avoids. Berlin, the pluralist, thus tends to present himself as a fox, and certainly he knows many things. As his biographer Michael Ignatieff writes, 'no other major figure in twentieth-century Anglo-American letters made contributions across such a range of disciplines: in analytical philosophy, in the intellectual history of Marxism, the Enlightenment, and the Counter-Enlightenment, and in liberal political theory'.[1]

Yet Berlin is also, and perhaps more deeply, a hedgehog. The great bulk of his work, however varied its immediate focus, can be understood as dedicated to a single, dominant project, namely the liberal struggle against twentieth-century totalitarianism, in particular in its Communist form. Berlin is explicitly a partisan of liberal democracy in the Cold War. His contribution to that cause is to trace the origins of the totalitarian disease to its intellectual roots, which he finds not in any wholly new outlook peculiar to the twentieth century but in conceptions of freedom and morality deeply embedded in the history of Western thought. The cure he prescribes is a tougher, more realistic version of liberalism, disabused of what he sees as the complacent expectations of the eighteenth and nineteenth centuries, and dedicated not to the creation of a cosmopolitan utopia but to the defence of the humane management of the hard choices that are inseparable from the human condition. Berlin is scarcely a one-dimensional thinker, or one whose interests are confined to a narrow range. Nevertheless, his thought is very far from being a mere series of unrelated claims and insights. His work has a discernible shape, with a distinct centre, and its development follows an intelligible trajectory.

Three themes

Within Berlin's overarching concern with the conflict between liberty and totalitarianism, three principal themes stand out in his work. These all involve contrast and conflict: between negative and positive conceptions of liberty, between the Enlightenment and the Counter-Enlightenment, and between monist and pluralist understandings of morality.

First, Berlin finds the origins of totalitarian thinking most immediately in what he calls 'the betrayal of freedom'. This is the idea not of a simple rejection of liberty but of a systematic distortion of what freedom truly is. Negative liberty, the absence of coercive interference, is contrasted with positive liberty, the freedom of self-mastery, where a person is ruled not by arbitrary desires but by the 'true' or authentic self. While both negative and positive ideas represent genuine and important aspects of liberty, history shows that the positive idea of freedom is peculiarly vulnerable to abuse. That is because it leaves open the possibility that the person's authentic wishes may be identified with the commands of some external authority, for example, the state or the Party. Freedom is then defined as obedience, and in effect is twisted into the very opposite of freedom. Berlin does not reject positive liberty entirely, but he warns against its potential for distortion. He recommends negative liberty, which he sees as the characteristically liberal conception of freedom, as the safer option.

The second of Berlin's major themes is the conflict between the Enlightenment on one side and the 'Counter-Enlightenment' and romanticism on the other. Berlin originally distinguished negative and positive liberty as 'liberal' and 'Romantic' conceptions of liberty respectively.[2] One source of the positive conception, with its emphasis on personal authenticity, is the romantic stress on the uniqueness of individuals, and of whole cultures, in reaction to the universalism of the Enlightenment. Romanticism is the cradle of modern nationalism, and of the irrationalism with which it combined in the right-wing totalitarianisms of Berlin's time. However, the Enlightenment too, on Berlin's view, is not without its share of blame for the ills of the twentieth century. As a liberal, Berlin considers himself a defender of the Enlightenment, with its faith in reason, personal liberty and toleration. But certain strains of Enlightenment thought take the claims of reason and science to utopian extremes, and these play a significant part in the genesis of the totalitarianism of the left, which is Berlin's principal target. For Berlin, Stalinism can be traced back to Marx, and from him to the hyper-optimistic scientism of well-meaning eighteenth-century *philosophes* like Helvétius, Holbach and Condorcet. The scientistic strain in the Enlightenment is, moreover, usefully opposed by the Counter-Enlightenment predecessors of the romantics. Vico, Herder and Hamann, in particular, raise important questions about the adequacy of the objective methods of the natural sciences for understanding distinctively human conduct. Consequently, Berlin looks to the Counter-Enlightenment not only for the origins of fascism but also for inspiration in the fight against communism. The totalitarian disaster has roots in both the Enlightenment and its critics, but each also provides weapons against the excesses of the other.

Berlin's third theme, the opposition between monist and pluralist conceptions of morality, is his deepest. The scientistic, utopian side of the Enlightenment is really a modern instance of a more deep-seated tendency in Western thought as a whole. This is to suppose that somehow, at some level, all genuine moral values must fit together in a single coherent system capable of yielding a single correct answer to any moral problem. This is moral 'monism'. Its political implication is utopian: that the true moral system, once known, will enable us to iron out all political conflicts and make possible a perfected society in which there will be universal agreement on a single way of life. Such a view, Berlin protests, does not do justice to the depth and persistence of conflict in the moral experience of human beings. That experience teaches that we are frequently faced with choices among competing goods, choices to which no clear answers are forthcoming from simple monist rules. Moreover, the monist outlook is positively dangerous. To suppose that moral and political perfection is possible, even in principle, is to invite the thought that its realization justifies the employment of any efficient means. There is a distinct, historically detectable association, Berlin believes, between moral monism and political totalitarianism by way of utopianism.

The truer and safer view of the deep nature of morality is that of 'value pluralism'. There are many human goods, we can know objectively what these are, and some of them are universal. But they are sometimes 'incommensurable', meaning that they are so different from one another that each has its own character and force, untranslatable into the terms of any other. When they come into conflict, as they often do, the choices between them will be hard choices, in part because in choosing one good we necessarily forgo another, and also because we will not be able to apply any simple rule that reduces the rival goods to a common denominator or that arranges them in a single hierarchy that applies in all cases. For example, liberty and equality are incommensurables on Berlin's view. Each is valuable for its own sake, on its own terms; no amount of one entirely compensates for any amount of the other. When they collide in particular cases, we are consequently faced with difficult, perhaps tragic, choices. Those choices cannot be resolved by a neat decision procedure such as utilitarianism, since 'utility', however understood, is simply another incommensurable good potentially in competition with liberty and equality. This does not mean that choices among incommensurables are necessarily non-rational or that no such choice can be more justified than any other, as I shall argue later. It does mean that pluralist choices tend to be complex and often painful.

What, if anything, are the political implications of value pluralism? Berlin believes that pluralism points us towards liberalism. Pluralism in his sense implies the inescapability of choice in human experience, hence, he argues, a case for freedom of choice. Pluralism also entails, as already mentioned, the impossibility of moral and political perfection and the inevitability of disagreement and conflict. A humane and viable politics will therefore accept fundamental disagreement about the good, and seek to contain and manage that disagreement rather than transcend it. This is what liberalism does in contrast to utopian doctrines such as Marxism. Utopian thinking, made possible most fundamentally by moral monism, is an invitation to justify any means by reference to an end that is, by definition, ultimately and absolutely desirable. The value-pluralist view denies that there can be any such ultimate end, insists rather that there are many different ends to be balanced, and counsels care and moderation in seeking that balance. Pluralism thus recommends liberalism in the political field, as a humane response to human imperfection and disagreement. Berlin is a hedgehog whose single underlying message is, ironically, that of value pluralism: 'Beware hedgehogs; imitate the fox'.

Life and times

The case for liberal moderation is, for Berlin, not merely academic but the fruit of personal experience and conviction. His was a life lived close to some of the major events and personalities of the twentieth century. Berlin was born, in 1909, into a middle-class Russian-Jewish family in Riga, in what is now Latvia, then part of the Russian Empire. His father was a successful timber merchant, and the family's circumstances were comfortable. In 1916, however, the Berlins moved to Petrograd (now, as earlier, St Petersburg), and there, the following year, they witnessed at first hand the revolutions of February and October. Isaiah was seven when he saw a Tsarist policeman, 'pale and struggling', being dragged away by a crowd, apparently to his death (*Conv.*, 4). This image stayed with Berlin for the rest of his life, crystallizing his abiding fear of revolutionary violence and of political extremism in general.

With the Bolshevik regime taking root, the family left Russia, eventually settling in England in 1921. Berlin was educated at St

Paul's School in London, before winning a scholarship to Oxford, which he entered in 1928. Oxford remained his home for the rest of his life, with the exception of the War years. He began by reading Classics, but the philosophy component of the curriculum soon came to preoccupy him, and he joined a lively circle of young philosophers attracted to the logical positivism championed by A. J. Ayer. Berlin was initially drawn to the no-nonsense empiricism of the logical positivists, but became frustrated by their abstract and ahistorical approach to philosophy. His move away from this kind of thought was accelerated when, soon after his election as a Fellow of All Souls (he was the college's first Jewish member), Berlin accepted a commission in 1933 to write a brief study of Marx for the Home University Library. His research for the book introduced him not only to the writings of Marx but also to those of the eighteenth-century French *philosophes* who formed part of Marx's intellectual background. As Berlin's reading progressed he became increasingly alienated from the dry rigours of 'Oxford philosophy', and increasingly attracted to the historically and socially richer fields of the history of ideas and political theory.

During the Second World War Berlin served as a British official, working at first for the Ministry of Information in New York, and then for the Foreign Office in Washington. His principal task was to write weekly reports on American public opinion, initially as part of the effort to encourage the Americans to enter the War on the side of Britain. Berlin's reports gained him a reputation as an astute and lively political observer, and his experiences close to the corridors of power helped him to grow in maturity and confidence. In 1945 he was briefly transferred from Washington to the Soviet Union (he had remained fluent in Russian), where he came into contact with dissident Russian writers, most notably Boris Pasternak and Anna Akhmatova. These meetings sharpened his sense both of the fate of the individual under Soviet communism and of the Russian element of his own identity.

After the War Berlin returned to teaching philosophy at Oxford, but he soon acquired a more public profile as a leading commentator on the intellectual dimensions of the developing Cold War. Throughout the early 1950s, he produced a steady stream of essays, lectures and radio broadcasts that brought out his central theme of the modern betrayal of freedom. These culminated in his appointment, in 1957, as Chichele Professor of Social and Political Theory at Oxford, a post he held until 1966. His inaugural lecture in 1958 was the famous 'Two Concepts of Liberty', which remains his most influential piece, and must be one of the most frequently cited works of twentieth-century political philosophy. In the latter part of his active career, Berlin was founding President of Wolfson College, Oxford, a new college for graduate students, from 1966 to 1975. He was elected Fellow of the British Academy in 1957, and President from 1974 to 1978. By the time he retired, he had become one of Britain's most prominent public intellectuals and a figure of international significance. He had known many of the most famous people of his time, among them world leaders such as Winston Churchill, Franklin Roosevelt, John F. Kennedy and Chaim Weizmann (the first president of Israel). Among the many honours he received were a knighthood (1957), the Order of Merit (1971), the Jerusalem Prize (1979), the Erasmus Prize (1983), and the Agnelli International Prize for Ethics (1988).

For and against Berlin

By the standards of institutional and popular acclaim there can be no doubt that Berlin was one of the major intellectual figures of his century. When he died in 1997 a flood of obituaries appeared, many in popular publications that would seldom acknowledge the passing of a political philosopher. Moreover, the content and tone of the great majority of these testified to the very high regard, indeed affection, in which Berlin was widely held. In the *Guardian Weekly*, for example, Bernard Crick described Berlin as 'the most famous English academic intellectual of the post-war era, outstanding lecturer, peerless conversationalist and superlative essayist'.[3] On the other side of the Atlantic *Time Magazine* declared that Berlin's death had brought to a close 'one of the most illustrious intellectual adventures of this century'.[4] The political theorist Alan Ryan noted of Berlin's passing that 'an astonishing number of people felt it as a personal loss'.[5] Berlin was eulogized not only for his remarkable range of knowledge but also for his ability to understand and explain ideas 'from the inside', as if he shared the mental world of their proponents. 'Beyond almost any of his contemporaries', Robert Wokler wrote, 'Berlin rendered the ideas and personalities of both past and present figures vivid and compelling, because in his fashion he came close to entering their own minds and conveying their thoughts.'[6] He was able to achieve these feats of empathetic understanding even – perhaps especially – with those views most alien and repugnant to his own, such as the

arguments of Counter-Enlightenment figures like Hamann and
Maistre.

The widely admired vividness and colour of Berlin's work was
made possible not only by an immense body of learning, but also
by a general approach to ideas that was highly distinctive. Anglo-
American philosophers and political theorists tend on the whole to
employ a coolly impersonal technique, focusing on the analysis of
language and the close examination of abstract chains of argument.
Berlin was capable of operating in this way, as he showed in his
work on logical positivism early in his career. But his more natural
and characteristic idiom emphasizes synthesis rather than analysis,
and his work typically depicts in bold, sweeping strokes broad com-
monalities and distinctions among many thinkers and outlooks. He
was drawn to the deeper currents underlying the surface multiplicity of human thought, and to the general spirit animating a
particular culture or historical period. Perhaps above all he was
fascinated by the interplay between a thinker's thought and personality, drawing out, for example, the link between Marx's system
and his authoritarian character, and between Turgenev's personal
ambivalence and the inner conflicts of the heroes in his novels. His
talent for entering into the personality of his subjects and seeing
with their eyes has already been mentioned.

Berlin's personal and free-flowing approach to thought is
reflected in his literary and personal style. His writing is full of long,
mellifluous sentences, bristling with sub-clauses, qualifications and
asides, which sweep the reader along with the writer's rapid
sequence of thoughts. That could hardly be otherwise, since much of
Berlin's work was dictated, and he was a famous talker. T. S. Eliot
commended Berlin's 'torrential eloquence', as irrepressible in formal
lectures and radio broadcasts as on the social circuit, and Michael
Oakeshott once introduced him as 'the Paganini of the lecture platform' (*FIB*, X). Ignatieff writes that 'Those who heard him lecture
[at Oxford] never forgot the experience ... Listening was like an
"airborne adventure", in which Berlin took the audience on a
swooping flight over the intellectual landscapes of the past, leaving
them at the end of the hour to file out onto the High Street "slightly
dazed", their feet not quite touching the ground' (*Life*, 225).

Yet Berlin also has his detractors. His distinctive method of
inquiry, for example, does not please everyone. Analytical philosophers sometimes regard his interest in historical personalities and
epochs as evading hard questions of truth and justification; intellectual historians have complained that his focus on broad patterns

of ideas obscures or neglects too many important historical details. But Berlin did not appear to be fazed by such criticisms. Inconsistency and neglect of detail seemed to be a price he was willing to pay in order to convey what he thought most important about ideas: namely, their powerful presence in, and influence over, actual human lives. Whatever the precise balance of strengths and weaknesses in Berlin's approach (I shall return to this in chapter 8), his defenders could refer the critics to those thousands of readers, including many non-specialists, whose interest in political thought and the history of ideas he captured and stimulated.

There are political detractors too. On the left, Berlin has been seen as a one-dimensional Cold Warrior in the service of the United States, an apologist for the Vietnam War, a complacent supporter of the capitalist *status quo*, a diner at high tables who was less concerned with speaking truth to power than with ingratiating himself with the powerful.[7] On the right, he has been condemned as a moral relativist, unable or unwilling to use his position as a prominent public intellectual to stand up against the erosion of civilized standards, in society and in the academy, that began in the 1960s.[8] From both left *and* right he has been criticized for his silence on the fraught subject of Israel and Palestine: from the left, for his refusal, until the end of his life, publicly to condemn the more aggressive forms of Zionism and to support the claims to self-determination of the Palestinians; from the right, for his failure to extend to those same Zionist policies his whole-hearted support.[9]

Behind many of these complaints lies the more personal allegation that Berlin did not use his public authority to stand up for the principles he supposedly professed. The charge of moral cowardice was one he felt keenly, and there seem to have been occasions when he recognized in it an element of truth (*Life*, 188, 193, 293). Perhaps his perceived failings in this regard had their source in the desire of the Jewish outsider to be accepted by an insular British establishment; the psychology of the Jewish struggle for acceptance is a subject perceptively discussed by Berlin himself.[10] It may be that he tried too hard to please, and that the same talents that made him such good company sometimes robbed him of the courage of his convictions. But perhaps, too, the critics were disappointed in Berlin because they did not always understand what his views really were, or because they were trying to hijack him for purposes of their own. Ignatieff rightly points out that the general content and character of Berlin's published work hardly fits the portrait 'of a man eager to please at any cost' (*Life*, 257). Berlin was unyielding in his defence of negative liberty, of value pluralism, and of liberalism more generally, at a time when so many Western academics and students were attracted enthusiastically to the ideas of the anti-liberal left. Moreover, his embracing of the history of ideas, and the synthesizing style in which he wrote on that subject, went very much against the tide of philosophical fashion in the Oxford of his day. Nevertheless, Berlin was himself troubled throughout his life by the thought that he had been over-estimated, worrying that his work lacked coherence, direction and originality: 'I am an intellectual taxi; people flag me down and give me destinations and off I go' (*Life*, 7). Much of this self-deprecation may have been, as Ignatieff suggests, a defence mechanism, the pre-empting of genuinely hostile critics; but it seems, too, that Berlin suffered from genuine self-doubt.

Here ends the psychological speculation. My concern is with Berlin as a thinker, and my focus will be on the evidence of his published writings. Here, too, there are hard questions to be asked. Berlin never produced a book-length statement of his position to compare, for example, with John Rawls's *A Theory of Justice*. Ignatieff reports that he tried in his later years to marshal his thoughts on romanticism in this way, but found the task beyond him (*Life*, 275–6). Berlin's preferred form was the essay, and his most widely read book is a collection of four of these: *Four Essays on Liberty* (1969), now incorporated into the expanded *Liberty* (2002). Many of these pieces are among the most stimulating one can read in political theory or the history of ideas. But Berlin's failure to publish a more extended development of his views has been taken by some as evidence 'that he was incapable of a work of grand synthesis' (*Life*, 276), or even of sustained systematic thought. Further questions have been raised, as I shall show, about the merits of Berlin's account of liberty, the accuracy of his history of ideas, and the validity of his whole empathetic approach to political ideas.

More fundamental still is the question of how Berlin's liberalism relates to his pluralism. I believe there is a major tension between these ideas, as Berlin presents them, that places a question-mark over his entire enterprise. On the one hand, he steps forward as a defender of liberalism against the threat of totalitarianism, adopting a position in which liberal values are apparently advocated as universal, the essential preconditions for a decent human life. On the other hand, Berlin's pluralism seems sometimes to shade into relativism, to imply that between one set of fundamental values and another no single choice can be shown to be better founded than another. In the face of pluralism, why should liberal values be ranked ahead of others, even those of totalitarians? Is it not true that one can be a liberal universalist or a value pluralist, but not both?

I shall argue that Berlin never provides a wholly satisfactory answer to this central problem, but also that he does leave us the necessary materials with which to construct such an answer. It is true that the tension between liberalism and pluralism is a problem he not only fails adequately to confront but scarcely acknowledges. In this regard his later work represents little real advance on his earlier work. In essay after essay he repeats, in his learned and elegant periods, his faith in both liberalism and pluralism, but so far as he does address the relation between them, his arguments are either flawed or crucially limited in scope. At various times he asserts that a commitment to liberalism is compatible with an acceptance of pluralism, or even that a case for liberalism is entailed by pluralism, but he offers no concerted or convincing defence of either claim. Worse still, some of Berlin's formulations of pluralism and its ethical implications have opened the way to expressly anti-liberal interpretations of the idea, such as that championed by John Gray (see chapter 7). Nevertheless, I shall also argue that, in what he does say, he provides us with the tools needed to make a substantial pluralist case for liberalism that is in keeping with his overall outlook. Scattered throughout his writings are clues to the development of a more coherent and persuasive defence of liberalism on pluralist grounds than the one he actually offers.

Unusually among philosophers, Berlin's significance rests not so much on his powers of argument as on his capacity for vivid exposition and fruitful suggestion. More specifically, we should look to Berlin for his express formulation of the idea of value pluralism, his deepening of that idea through his historical researches, his opening up of the question of pluralism's moral and political implications, his subsequent challenge to liberals to rethink liberalism in pluralist terms, and finally his scattered hints about how to do this. It is in these achievements that Berlin's deepest originality and significance as a political thinker consists.

Overview

The organization of this book is both thematic and loosely chronological. I discuss Berlin's earlier work, up to the mid-1950s, in chapter 2, connecting the emerging themes of his philosophical outlook with the three principal strands of his complex personal identity: English, Russian and Jewish. In the 1950s Berlin explored the idea of freedom in post-Enlightenment thought and its fate in the twentieth century. This is the subject of chapter 3, which situates Berlin's treatment of freedom in the context of the Cold War, and goes on to examine his essays on free will and determinism in history, and on the 'enemies of human freedom' in modern political thought. Chapter 4 focuses on Berlin's seminal 'Two Concepts of Liberty', analysing its argument and evaluating some of the main lines of criticism to which it has been subjected. In chapter 5 I trace Berlin's deepening investigation, from the 1950s to the 1970s, of the debate between the Enlightenment and its critics and of the broader implications of that debate for modern intellectual history and political thought. Chapter 6 tackles the key distinction between moral monism and pluralism, and opens up the tension between Berlin's commitment to pluralism and his liberalism. This central issue is pursued in chapter 7, where I consider some of the competing interpretations and extensions of Berlin's position on the pluralism–liberalism nexus. In chapter 8 I locate Berlin within the modern liberal tradition, examine the implications of his ideas for social justice and cultural rights, and assess his overall achievement.

2

Three Strands

To do justice to Berlin as a thinker is necessarily to apply to him his own method of empathetic understanding. As Alan Ryan writes, 'because Berlin practiced the history of ideas in a highly personal and imaginative fashion, the student of his analysis is also a student of his sensibility'.[1] In particular, his sense of human values as multiple, conflicting and incommensurable reflects his own experience of inner division and conflict.

A useful introduction to the influence of Berlin's personal experience on his thought is provided by his own brief sketch, 'The Three Strands in My Life' (1979). Looking back on his career, he agrees with the suggestion of an interviewer 'that I had been formed by three traditions – Russian, British and Jewish' (*PI*, 255). In this chapter I trace the way these three strands of identity impress themselves on Berlin's early work. I start in the 1930s with his English background: his basic empiricism, his initiation into the hermetic world of Oxford analytical philosophy, his brush with logical positivism, and the beginning of his turn towards the history of ideas with the writing of *Karl Marx* (1939). Berlin's Russian identity is revived by his meetings in 1945 with Pasternak and Akhmatova, and expressed in his post-War studies of the great Russian writers of the nineteenth century. There, he works out many of his characteristic political views. His Jewish heritage comes to the fore with the creation of Israel in 1948, reinforcing his sense of the human need for cultural belonging. Each of these three strands makes a distinctive contribution to Berlin's outlook, and their combination helps to explain his unique cast of mind. Together they provide a way into all of his principal themes.

Oxford and philosophy

Berlin was not a native Briton, but he loved his adopted home and saw himself as, in part, a characteristically British thinker. His basic philosophical platform is British empiricism. In 'Three Strands' he confesses

> to a pro-British bias. I was educated in England and have lived there since 1921; all that I have been and done and thought is indelibly English. I cannot judge English values impartially, for they are part of me: I count this as the greatest of intellectual and political good fortune. These values are the basis of what I believe: that decent respect for others and the toleration of dissent are better than pride and a sense of national mission; that liberty may be incompatible with, and better than, too much efficiency; that pluralism and untidiness are, to those who value freedom, better than the rigorous imposition of all-embracing systems, no matter how rational and disinterested, or than the rule of majorities against which there is no appeal. All this is deeply and uniquely English, and I freely admit that I am steeped in it, and believe in it, and cannot breathe freely save in a society where these values are for the most part taken for granted. (*PI*, 257)

When Berlin began his philosophical career in Oxford in the 1930s, those values seemed to be mortally threatened by the rise of German and Italian fascism on the one hand, and by the apparent promise of Soviet communism on the other. Yet Berlin's dominant philosophical interest, in these formative years, was not political philosophy or the history of political ideas, but the meaning of propositions such as 'All swans are white'. Why was this?

It was not because Berlin or his friends were ignorant of the political questions of the day; these were scarcely avoidable. Berlin's childhood experiences in Russia had made him well aware, and wary, of Soviet communism. As a Jew, he was under no illusions about Nazi Germany, which he saw at first hand on visits with his friend Stephen Spender. Nor was the general intellectual climate of Oxford unpolitical, especially after 1931 when the Great Depression began to affect even the families of the relatively privileged undergraduates (*Conv.*, 7–9). Berlin describes himself as broadly 'liberal-minded' in this period, an intuitive sympathizer with the cause of anti-fascism who packed parcels for the Republican government in Spain. Many of his friends, like Ayer and Stuart Hampshire, held broadly 'left-wing' or 'progressive' political views. But political concerns were largely absent from Berlin's earliest philosophical writing. In part, this reticence may have been a function of Berlin's personality: the Jewish outsider who was reluctant to make himself a critical target with excessively outspoken declarations of political allegiance. Even more important, however, was the character of the 'Oxford philosophy' of the period: abstract, unhistorical and in some cases not only detached from, but positively dismissive of, moral and political claims. In spite of all this, Berlin's early encounter with Oxford philosophy was a vital influence on his mature political thought.

According to Berlin, the dominant form of philosophy in 1930s Oxford was 'a kind of philosophical realism' inspired by the work of G. E. Moore and Bertrand Russell and tracing its ancestry to the British empiricists of the seventeenth and eighteenth centuries – Locke, Berkeley and Hume (*Conv.*, 13).[2] Berlin describes this realism as claiming 'that the external world was a material reality which could be perceived directly, or misperceived as the case might be' (*POI*, 3). It took as its critical target the Hegelian idealism that had been influential in English intellectual life before the First World War, 'the view that our world was entirely created by human faculties – reason, imagination, and the like' (*POI*, 3). From the dominant realist (or empiricist) climate, Berlin inherited an abiding hostility to the sort of metaphysical speculation and system building associated with the names of Hegel and other German idealists like Fichte and Schelling.

The most vigorous and innovative form of the empiricist trend in Oxford philosophy was 'logical positivism', which immediately exerted a powerful influence on Berlin. Logical positivism was the doctrine of the Vienna Circle (Carnap, Schlick, Waismann and others), which was popularized in England after 1933 by Berlin's brilliant young friend and rival, A. J. Ayer.[3] The general purpose of the Vienna Circle was to cleanse philosophy of vague speculation and obscurity, and to re-establish it on the same methodological basis as that of the natural sciences. Philosophical method was henceforth to be scientific method, that is, a method for testing claims to knowledge by a standard of 'verifiability'. Genuine knowledge could only be of propositions that were meaningful, and only those propositions had meaning which could pass the test of verification. Verification was possible only in two ways: empirical observation or logical inference (e.g. mathematical proof). It followed that only two kinds of proposition were meaningful: either claims of empirical fact or statements of logical relations. The effect of this was to sweep the field of all 'metaphysical' claims, including not only claims about such notoriously unverifiable entities as God, but also all moral and political judgements as well. Ayer famously regarded moral judgements as mere expressions of emotion, either of approval or disapproval, which, amounting neither to empirical nor logical propositions, could possess no meaning. For Ayer, to say that 'X is morally wrong' was merely to say, 'I have a feeling of disapproval for X', or, more concisely, 'X: boo!' The task of philosophy, on this view, was merely that of handmaiden, or gatekeeper, to science.

Berlin was interested in logical positivism, but from the beginning he also had reservations, and these deepened over time. At a personal level he recognized in the logical positivists some of the outstanding philosophers of his generation, and he naturally wanted to test himself in their company. Philosophically, he saw them as rightly preferring conceptual clarity to Hegelian obscurity. On the other hand, he was sceptical, from the start, of the 'verification' standard. From the mid-1930s until about 1950, Berlin's principal philosophical essays were painstaking dissections of logical positivism which press a single, central point: could there not be propositions or utterances which were not verifiable but still meaningful? For example, the sentence 'All swans are white' can never be verified conclusively, since no matter how many white swans we see, some further observation may always turn up a black swan; yet such a sentence is obviously meaningful (*CC*, 18; *POI*, 2). Berlin patiently proposes a stream of examples of this kind which the verification standard, no matter how refined, does not adequately account for. His conclusion, in effect, is that verification, and therefore logical positivism, is too narrow in its view of meaning and therefore of the proper objects of knowledge. Berlin remains an empiricist, but his empiricism takes a more relaxed form than that of logical positivism.

Berlin's ultimate rejection of logical positivism, arrived at in debate with the Oxford philosophers of the 1930s, might seem to be of no more than antiquarian interest, but in fact it remained a central reference point for him thereafter.

I have never departed from the views I held at that time, and still believe that while empirical experience is all that words can express – that there is no other reality – nevertheless verifiability is not the only, or indeed the most plausible, criterion of knowledge or beliefs or hypotheses. This has remained with me for the rest of my life, and has coloured everything else I have thought. (*POI*, 2–3)

Indeed, the joust with logical positivism is the starting point for Berlin's distinctive understanding of the role and character of philosophy in general, and so the starting point for the general orientation of his ethical theory. He retains from the logical positivists their commitment to clarity and mistrust of obscurity, speculation and grand system building. To the end of his life the name of Hegel is something of an anti-icon for Berlin: 'The Hegelian system seems to me a dark, deep cave of Polyphemus, from which few return – all the footsteps point one way, as the Latin poet pointed out' (*Conv.*, 30). What he rejects in the logical positivists is their positivism or scientism, their assumption that the methods of the natural sciences are the only routes to understanding. This is a crucial theme for Berlin, to which he returns many times. Indeed, it appears even more strongly in his mature political theory, where scientism is presented not merely as mistaken but as positively dangerous. Enlightenment scientism generates, Berlin comes to believe, one of the most powerful streams of the utopianism that has led historically to the totalitarian horrors of the twentieth century.

Berlin's anti-scientistic bent is strongly expressed in the later, widely read essays 'Does Political Theory Still Exist?' (1961) and 'The Purpose of Philosophy' (1962). There he defines the field of philosophy as precisely that area of inquiry which is *neither* empirical *nor* strictly deductive. Rather, it deals with 'queer questions', like 'What is time?', which cannot be answered either by empirical observation or by logical deduction (*CC*, 2). It is exactly in cases such as these, when it is not obvious where or how we should look for answers, that we know we have a philosophical question on our hands. Most people regard such cases with bewilderment and suspicion, and the natural tendency, Berlin believes, is to try to restate them as questions that can be solved by empirical or formal methods. The history of thought is thus a 'long series of parricides' in which new, 'scientific' disciplines try to kill off the parent subject, philosophy (*CC*, 5). This had been the dream of much of the eighteenth-century Enlightenment: to extend the methods of the natural sciences to the study of human behaviour and institutions, thus replacing the unanswerable questions of philosophy with the orderly data and laws of the 'social sciences' (*CC*, 5–6, 161–2). But 'this programme was doomed to failure', because it misconceived the nature of the questions it was trying to answer (*CC*, 7). The parricide of philosophy by science can never be completed, because there always remain awkward questions that science cannot subsume. Prominent among these are questions of value, especially questions concerning the 'ultimate ends' of human beings, that is, what goods are desirable for their own sake (*CC*, 147). This is why, Berlin argues, normative political theory can never wholly disappear, despite what seem to be the doldrums it has entered in the mid-twentieth century (*CC*, 172). As a sub-branch of philosophy, political theory deals with questions that can never be answered satisfactorily by the methods of the natural or formal sciences.

More precisely, the distinctive subject-matter of philosophy, for Berlin, 'is to a large degree not the items of experience, but the ways in which they are viewed, the permanent or semi-permanent categories in terms of which experience is conceived or classified' (*CC*, 9). He has in mind, to begin with, Kant's idea that our knowledge of the world is unavoidably conditioned by natural mental 'categories' like space and time, filters or frameworks by which we make sense of experience but which are themselves beyond empirical observation or logical confirmation (*CC*, 7, 165). But a crucial thought for Berlin is that in addition to these 'natural' or 'permanent' categories, we also see the world through moral, political and cultural categories. Our 'category-spectacles' include patterns of belief and value characteristic of particular cultures or civilizations. These cultural lenses are, of course, more subject to change than the natural mental furniture to which Kant refers. Although enduring over long periods of time, they are only 'semi-permanent'.

This semi-permanence of the cultural categories connects with a central feature of Berlin's outlook, namely his view of the *historicity* of philosophical thought. One of his deepest sources of dissatisfaction with the logical positivists was the abstractness of their approach, their lack of interest in the historical context of ideas. For Berlin, history is crucial.

> If you are interested in ideas and they matter to you, you cannot but be interested in the history of these ideas, because ideas are not monads, they are not born in the void, they relate to other ideas, beliefs, forms of life, outlooks – outlooks, *Weltanschauungen*, flow out of one another and are part of what is called 'the intellectual climate',

and form people and their actions and their feelings as much as material factors and historical change. (*Conv.*, 24–5)

Historical context must be of the first importance for philosophers, because it is historical context that forms the cultural category-spectacles through which we understand and evaluate our world, and those cultural category-spectacles are part of the distinctive subject-matter of philosophy. Moreover, since the natural, Kantian categories are themselves accessible only through our cultural lenses, it may not be going too far to say that, on Berlin's view, the study of historical and cultural context is philosophy's primary task. It is for this reason that Berlin famously emphasizes the need to try to understand ideas and arguments, no matter how alien, from the inside.

> The history of ideas is the history of what we believe that people thought and felt, and these people were real people, not just statues or collections of attributes. Some effort to enter imaginatively into the minds and outlooks of the thinkers of thoughts is indispensable, an effort at *Einfühlung* is unavoidable, however precarious and difficult and uncertain. (*Conv.*, 28)

The emphasis on historicity raises an important issue that arises frequently in Berlin's thought: is his position a form of relativism? It might seem from what has just been said that Berlin is indeed a relativist. If he is saying that beliefs and values are wholly determined by their historical and cultural context, and that there is no universal or non-relative perspective from which to perceive or judge, then he is a cultural or historical relativist and must be seen as rejecting any notion of concepts or values as having universal validity. In that case his view of ethics is clearly at odds with his political commitment to the universal validity of liberal values and institutions. Berlin has indeed been interpreted as occupying this confused position.[4]

Whether or how far the allegation of relativism is really deserved is a difficult and crucial question that I leave open for the present. What does need to be said straightaway is that Berlin clearly does not *intend* his view to be a wholly relativist one. It is true that he stresses the historically and culturally situated nature of human thought and evaluation, and consequently the wide range of historical and cultural variation in perception and values. Moreover – a point that I shall develop later in connection with the notion of value pluralism – he also insists that much of this variation in values is not merely a function of belief but is also morally legitimate, that many different values, outlooks and forms of life are ethically valid. However, he always adds that there is a limit to the acceptable range of moral outlooks. The question of where precisely that limit lies receives various answers in Berlin's work, and its exact contours are unclear. Roughly speaking, however, the limit is marked by Berlin's conception of what it is to be human – or perhaps, more tentatively, by his belief that we must have some such conception of the human in order to make sense of the world. The category of the human includes the notion of certain basic ends or values as common to human beings. This thought is confirmed, Berlin believes, by the fact that people from different cultures and historical periods are not entirely incomprehensible to one another (*L*, 152; *CTH*, 80–90). Trans-historical and cross-cultural understanding presupposes some kind of common language. Berlin's own understanding of the thinkers of the Counter-Enlightenment is evidence of that common ground. Historicity, therefore, while of the first importance, has its limits; there are certain underlying universals, of behaviour, under-standing and valuation. Or at least, Berlin would say, there must be some such universal limits, however difficult these may be to for-mulate precisely, if we are to make sense of the category of 'human' (*CTH*, 80).

Berlin's view of philosophy, and consequently his view of ethics and politics, can be seen as an attempt to strike a balance between the opposed tendencies he encountered at the beginning of his career, in the Oxford of the 1930s. These tendencies are represented by the logical positivists on the one hand, with their abstract, sci-entistic universalism, and Hegel on the other, standing for a richly situated historical relativism. Mention of the latter may seem out of place as any sort of positive influence on Berlin in view of his fre-quently expressed anti-Hegelianism. Nevertheless, the historicist aspect of Hegel has affinities with the outlook of several of the thinkers whom Berlin mentions as alerting him to, or confirming, his sense of the historicity of ideas. Those historicist thinkers include, most notably, Vico and Herder, but also Marx. In the case of Marx, whom I shall come to in a moment, Hegel is, of course, acknowledged as a crucial influence (*KM*, ch. 3).

On the other hand, Berlin sees the logical positivists' search for clarity in language, and perhaps the universalism of the British empiricist tradition more broadly, as counterbalances to the exces-sive obscurity of Hegelianism and to the excessive relativism of some among Hegel's idealist and romantic successors. Philosophy itself is eternal, because it deals with questions raised by the permanent and universal categories of human experience. But philosophy is also historical, because the form those questions take, and the answers proposed, are peculiar to their time and place. The balance that Berlin seeks, between universality and relativism, and between abstraction and particularity, is a key preoccupation in his thought, resurfacing many times. How far he succeeds in achieving that balance is a question I shall consider in its place (see especially chapters 5–7).

Karl Marx

Berlin's concern with the historical dimension of ideas has its origins not only in his response to Oxford philosophy, but also in his study of Marx. First published in 1939, *Karl Marx: His Life and Environment* is now in its fourth edition and remains one of the most readable, and widely read, introductions to Marx in print. Berlin accepted the commission initially as an exercise in self-education, conceding that he knew little about Marx but reasoning that 'Marxism was obviously going to be more important and influential, not less' (*Conv.*, 11). What attracted him to the project, according to Ignatieff, was the opportunity

> to join the swim of the major ideological current of his age and to take the measure of the challenge that it represented to his own inchoate liberal allegiances. What fascinated him was Marx's loathing for the very civilisation he himself admired. This set a pattern that was to last for the rest of his life: he defended his own commitments by writing about those who were its sworn enemies. (*Life*, 70–1)

The book on Marx represented a turning point for Berlin, because it was there that he began to confront the leading intellectual rival to the liberalism of the period, and also because it marked the beginning of his transition from analytical philosopher to political theorist and historian of ideas. Beyond the engagement with Marx himself, Berlin was brought into contact with most of the figures who would preoccupy him later: first, Marx's forerunners, the Enlightenment *philosophes*, and then in turn the Enlightenment's critics. *Karl Marx* exhibits, in embryo, many of the attitudes and themes that would become characteristic of the work of his maturity.

Central to Berlin's approach is the attention to Marx's 'environment' that is signalled by the book's subtitle. In contrast with the disembodied reasoning of the logical positivists, Berlin richly situates the ideas he discusses in Marx's personal life and in the intellectual, social and political ferment of the nineteenth century. Indeed, the book is an early example of Berlin's capacity to explain a thinker from the inside. 'When I was working on Marx, I tried to understand what it was like to be Karl Marx in Berlin, in Paris, in Brussels, in London, and to think in terms of his concepts, categories, his German words. It was the same thing with Vico and Herder, Herzen, Tolstoy, Sorel, whoever' (*Conv.*, 28). The result is a much more nuanced and balanced treatment of Marx than might have been expected from someone with the Cold Warrior reputation Berlin acquired later. Although he is far from uncritical, his principal concern is to give Marx a fair hearing in order to explain the source and power of his influence. Berlin's critical comments, whether of blame or praise, are brief and balanced, even muted, and confined to the margins of the discussion.

Berlin is, in fact, surprisingly sympathetic to Marx in a number of respects. Much of this sympathy is expressed only obliquely, and there is a danger of reading into the text of *Karl Marx* views that Berlin came to hold only later.[5] But the least that can be said is that several Marxian themes emerge in the book that would reappear prominently in Berlin's own thought as it developed. The first of these is a contempt for the kind of optimistic rationalism preached by Enlightenment philosophers like Voltaire and Condorcet, and inherited in the nineteenth century by radical reformers like Proudhon and liberal-minded people like Marx's own father. According to this view, the power of human reason, allied with moral conviction, is sufficient, in the fullness of time, to defeat the evils oppressing humanity. Social and political problems are so many temporary obstacles which will inevitably be swept away by the progress of truth and justice propelled by the agency of rational education. 'To Marx', Berlin writes, 'this was the oldest, most familiar, most outworn of all the rationalist fallacies . . . the belief of his own father and his contemporaries that in the end reason and moral goodness were bound to triumph, a theory which had long become discredited by events during the dark aftermath of the French Revolution' (*KM*, 128). Although Berlin does not say so directly, his tone in reporting this aspect of Marx suggests more than a hint of approval

– as when he refers to the contemporary inheritors of Enlightenment radicalism ('democrats of all shades and hues') as even less convincing than their ancestors (*KM*, 48). In a similar vein, Berlin later paints a dark picture of the prospects of social and political improvement. Although his vision, unlike Marx's, is a liberal one, it is a vision of liberal values and institutions as permanently embattled, holding the line of civilization against tides of irrationalism, injustice and conflict that can never be wholly dissolved (see chapter 8). The confidence, characteristic of eighteenth- and nineteenth-century liberalism, that reason and virtue alone would bring about moral progress is, on Berlin's view as well as on Marx's, a utopian dream.

Consequently, Berlin shares with Marx a belief in the historicity of ideas and values. He seems to accept Marx's view that the mere preaching of the rights of man is inadequate as a means to progress because ideas and values have real power only when the historical conditions for their realization are ripe. Marx calls us away from moral prescription to the study of history, and Berlin, to some extent, follows him. The background to Marx's historicism is, of course, that of Hegel, for whom Berlin's sympathy, within limits, has already been noted. In *Karl Marx*, Berlin places considerable emphasis on Marx's Hegelian framework, taking time to set out Hegel's understanding of human institutions as necessarily moulded by their historical epoch and cultural context. This, says Berlin, amounts to a revolution in human thought, the effect of which 'is inestimably great' (*KM*, 56). Berlin, too, believes that ideas and values can be fully understood only within their historical and cultural context.

Another Hegelian theme that gains Berlin's qualified sympathy is 'the dialectic', the idea that historical progress is not linear but proceeds by way of successive states of conflict, the resolution of which leads to a new and higher level of conflict (*KM*, 57–9). This is not to say that Berlin accepts the dialectic in precisely the Hegelian and Marxist sense of a historical law; he is highly suspicious of any attempt to impose law-like patterns on history. What he accepts in the notion of the dialectic is its emphasis on the role of conflict in human affairs. Indeed, he takes this further, for while Hegel and Marx project an ultimate end to history-making conflict, Berlin regards human conflict, rooted in the collision of fundamental values, as ineradicable. Yet he may have been given a clue to this by Marx's insistence (against Proudhon) that the dialectic is not 'a simple struggle between good and evil', since 'both aspects are equally indispensable for the development of human society' (*KM*, 113). The dialectic suggests a conflict between good and good. It may not be going too far to see this as foreshadowing Berlin's mature value pluralism.

Finally, the distinctively materialist twist which Marx imparts to Hegel's pattern of human history is yet another Marxist theme of which Berlin seems tacitly to approve, at least to a degree. Marx's insistence on the role of material conditions in determining ways of life and their cultural expressions is presented by Berlin as a necessary correction to the Hegelian's tendency to 'attribute anything he wishes to the unobservable activity of an impalpable world-substance' (*KM*, 119). Berlin on several occasions describes Marx's outlook as fundamentally empirical, in a tone of tacit endorsement (*KM*, 13–14, 87, 88, 119–20). Marx's attempt to combine the historical outlook of Hegel with the empiricism of the French socialists and English economists anticipates Berlin's own attempt to balance history and empiricism, and fact and value.

In the end, however, there is little doubt that Berlin's overall judgement on Marx, however oblique, is hostile. Marx's attention to history is a salutary corrective to the scientistic abstractions of the Enlightenment, and his empiricism is a necessary antidote to Hegelian metaphysics. But in both respects he goes too far, to the point where his ideas become not only mistaken but dangerous. Marx's empiricism becomes a narrow materialism that diminishes the role of values and ideals almost to zero. Economic factors are presented not merely as playing a central role but as 'the single operative cause' of social structures and change (*KM*, 123). Consequently, Marx's historicism generates a scientism of its own, in which laws of economic development are seen as determining all human actions and therefore as predicting the coming revolution regardless of moral arguments – 'Hence', Berlin writes, 'the almost complete absence in Marx's later works of discussions of ultimate principles, of all attempts to justify his opposition to the bourgeoisie' (*KM*, 15–16). Marx's position tends to avoid and even to denigrate the language of moral justification (*KM*, 8, 9). This is in keeping with the logic of his system, according to which values and ideals are merely the superstructural expressions of more fundamental material causes. The danger in this is that ethical concerns will be sacrificed to an exclusive and ruthless commitment to whatever goals are seen as 'given' by the movement of history, goals that are not themselves questioned.

How persuasive is Berlin's criticism of Marx? It would be very unpersuasive if his point were simply that Marx's system is wholly amoral. Against such a reading, G. A. Cohen points to the evidence of ethical concerns in Marx, albeit often implicit, in concepts such as exploitation and alienation.[6] But Berlin is well aware of an ethical dimension to Marx; his attack goes deeper. First, even allowing that Marx does have deep moral concerns, it remains the case that these are largely submerged by his 'materialist' apparatus, according to which ethical values are merely superstructural. The door is thus left open to those who would go one step further and exclude ethical considerations from political decision making altogether.

Secondly, and more significantly, Berlin hints, even in this early work, at the problem he will analyse later under the label of 'moral monism'. The deeper problem with Marx is not that his system is amoral, but rather that it is informed by a particular kind of morality, one directed to the realization of a single end that overrides or subsumes all others. The more immediate, practical goal is the revolution of the proletariat. To this effect, Berlin quotes Marx's Inaugural Address to the First International (1864): 'The economic emancipation of the working class is therefore the great end to which every political movement ought to be subordinate as a means' (*KM*, 198). Behind this lies the Hegelian notion that history is tending towards a particular goal, the details of which we cannot predict, but the eventual coming of which is guaranteed by the laws of history. There is a sense in which the end of history must be for Marx not only a chronological but also a moral end: the historical pattern is ultimately, despite the ups and downs of the dialectic, a trajectory of progress, so the terminus of the upward curve must be a condition of improvement. Indeed, Berlin believes that the Marxist goal is not merely improvement but perfection, the complete realization of humanity's potential. Later, in 'Two Concepts of Liberty' (1958), he implicitly includes Marx among those who hold the 'ancient faith . . . that all the positive values in which men have believed must, in the end, be compatible, and perhaps even entail one another', and who dream 'of a final harmony in which all riddles are solved, all contradictions reconciled' (*L*, 213). For Berlin, Marx's system is informed by a utopian morality, anticipating the creation of a new society in which all legitimate human goods will at last be realized.

The crucial consequence is that Marx's goal, thus understood, necessarily outranks every other consideration, and so justifies any sacrifice made in its name. The goal of the final revolution which will defeat capitalism and usher in the new world is by definition the highest of purposes, and necessarily justifies any sacrifice. Thus, Berlin writes, it follows from Marx's view that

> the only sense in which it is possible to show that something is good or bad, right or wrong, is by demonstrating that it accords or discords with the historical process, assists it or thwarts it, will survive or will inevitably perish. All causes permanently lost are by that fact made bad and wrong, and indeed this is what constitutes the meaning of these terms. (*KM*, 134)

Whatever is done against the grain of history is wrong, whatever is done with that grain is right. As long as one is acting with the current of history, anything is justified.

G. A. Cohen objects that this picture assumes a degree of utopianism in Marx's view of the end of history that is not truly present there. Marx does not predict the harmonization of all human aspirations, Cohen argues, as shown by the fact that he does not predict the end of all human conflict, but only of 'specifically class conflict . . . There remains, after all, "individual [non-class] antagonism", and consequently room for the persistence of "human misery" and even "tragedy".'[7] But Berlin gives us good reason to be suspicious of Marx in this respect when he cites the Marxist dismissal of natural rights as 'but the ideal aspect of the bourgeois attitude to the sanctity of private property' (*KM*, 133). This dictum inaugurates a Marxist tradition in which human rights are typically regarded as mere temporary correctives necessitated by capitalist alienation and exploitation, the implication being that in a post-capitalist society they will no longer be necessary. But that will be true only if post-capitalist society is indeed a realm of harmony to a degree unrecognizable from human experience. At the very least, Berlin might argue, Marx's explicit doctrine is open to malign interpretation. It is a hostage to fortune, and in the twentieth century such hostages have frequently been abused.

Marx's understanding of history and morality eventually becomes, for Berlin, the very model of what he will later call 'monism'. Here in his first book he already tentatively identifies the enemy: the belief in a single overriding end to which everything else must be subordinated. Berlin sees Marx's monism as in part an expression of Marx's personality: an imperious, dogmatic nature which brooked no disagreement from others and regarded compromise as weakness. In a memorable passage Berlin summarizes the character and basic tendency of Marx as follows:

> The nineteenth century contains many remarkable social critics and revolutionaries no less original, no less violent, no less dogmatic than Marx, but not one so rigorously single-minded, so absorbed in making every word and every act of his life a means towards a single, immediate, practical end, to which nothing was too sacred to sacrifice . . . [H]is rigid belief in the necessity of a complete break with the past, in the need for a wholly new social system, as alone capable of saving the individual, who, if left to himself, will lose his way and perish, places him among the great authoritarian founders of new faiths, ruthless subverters and innovators who interpret the world in terms of a single, clear, passionately held principle, denouncing and destroying all that conflicts with it. (*KM*, 25–6)

Fittingly, these tendencies are the very opposite of Berlin's own: Marx is Berlin's archetypal critical target. But there is already in this passage, in the reference to other 'great authoritarian founders', evidence that Marx is not Berlin's sole target, that the problem of monism is not unique to Marx, but lies deeper in the history of Western thought. Indeed, Berlin explicitly observes that in these respects Marx 'embodies one of the oldest of European traditions' (*KM*, 25). The tracing of that tradition is the central task of Berlin's maturity.

Russian thinkers

'To my Russian origins', Berlin writes, 'I think I owe my lifelong interest in ideas. Russia is a country whose modern history is an object-lesson in the enormous power of abstract ideas' (*PI*, 255). Berlin was a native Russian speaker and an avid reader of the great Russian writers of the nineteenth century: Tolstoy, Dostoevsky, Pushkin, Turgenev, Chekhov and others. This part of his background contributed to his secondment, in 1945, from the British Embassy in Washington to the embassy at Moscow. Berlin's brief return to Russia was a pivotal episode in his life. There he made contact with a number of Russian writers and artists, most significantly with Boris Pasternak and Anna Akhmatova. Berlin's encounters with them, and his observation of the oppressive conditions they were forced to endure under Stalin, moved him deeply. Pasternak had seen most of his friends liquidated or sent to labour camps in the purges of the 1930s, and had himself survived only by dissembling a humiliating appearance of support for the regime. Akhmatova's husband had been executed, and her son arrested, and she had been forbidden to publish anything since 1925. Years later Berlin recalled that

> my realisation of the conditions, scarcely describable, under which they lived and worked, and the treatment to which they were subjected, and the fact that I was allowed to enter into a personal relationship, indeed, friendship, with them both, affected me profoundly and permanently changed my outlook. (*PI*, 252)

Berlin's meetings with Pasternak and Akhmatova affected him in two ways. The more obvious is that he saw at first hand the effect of a totalitarian regime on actual individuals for whom he cared deeply. Berlin had never been an admirer of the Soviet Union, but his concerted hostile engagement with Soviet communism dates from this post-War period. Secondly, the Russian visit opened his eyes to what a totalitarian system could do not just to the individual in general but specifically to the artist, and, through the artist, to an entire culture. Berlin saw Pasternak and Akhmatova as the last representatives of a pre-Revolutionary cultural tradition which combined an authentically Russian temperament with the best of Western civilization. This tradition had been submerged since the 1920s, when Russia had been, as Pasternak put it, severed from the rest of Europe (*PI*, 216). The recovery of this lost cultural voice became one of Berlin's central preoccupations in the late 1940s and early 1950s.

In the essays eventually collected as *Russian Thinkers* (1978), Berlin explores a number of nineteenth-century writers, in particular Tolstoy, Belinsky, Herzen and Turgenev. His purposes are multiple and are pursued with his characteristic indirectness. One such purpose has just been mentioned: the rescuing of the liberal, Westernizing voices of nineteenth-century Russia. In addition, Berlin is surely engaged, although he never quite says so, in a hunt for the intellectual origins of Soviet communism, and in the course of this he offers an implicit critique of contemporary Soviet tyranny. The parallels are obvious between the predicament of those nineteenth-century liberals and radicals most opposed to Tsarist autocracy and the plight of political dissidents in the Soviet period. Further, Berlin is also, in part, writing about himself, trying on a succession of outlooks as a way of finding his own voice as a political theorist. In the process, he is moving decisively away from Oxford-style analytical philosophy and towards his developing vocation as a historian of ideas.

What were the intellectual roots of the Soviet disaster? The orthodox answer given by Western Soviet studies throughout the 1950s and 1960s blamed the Bolshevik Revolution on the extremism of the nineteenth-century Russian intelligentsia.[8] According to this view, the influential writers and thinkers of mid-nineteenth-century Russia shared a tendency to seize on the most dramatic ideas from the West, and to pursue them to their logical extremes without regard to the consequences for actual people and institutions. Berlin agrees with this orthodoxy to some extent, but he also enters a significant qualification. The generation of the 1840s, which included Belinsky, Herzen and Turgenev, did indeed exhibit passion and commitment, but there was also a more questioning, ambivalent side to them, that of the moderate liberalism submerged in 1917.

Both orthodoxy and dissent are to be found in Berlin's essay sequence, 'A Remarkable Decade' (1955–6), his study of the heroes of the 1840s. Their common background is examined in the first two pieces, 'The Birth of the Russian Intelligentsia' and 'German Romanticism in Petersburg and Moscow'. There Berlin sets out the social and political context of mid-nineteenth-century Tsarist Russia: economically and socially backward, politically authoritarian, riven by an immense gulf between the educated elite and the masses of illiterate and impoverished peasantry, many of whom retained the medieval status of serfs, the 'baptised property' of landowners (*RT*, 265). Those younger members of the elite who were critical of the system were prevented by a crushing political censorship from promoting reform openly. They became, in Turgenev's phrase, 'superfluous men', unable to find a place for themselves in a society they could neither change nor accept (*RT*, 187–8, 265; also *L*, 343n.). For many young intellectuals, frustrated political energies were consequently channelled into the ostensibly non-political fields of literature and literary theory: on this view, the great flowering of Russian literature was in part owed to Tsarist censorship. But, as Berlin points out, the result was a literature rich in political themes and in many cases a vehicle for radical political protest. 'Hence the notorious fact that in Russia social and political thinkers turned into poets and novelists, while creative writers became publicists. Any protest against institutions . . . under an absolute despotism is *eo ipso* a political act' (*RT*, 265). One does not have to stretch Berlin's meaning too far to read him as referring to the Russia of the twentieth century as well as that of the nineteenth.

Another consequence of Tsarist oppression was the emergence of a distinctive intellectual climate among the young generation of liberals and radicals. This was in part borrowed from or reacting against German romanticism but, either way, it was intensified in what Berlin sees as a typically Russian manner. Since Paris, with its Enlightenment heritage, was declared off limits by the Tsar's government, Russian students who wished to study abroad tended to go to Germany. There they came into contact with even more incendiary ideas: namely, those of anti-Enlightenment romanticism. Romanticism, with its emphasis on the power and value of the emotions and the authentic will, is open to extremes of political interpretation, both radical and reactionary, in a way that the cooler, rationalist doctrines of the Enlightenment are not. This is not to deny Berlin's mature view that Soviet communism should be traced less to romanticism than to the Enlightenment. In 'A Remarkable Decade' the role of romanticism is that it set the scene for later developments by whetting the Russian appetite for extremes. Such extremes, Berlin believes, tended to appeal to the Russian intelligentsia of the nineteenth century, whom he describes as 'exaggerated Westerners' (*RT*, 125). Starved of more regular and normal contact with the West, Russian thinkers of the period tended to lay hold of the more radical Western notions with a passion. This tendency on the one hand produced an exceptionally vibrant intellectual climate among those affected, marked by an intensity, sincerity and freshness of response not so common in the West. On the other hand the same traits could lead to fanatical views and actions, in which a realistic sense of proportion and of real-life consequences was lost to sight. Here, Berlin hints, lie the intellectual roots of the Bolshevik Revolution.

Berlin sees this characteristically Russian, potentially explosive combination of intellectual enthusiasm and moral dedication as embodied most dramatically by the literary critic Vissarion Belinsky. For Berlin, Belinsky is the stern conscience of the 1840s intelligentsia, the original of a familiar character-type in the novels and plays of Turgenev, Dostoevsky and Chekhov. This is the dedicated young radical crusader: idealistic, passionate, possessing a profound inner dignity and firmness of purpose (*RT*, 150–2). For Belinsky, a work of literature should be not merely enjoyed for its own sake but mined for the ideas it embodies, the most important of which are its moral values. The artist has a duty not merely to satisfy the audience aesthetically, but to tell the truth – in particular the moral truth. Marxist critics later identified this doctrine of 'social criticism' as anticipating their own view that the function of literature is fundamentally ideological. But Belinsky's claim is not that artists should be self-conscious preachers, rather that moral illumination should emerge unforced from their sincere account of experience. Sincerity and commitment to the truth are Belinsky's watchwords, and this is what makes him both the moral leader of a generation and also a model for later generations of single-minded, puritan revolutionaries, a tradition culminating in Lenin and the Bolsheviks (*RT*, 181).

The origins of Soviet ruthlessness, however, are only part of what Berlin is after in his Russian essays. He is also trying to re-establish contact with a less single-minded, more liberal strain of Russian thought. The orthodox view is only partly right to find in the men of the 1840s the beginnings of Soviet fanaticism; there is another side to them. In Belinsky's case, the tendency to extremism is counterbalanced by a willingness, if truth requires it, to subject even his most fundamental beliefs to revision, as he did twice when passing into and out of a conservative phase (*RT*, 166–9). Belinsky's distinctively Russian intellectual and moral fervour remains admirable for Berlin, but even more admirable is his honest willingness to admit the force of other views when these are persuasive, and to change his mind accordingly.

A similar honesty in the face of complexity and ambivalence is what attracts Berlin to his other principal subjects in the Russian essays. One of these is Tolstoy, the main focus of the celebrated piece 'The Hedgehog and the Fox' (1953), with which I began this book.[9] Berlin portrays Tolstoy as a fox who wants to be a hedgehog. By nature, Tolstoy is a masterful observer of the concrete details of human life, its precise contours and textures: this foxy quality is what makes him a great novelist. But we also see Tolstoy straining, especially in *War and Peace* (1863–9), to extract from his observations an underlying philosophy of history. Surely, Tolstoy thinks, there must be some discernible pattern beneath the flux and chaos of events if human experience is not to be regarded as wholly random and meaningless. Yet his intellectual integrity compels him to confess that if there is such an underlying order, he cannot say what it is. Against the systematic ambitions of the hedgehog, the fox's sensitivity to the irreducible multiplicity and complexity of human life reasserts itself. The result is Tolstoy's anguished, anti-scientific view of history as implying *some* deep pattern which is

nevertheless inexpressible. Wisdom prescribes an attitude of submission to this sensed but ineffable force. This sounds like a final
reconciliation, but Berlin does not believe that it is. Tolstoy, he
insists, is never wholly satisfied with his official doctrine of surrender to fate, and remains to the end of his life torn between his yearn-
ing for system and his recognition that system is elusive (*RT*, 81).

Tolstoy appeals to Berlin because of the deep intellectual and
emotional honesty that prevents him from denying the conflicts and
contradictions thrown up by his thoughts and feelings. Yet Tolstoy
is in the end too much the angry prophet, the authoritarian
preacher, to be a truly Berlinian figure. Closer to Berlin's heart
is another powerfully ambivalent thinker, Alexander Herzen.
Champion of individual liberty against Russian autocracy, great
revolutionary publicist, Herzen is for Berlin 'the Russian Voltaire'
(*RT*, 189). But he is also a revolutionary assailed by deep misgiv-
ings about the human costs of revolution. Herzen is profoundly
averse, for example, to the language of 'sacrifice' that was fashion-
able in the radical and nationalist circles of his day, the sacrifice
required of the individual for the sake of justice or the nation or
humanity (*RT*, 197). What this kind of talk really contemplates is
the loss of actual, living human beings for the sake of mere abstractions: 'the despotism of formulas', as Berlin puts it (*RT*, 200). 'If only
people wanted', Berlin quotes Herzen as saying, 'instead of liberating humanity to liberate themselves, they would do much for . . .
the liberation of man' (*RT*, 200). This 'sense of reality' (*RT*, 111, 207),
a concern for the real-world consequences of ideas for real people,
becomes one of Berlin's persistent themes. Behind it one can detect
the feelings awakened by his meetings with Pasternak and Akhmatova, whose persecution was authorized by the abstract and distant
goals of the Soviet Union. An intellectual distaste for abstraction is
already present in Berlin's outlook, awakened by his encounter with
logical positivism. This is now reinforced at a visceral level in his
thinking about Russian morals and politics.

The ambivalence Berlin finds in Tolstoy and Herzen is still
more pronounced in Ivan Turgenev, who of all the Russian thinkers
is closest to Berlin in both politics and temperament. Indeed, the
picture Berlin presents in 'Fathers and Children: Turgenev and the
Liberal Predicament' (1972) is virtually a self-portrait. The conventional view of Turgenev, Berlin reports, is that of a fundamentally
non-political artist who is dragged into public debate only reluc-
tantly. Berlin disagrees, arguing that Turgenev's central preoccupations are no less political than those of his friends, Belinsky and

Herzen, and that Turgenev's opposition to the Tsarist regime permeates his writing from the beginning. Like Berlin, Turgenev is haunted by a single image of violence, in Turgenev's case that of his stepmother murdering a serf (*RT*, 267–8). But that image condemns the violence of the revolutionaries almost as much as that of the existing regime, and makes Turgenev less confident even than Herzen that radical revolution is the answer to Russia's troubles. The puritan values of Belinsky's radical descendants, of the type embodied by the character of Bazarov in Turgenev's *Fathers and Children* (1862), promise to uproot from Russia not only the choking weeds of Tsarist autocracy but also the tender shoots of Western civilization.

'Fathers and Children' is not only a subtle treatment of Turgenev, but a key statement of Berlin's own liberalism. Turgenev is portrayed by Berlin as caught between the authoritarian order he detests and the revolutionary cure that threatens to be worse than the disease. The younger generation of revolutionaries is riding a whirlwind that could destroy humane values along with others. This is 'the liberal predicament' of Berlin's subtitle, and he explicitly extends the problem beyond Turgenev's time and place to his own: 'the painful predicament of the believers in western values, a predicament once thought peculiarly Russian, is today familiar everywhere' (*RT*, 302). In Berlin's case, in the 1970s, liberals are caught not so much between autocracy and revolution as between the managerial, bureaucratic state on the one hand and the vehement but ill-directed resistance of New Left radicalism on the other. The characteristic middle-ground position of the liberal remains the same, torn between life-destroying authoritarianism and justified fear of ill-conceived radical alternatives.

Several other themes in Turgenev are central concerns for Berlin, too. The 'sense of reality' features in Turgenev as it does in Herzen, along with a similar distrust of abstraction (*RT*, 269, 294). By contrast with the vague and dangerous generalities of the revolutionaries, Turgenev's novels, Berlin argues, are models of concrete, sharp and delicate observation. They are also witty, satirical and ironic, displaying a lightness of touch with serious questions of a kind that Berlin tries to emulate, in contrast to the thundering preachiness of Tolstoy and Dostoevsky (*RT*, 263). Above all, Turgenev surpasses even Herzen in his dedication to understanding and empathy with different ideals and personalities, including those of the conservatives and (especially) the radicals whose views collide with his own (*RT*, 263). As a result he is fiercely criticized from both extremes for being half-hearted, timid, vacillating, too detached and lacking the courage to declare more emphatically where he stands. But this is unfair, Berlin replies in effect, because where Turgenev stands is precisely on the middle ground of toleration, compromise and moderation. This is a position underpinned by its own deep value commitments, and one which it takes no little courage to defend in troubled times.

All this holds equally as a description and defence of Berlin's own position, and the same judgement applies to his account of Turgenev's gradualism. The grand gestures and striking postures of radical politics invite us to leap into an unknown future in which much more may be lost than gained. By contrast, 'only education, only gradual methods, [and in Turgenev's words] "industry, patience, self-sacrifice, without glitter, without noise, homeopathic injections of science and culture" could improve the lives of men' (*RT*, 295). This is an important part of Berlin's credo as a liberal. Our purposes should be the modest ones of meeting basic needs and removing specific injustices to the extent required for the creation of 'a decent society':

> these goals are less glamorous, less exciting than the glittering visions, the absolute certainties of the revolutionaries; they have less appeal to the idealistic young, who prefer a more dramatic confrontation of vice and virtue, a choice between truth and falsehood, black and white, the possibility of heroic sacrifice on the altar of the good and the just – but the results of working for these more moderate and humane aims lead to a more benevolent and civilised society. (*PI*, 257)

Berlin's explorations of these nineteenth-century Russian thinkers occupy a place of central importance not only in his work as a historian of ideas but also in his political thought more generally. For it is there that he works out or confirms some of his most characteristic themes: 'the power of ideas', especially moral ideas, to shape people's lives for good or ill; the consequent imperative to take those ideas seriously and to assess their intellectual and moral force; the value of trying genuinely to understand, empathetically, all significant points of view on a question, not just one's own; the preference, as a result, for a degree of critical and perhaps ironic detachment as opposed to wholesale immersion in a particular outlook; and finally, the rejection of both reaction and revolution in favour of gradualism, and the idea that the liberal modes of caution, moderation and compromise should be seen not as weaknesses in politics but as strengths, not as abdication but as commitment.

Berlin need not be taken as insisting that all these ideas are distinctively 'Russian'. After all, the tendency Berlin most frequently identifies as characteristically Russian seems to lead in the opposite direction from liberal moderation. Russian intellectual passion and the urge to follow through the logic of a view irrespective of its consequences have less in common with liberalism than with Bolshevism. Rather, he is focusing on a unique group of Russian thinkers in a particular set of historical circumstances. The effect of this is to render concrete, and to dramatize, a universal political choice between reaction and revolution and a broadly liberal middle way. Characteristically, Berlin presents this choice through the lives of particular thinkers rather than patterns of abstract reasoning. To that extent, Berlin's Russians are as much a vehicle for his own thought as he is a product of theirs.

Jewish identities

One of the most striking characteristics of Berlin's liberalism, unusual for its time, is his explicit attention to the role and value of cultural identity. The principal source of this is his Jewishness.

> As for my Jewish roots, they are so deep, so native to me, that it is idle for me to try to identify them, let alone analyse them. But this much I can say. I have never been tempted, despite my long devotion to individual liberty, to march with those who, in its name, reject adherence to a particular nation, community, culture, tradition, language – the myriad unanalysable strands that bind men into identifiable groups. (*PI*, 258)

Berlin's Jewish background makes him acutely aware of the damage inflicted on human beings when their need for cultural belonging is denied. 'Two thousand years of Jewish history have been nothing but a single longing to return, to cease being strangers everywhere' (*PI*, 258). In particular, he emphasizes the role of identification with the nation. Against what he sees as the facile cosmopolitanism of the Enlightenment tradition, Berlin insists that nationalist identities are ineradicable in the modern age. The persistent power of nationalist movements, and the legitimacy, within limits, of their claims, must be acknowledged by any form of liberalism that pretends to be realistic. Once again, this is a thought rooted in personal experience, in this case his Zionism. But Berlin's support for a Jewish state, although consistent and deeply felt, is justified on universalist rather than particularist grounds, and hedged by liberal qualifications. As ever, his view is complex and ambivalent, reflecting his own inner conflicts.

Berlin's Jewish identity was secular and cultural rather than religious. His parents were partly assimilated, Europeanized Jews, belonging to the relatively privileged class of Jewish merchants who were permitted to live and travel outside the traditional Pale of Settlement imposed on Russian and Polish Jews in the Russian Empire. Berlin was not given a religious upbringing, and he remained a sceptic in matters of faith all his life. Nevertheless, he identified deeply with his Jewish roots, which he never denied or concealed. He cheerfully combined with his personal scepticism a respect for the beliefs and rituals of Judaism and other religions, maintaining a regular observance of the main holy days (*Life*, 293–4).

The political expression of Berlin's Jewishness was his Zionism.[10] Throughout his life, he remained committed to the case for a Jewish homeland and state. That commitment, however, was a frequent source of inner turbulence for Berlin, since it often came into conflict with other components of his identity, in particular his adopted Englishness. Visiting Palestine in 1934 and 1947, he found himself torn between his loyalties to his British friends and colleagues on the one hand and his Jewish relatives and Zionist associates on the other – one of his relatives was Yitzhak Sadeh, a leading figure among those favouring the use of violence against the British authorities. In this period, British policy in Palestine, which it had administered since the First World War, was largely devoted to restraining the ambitions of the Zionists, who were seen to be threatening the legitimate interests of the Palestinian Arabs. The Zionist cause had been gathering momentum since the late nineteenth century, under the leadership first of Theodor Herzl and later of Chaim Weizmann. The latter, in particular, stood for the more liberal, gradualist wing of Zionism, in contrast with the violent, revolutionary approach endorsed at that time by leaders such as Sadeh and Menachem Begin. Berlin sided with the gradualist faction, meeting Weizmann in 1939 and becoming a close friend and ally. During the War he went so far as to use information gained in his official capacity to tip Weizmann off (anonymously) about confidential proposals for a joint US–UK declaration condemning Zionist agitation.

When Israel was founded in 1948, Weizmann became its first president and offered Berlin a career as a government adviser in Israel. Berlin declined. In part this may have been out of concern for his personal safety, but his decision also reflected, first, his dismay that the real power in the new state had been captured by the more militant leaders, and, secondly, his feeling that as a liberal Westerner he was out of place among the new Israelis, the majority of whom were 'Middle Eastern, Hebrew-speaking and instinctively anti-British' (*Life*, 179). These concerns suggest the main features of Berlin's distinctive approach to Zionism: his celebration of the resilience and value of Jewish identity, balanced by his recognition of the multiplicity of legitimate ways of being Jewish, and by his insistence on the need for liberal restraints.

All of these themes are present in Berlin's principal treatment of Jewish identity, the article 'Jewish Slavery and Emancipation' (1951). Since the ancient diaspora, Berlin writes, the central peculiarity of the Jewish identity has been its insecurity. 'The Jewish problem', as formulated by Berlin, is that of how the Jewish people can feel at home in the modern world, and how the modern world can feel at home with the Jews. One possibility that must be rejected immediately is the maintenance, unchanged, of the traditional Jewish way of life: that is simply not a realistic option in a world irreversibly transformed by the Enlightenment (*POI*, 163). Nor, however, does Berlin believe that complete assimilation is a real alternative. The Jews, Berlin writes, are like a group of strangers visiting an alien culture. In order to survive, they become expert interpreters of the culture, often more learned in its ways than the natives themselves. But they never quite *belong*, and are never accepted as wholly belonging by the natives.[11] In an extraordinary image, Berlin compares different kinds of assimilated Jewry to different kinds of hunchback. Some deny they have humps at all, some glory in their humps, and some try to ignore their humps, or to disguise them, or to reduce them by applying 'various kinds of ointment' (*POI*, 175–6). Eventually, however, other hunchbacks propose cutting off the hump completely. This is the Zionist solution: to live in a separate community with its own political authority, where one's identity is no longer seen, by oneself or others, as a deformity. 'The Jews of Israel, certainly those born there in recent times, are, whatever their other qualities and defects, straight-backed' – they fit in, they are no longer strangers (*POI*, 176).[12]

Does it follow, however, that a satisfying life for Jews can *only* be lived as a citizen or resident of Israel? Berlin is in part writing in reply to Arthur Koestler, who argued that his fellow Jews must either identify completely with Israel or assimilate completely with the local majority culture wherever they find themselves.[13] Such a black-and-white, either-or solution, Berlin replies, must be rejected. First, people cannot assimilate at will: genuine identification cannot be forced but must be felt. Moreover (a thought implicit in the 'strangers' analogy), recognition of belonging is not a unilateral act, but can only be arrived at by negotiation with others.[14] Secondly, the liberation offered to Jews by the founding of Israel is not contingent on physical emigration. The existence of Israel emancipates Jewish people, wherever they are, because it gives them a choice: 'their problem of whether to go or stay, to assimilate or to remain in a betwixt-and-between condition, is now a purely individual problem which each Jew is free to solve as he chooses, and for which he bears responsibility not as a member of a nation but as an individual human being' (*POI*, 179). Before the founding of Israel, 'the tragedy of the Jews' – and the source of their 'slavery' – 'was that no real choice was open to them' (*POI*, 179). Israel has liberated the Jews not by making it possible to live out a single, authentic Jewish identity, as Koestler supposes, but by freeing them on a human level, giving them the freedom of choice that is the right of every human being: 'his right to live as he chooses, unless thereby he brings too much pain or injustice into the world' (*POI*, 179).

'Jewish Slavery' is not only Berlin's most extended treatment of Jewish identity and Zionism, it also has a number of broader implications. First, it is one of Berlin's clearest statements of his view of the role, value and resilience of cultural identity in general. The need for belonging and for recognition – the need to be relieved of one's 'hump' – is felt with especial force by the Jewish people because of their unique historical situation. But the need itself is universal. Belinsky, for example, feels at home only in his native Russia, despite his longing for the intellectual life of the West (*RT*, 179). Berlin himself reports that he can 'breathe easily' only in a society that cherishes the values of tolerance and liberty that he associates with England (*PI*, 257). Security of cultural belonging is, for Berlin, a human right. In this he takes issue with those Enlightenment thinkers who appear to neglect or denigrate the role of particular cultural bonds, believing that these could, and eventually would, be superseded by convergence on a single, rationally based culture of cosmopolitanism.[15]

Berlin's position anticipates those recent liberal thinkers who emphasize the role of cultural membership in providing a secure basis for personal liberty.[16] But, unlike them, Berlin does not go as far as advocating special rights for the members of minority cultures. That is, he does not advocate 'multiculturalism', the view that the state should extend official recognition – which could take various forms, ranging from legal exemptions to self-determination – to minority cultures within its jurisdiction. Indeed, in 'Jewish Slavery' Berlin expressly rejects such claims, at any rate in the Jewish case. Jews, he writes, should be accorded no less than all the entitlements of human beings, 'but neither, unless they go to Israel, have they a right to ask for more: for example, for even an attenuated version of a State within a State, or the enjoyment of any status and privileges in non-Jewish communities' (*POI*, 184). Berlin does not explain why he takes this view, but he probably thinks that special rights to cultural preservation are simply unnecessary. That is because he tends to see cultural identities as, on the model of the Jewish identity, persistent and resilient, part of the furniture of the human universe and needing no artificial refurbishment. 'He always said', Ignatieff writes, that 'origins . . . are a fact, full stop; but nothing to be proud of. To take pride was to surrender to the dubious determinism of the blood' (*Life*, 15). What this ignores, it may be objected, are cases where a culture is fragile, ailing or in a minority position that makes it vulnerable to forces imposed on it by the majority – the position, for example, of many indigenous cultures. To this Berlin might reply, in line with his remarks about the fate of the traditional Jewish way of life, that such cultures are ill-suited to the modern world, and that attempts to perpetuate them are futile.

Another reason why Berlin rejects policies of deliberate cultural preservation may be implied by his observation that cultures are not internally uniform but protean. If a culture is capable of many different expressions and interpretations, the argument might run, then it cannot be reduced to the kind of formula required for its preservation as a matter of public policy. There is, for example, more than one way of being Jewish: Koestler is wrong to identify Jewishness solely with citizenship of Israel. Similarly, Berlin takes issue with T. S. Eliot's view that the presence within fundamentally Christian civilizations of 'any large number of free-thinking Jews' is 'undesirable' because it undermines the cultural integrity of both Christianity and Judaism.[17] For Berlin, Koestler and Eliot are united in their desire to iron out all the creases of modern societies, to eliminate differences, and so to impose a uniformity of culture. In so doing they reveal themselves to be 'in this respect, true children of the new age which, with its totalitarian systems, has tried to institute just such an order among human beings, and sort them out neatly, each to his own category, and has suppressed civil liberties in varying degrees in order to achieve this purpose' (*POI*, 181). The goal of cultural purity, like that of 'ethnic cleansing' more recently, is a fundamentally totalitarian project.

Whether these arguments altogether justify Berlin's rejection of multiculturalism is doubtful. The goal of cultural 'preservation' does not necessarily imply the 'freezing' of a culture, still less the denial of its members' individual liberty. After all, Berlin is happy to support liberal forms of nationalism without supposing that the national cultures concerned will be frozen by the states that protect them. (I shall return to Berlin's nationalism in chapter 5, and to the issue of multiculturalism in chapter 8.) The more valuable point that emerges from Berlin's attack on Koestler and Eliot is the principle that cultural identity, although important, is in general subordinate in value to freedom of choice. There is more than one legitimate way of being Jewish, because more important than living any particular form of Jewish life is the liberty of the individual to choose between that form of life and others. This is a crucial point, which gives Berlin's view of Jewishness, of Zionism, and of culture more generally, its fundamentally liberal cast. Berlin's defence of Israel is based not on the particularist (or relativist or communitarian) idea that the Jewish outlook is authoritative for Jews, but on the universalist ground that the existence of Israel guarantees to the Jewish people their right to choose how to live, which is a right common to all human beings.

Brian Barry has objected that this is a poor justification of Israel, because for many Jews still in the diaspora, with interests and allegiances in other societies, emigration to Israel is not a realistic or desirable option.[18] But there can be no doubt that the existence of Israel added to the options of many Jews if not all. Moreover, it is not just that the founding of Israel enables Jews to live in a Jewish state, but also that Jews are free *not* to live in Israel. They may decide, as did Berlin himself, that other considerations besides Jewish solidarity are equally or even more important to them. For those who choose to remain in the diaspora, feelings of social uneasiness may remain, but at least this is now a condition they have chosen rather than had thrust upon them. This is what Berlin means when he says that the creation of Israel 'has restored to Jews not merely their personal dignity and status as human beings, but what is vastly more important, their right to choose as individuals how they shall live – the basic freedom of choice, the right to live or perish, go to the good or the bad in one's own way' (*POI*, 182). This last idea, the right to 'go to the good or the bad in one's own way', lies at the heart of Berlin's conception of negative liberty, which I shall discuss later.

From Berlin's universalist, liberal justification of Israel's existence follows a universalist, liberal account of its mission and obligations. In 'The Origins of Israel' (1953), he robustly declares that the task of the new citizens of Israel is simply to live like normal human beings, a condition they richly deserve after centuries of abnormality. 'Normality' or well-being he defines as follows:

> The principal obligation of human beings seems to me to consist in living their life according to their lights, and in developing whatever faculties they possess without hurting their neighbours, in realising themselves in as many directions as freely, variously and richly as they can, without worrying overmuch whether they are measuring up to the peaks in their own past history, without casting anxious looks to see whether their achievements reach the highest points reached by the genius of their neighbours, nor yet looking at other nations, or wondering whether they are developing precisely as they expect them to develop. (*POI*, 157)

This passage, with its emphasis on personal autonomy and self-realization (and hostility to the more paranoid or aggressive forms of nationalism), is actually one of the relatively few occasions on which Berlin explicitly identifies human well-being with those distinctive liberal values. Elsewhere he is usually content to refer, more generally, to 'humane' values and a 'decent' human life. It is ironic that one of his clearest expressions of liberal universalism occurs as part of his case for the particular claims of Israel.

Berlin's universalism is also significant in this context, because it implies limits to his defence of Zionism. If the existence of Israel is ultimately justified by the human values of personal autonomy and self-determination, then those same basic goods underpin the claims of the displaced Palestinian Arabs too. Berlin is well aware of the implications of his argument: Israel should be a vehicle for human rights, not for cultural and political domination and exclusion. As time went on he became increasingly unhappy with the way the country was developing, in particular in its relations with the Palestinians. One of his last acts, only weeks before his death, was to issue a public plea to the Israeli government to resolve its differences with the Palestinians peacefully by arranging with them a final and just partition of the land.[19]

Summary

Berlin's earlier writings, up to the mid-1950s, introduce all of his principal themes: his broadly empiricist but historically informed approach to philosophy, in contrast with ahistorical scientism on the one hand and grand-theory historicism on the other; his opposition to Marxism as a dangerous combination of both scientism and historicism, and of authoritarianism and monism; his excavations among the Russian thinkers of the nineteenth century for the roots of both revolutionary fanaticism and its moderate liberal antidote; and his insistence, informed by his Jewish identity, on the universal role and value of cultural belonging. All of these concerns remained important to Berlin throughout his career, but it was the conflict with Marxism, in the name of individual liberty, that became his most pressing project as the 1950s unfolded.

3

The Betrayal of Freedom

In the middle part of Berlin's career, in the 1950s, his immediate focus was the threat posed to liberal democracy by Soviet communism.[1] His view that the Soviet system and the Marxist philosophy underlying it are fundamentally opposed to individual liberty is deeply felt and memorably expressed. Thus far, however, this was a position shared by many contemporaries, such as F. A. Hayek, Karl Popper and Jacob Talmon.[2] The originality of Berlin's anticommunism is twofold. First, he analyses the Marxist threat to liberty not merely as a rejection or devaluing, but as a hijacking and subsequent corruption of the idea. The problem is not outright opposition to freedom, but a more insidious betrayal of the very concept of freedom by political leaders and intellectuals. Secondly, Berlin hints that the roots of the betrayal lie deeper than the crude logic of Sovietism or even the more sophisticated system of Marx. Rather, the sources of Stalinist tyranny are to be found at the heart of modern political thought, in both its romantic and scientistic streams.

In this chapter I discuss Berlin's work of the early 1950s in three sections. First, I examine those of his pieces that are most explicitly shots fired in the Cold War. The second section traces Berlin's archaeology of Soviet totalitarianism at the deeper level of determinist historical theory. In the third section I set out his account of the most prominent 'enemies of human liberty' of modern times, preparing the ground for my treatment of 'Two Concepts of Liberty' in the next chapter.

Cold War

Berlin is a declared opponent of 'totalitarianism'. It is worth noting, however, that it is totalitarianism in its specifically Soviet rather than fascist form that usually concerns him – and this despite his Jewish identity. In part this may be because by the time he returned to Oxford after the War and began to emerge as a political thinker of note, fascism had been defeated militarily and replaced by communism as the greatest threat to liberty. Churchill's 'iron curtain' speech of 1946 announced the terms of the tense ideological stand-off between international communism and capitalist liberal democracy that was to last for the next forty years. Under these conditions Berlin, with his Russian background and his reputation for general political shrewdness established by the wartime dispatches from Washington, was well placed to become a prominent political commentator.

A sign of Berlin's growing status was an invitation to contribute to the prestigious American journal *Foreign Affairs*, for which he wrote two articles. One of these, 'Generalissimo Stalin and the Art of Government' (1952), published under the pseudonym 'O. Utis' to protect Berlin's Russian relatives and friends from reprisals, is representative of his more explicitly Cold War writings.[3] The essay analyses the classic Stalinist pattern of alternating waves of repression and liberalization, under which even (or especially) the Communist Party faithful are kept in a near-constant state of tension and fear. Failure to predict and adjust to the next shift in the 'general line' could have fatal consequences. This phenomenon had been vividly brought home to Berlin in his meetings with Pasternak and Akhmatova, and he notes that it is an especially agonizing problem for people such as writers and artists whose business it is to make public statements (*SM*, 103).

Berlin argues that these sudden, dangerous changes in the official Soviet view should be attributed not merely to Stalin's whims or to the shifting imperatives of national interest, but to a deliberate policy based on a new theory of government, which he calls the 'artificial dialectic' (*SM*, 107). Any revolutionary regime, Berlin explains, is threatened by two dangers. Either the revolution may go too far, striking at all institutions and authorities to a degree that menaces the revolutionary leadership itself, or it may, after achieving its initial goals, lose its momentum and gradually return to the *status quo* it sought to overturn. An additional problem for distinctively Marxist revolutions is that, according to their determinist theory of history, there is no escape from a 'dialectical' process in which peaks of revolutionary energy are followed by troughs of inaction. Marxist historical theory seems to invite submission to these peaks and troughs, yet any of these could lead to an excess or deficiency of action that would destroy the revolution and the regime. Stalin's solution, Berlin argues, is to take control of the dialectical process, deliberately stimulating the peaks of revolutionary activity – that is, suppressing opposition – and just as deliberately judging when to ease off the pressure and allow something of a return to normality. This artificial dialectic is 'Stalin's most original invention, his major contribution to the art of government' (*SM*, 114). It is this that enables the dictator to steer between the extremes that could ruin him, and of course it is this that explains the apparently arbitrary adjustments of the Party line. These shifts are necessary to maintain 'the perpetual tension – the condition of permanent wartime mobilization – which alone enables so unnatural a form of life to be carried on' (*SM*, 114).

'Generalissimo Stalin' is more an expression of Berlin's talent for dark irony than a serious analysis of Stalinism. It contains some important insights, nevertheless, not least concerning the logical and practical difficulties entailed by a thoroughgoing historical determinism. But these are matters Berlin discusses more fully elsewhere, and I shall come to them later in this chapter. The most striking feature of the piece is the directness of its focus on current political practice. In Berlin's better-known writings his approach is politically more oblique, evoking deeper intellectual sources and broader historical consequences.

Typical of this more characteristic approach is the lecture 'Democracy, Communism and the Individual' (1949), delivered at Mount Holyoke College, Massachusetts, while Berlin was a visiting fellow at the Russian Research Centre at Harvard. His surviving notes sketch or suggest most of the central themes of his characteristic analysis of communism. 'Eighteenth-century rationalism' is the root both of liberal democracy and of communism, since both draw on the notion that questions of morals and politics are susceptible to a scientific approach that will yield certain knowledge. In liberal democracy this rationalism is tempered by an acceptance of the fact that basic values such as liberty and equality are incompatible and must be traded off against one another in particular cases, and by the importance attached to the moral autonomy of the individual and the political expression of this in the idea of inalienable individual rights. The Communist view, on the other hand, places no such restrictions on the claims of rationalism. According to the 'scientific' account given by Marxism, ideals and values are merely expressions of class interests which are destined either to victory or to defeat by the inexorable laws of history. Those laws can be known with certainty by experts, whose scientific formulations provide infallible guidance for the state. Consequently, those who dissent from the state's directions 'necessarily place themselves in opposition to the juggernaut of history, that is to say, are behaving suicidally, which proves that they are irrational, blind, mad, not worth listening to, . . . to be swept away as an obstacle to progress'.[4] In education, for example, the Communist goal is not to encourage autonomous judgement, but rather to fit the individual to the social plan laid down by the authorities.

Later in the lecture Berlin introduces a warning for liberal democracies. Although Soviet communism expresses totalitarian tendencies in their most extreme form, the general 'rationalist' outlook at its root is also 'widespread beyond the confines of Russia today'.[5] In the West too, Berlin suggests, the liberty of the individual is under threat from rationalist planning. The difference is that while the Communists see society as 'a correctional institution, a cross between a reformatory and Dotheboys Hall', the 'more benevolent view' of the Western welfare state is that 'society is an enormous hospital and all men are inmates, each suffering in greater or lesser degree from some kind of malaise or maladjustment, which it is the duty of education to cure or at least to make bearable'.[6]

The Mount Holyoke lecture is to some extent no more than typical of the anti-communism of the period, but it also hints at some of Berlin's broader themes to come. The plea for individual liberty in the face of the totalitarian state is, of course, a staple of liberal writing. The fear that Western social democracy is not immune to the totalitarian contagion had also been expressed by Hayek in *The Road to Serfdom* (1944) and by George Orwell in *Nineteen Eighty-Four* (1949). But Berlin hints at concerns that go deeper than standard liberal views when he traces both communism and liberal democracy to a common root in Enlightenment rationalism, and again when he contrasts the attitudes of the two systems to value conflict. These points look forward to his later explorations of the relationship between the Enlightenment and romanticism, and of opposition between value pluralism and monism.

Berlin's intellectual net is cast wider still in the second essay he wrote for *Foreign Affairs*, 'Political Ideas in the Twentieth Century'

(1950). There he addresses the question: what is distinctive about twentieth-century political thought? His short answer is: its irrationalism. The great ideologies of the nineteenth century, liberalism and socialism, were opposed to each other in many ways but united in the rationalist optimism they both inherited from the Enlightenment. On this view, all significant human problems could be formulated rationally and, at least in principle, rationally resolved. The march of the human intellect, aided by the fundamental goodness of human nature, would triumph eventually. However, Berlin argues, as the nineteenth century wore on, rationalist reforms continued to be resisted by established institutions and interests, and in the face of this provocation a more militant approach to social change emerged. Marx is, of course, a key figure in this connection, rejecting the Enlightenment faith in reasoned argument on the ground that beliefs and values are merely reflections of more fundamental class interests, which are in turn determined by a society's economic structure. What is required is not disinterested reason, but revolutionary consciousness. Lenin takes this thinking a stage further. Disinterested inquiry is positively harmful to the revolution, since it merely divides the intellectuals and, through them, the people, and leads to the dissipation of revolutionary energy. For Lenin, the revolution will succeed only if an elite of informed leaders disciplines the masses to accept their authority unquestioningly. The goal of the revolution is still the Enlightenment dream of the rational society, but the means by which that goal is to be pursued involve a repudiation of reasoned judgement on the part of the unreliable masses, and its replacement by implicit devotion to the Party and its leaders.

The Communist method is also that of the Fascists: both aim at 'the training of individuals incapable of being troubled by questions' which would upset the system (L, 77). Such questions are regarded as symptoms of neuroses, to be cured rather than answered. Questions of this kind will not even be raised by people who have undergone the appropriate preparation, which is not education but psychological conditioning applied through the agency of institutions, myths and a general culture of conformity. The process may involve the use of old terminology, but this will be given new meanings in keeping with the requirements of the regime – a point anticipating Berlin's later discussion of the totalitarian distortion of the idea of freedom. The general atmosphere of the totalitarian state is hostile to questions other than the merely technical, concerning means to accepted ends. This is, Berlin notes, the age of the expert and the manager. Artists, on the other hand, are regarded with suspicion because of their propensity to raise disturbing issues and to imagine alternatives.

As in the Mount Holyoke lecture, Berlin sees the thought patterns underlying totalitarian societies as a problem for contemporary liberal democracies too. Hostility to the questioning of ends takes an extreme form under fascism, which openly celebrates a cult of the irrational, and under communism, which worships 'science', but only as providing the technical means to the achievement of ends rigidly enforced by the Party. The same basic pattern, although not so brutally embodied, is also present in the West, where the unquestioned end is that of economic prosperity, and public debate is largely confined to how this may be achieved most efficiently (*L*, 83). 'The great philanthropic foundations of the West' are genuinely concerned to promote human well-being, but conceive this 'almost entirely in therapeutic terms', that is, as the harmonization of human behaviour with a predetermined set of norms which are themselves taken for granted (*L*, 87). Once again, if the Fascist and Communist image of society is that of a prison or reformatory, the capitalist image is that of a hospital. Between the prison and the hospital, despite important differences, there is a certain commonality, namely the denial of the capacity of individual human beings to judge for themselves what matters to them and how they ought to live. 'Both these tendencies – which spring from a common root – are hostile to the development of men as creative and self-directing beings' (*L*, 88). Even the mild paternalism of the New Deal or European social democracy involves a significant loss of individual liberty in its tendency to narrow the individual's field of choice, which includes the freedom 'to commit blunders' (*L*, 91).

The undermining of the individual's capacity for choice becomes, in some passages of Berlin's thought, something like the supreme evil. In a letter to George Kennan (1951) he writes:

> [T]he one thing which no utilitarian paradise, no promise of eternal harmony in the future within some vast organic whole will make us accept is the use of human beings as mere means – the doctoring of them until they are made to do what they do, not for the sake of the purposes which are their purposes, fulfilment of hopes which however foolish or desperate are at least their own, but for reasons which only we, the manipulators, who freely twist them for our purposes, can understand. (*L*, 339)

But there is a problem here, one that bears on the relation between Berlin's liberalism and his value pluralism. Berlin's pluralism, as I shall show in more detail later, includes the idea that no single human good absolutely overrides all others. Yet if there is no supreme good, then there is no supreme evil either.[7] A consistent value pluralist cannot rule out the possibility that in some cases there may be good reason to exchange or diminish individual choice for the sake of some other good, for example social justice. In 1951 Berlin's express commitment to the idea of value pluralism still lay in the future. But the conceptual problem is already latent. Is Berlin's liberal devotion to a Kantian respect for persons in conflict with the pluralism that is already developing in his thought and that he will later embrace explicitly?

The tension between liberalism and pluralism in Berlin's thought will require further investigation (chapters 6 and 7), but the outline of his answer to the problem is already evident in 'Political Ideas'. Individual choice is a value that liberals must take very seriously indeed, but that does not mean they must fetishize it as an absolute. For this reason Berlin refuses simply to condemn the planned state in the name of individual freedom. A reduction of personal liberty may be a price that must be paid if we are to enjoy other important goods, such as security from social disorder and economic want. Berlin's conclusion is worth quoting at length:

The dilemma is logically insoluble: we cannot sacrifice either freedom or the organisation needed for its defence, or a minimum standard of welfare. The way out must therefore lie in some logically untidy, flexible and even ambiguous compromise. Every situation calls for its own specific policy, since 'out of the crooked timber of humanity', as Kant once remarked, 'no straight thing was ever made'. What the age calls for is not (as we are so often told) more faith, or stronger leadership, or more scientific organisation. Rather it is the opposite – less Messianic ardour, more enlightened scepticism, more toleration of idiosyncrasies, more frequent *ad hoc* measures to achieve aims in a foreseeable future, more room for the attainment of their personal ends by individuals and by minorities whose tastes and beliefs find (whether rightly or wrongly must not matter) little response among the majority. What is required is a less mechanical, less fanatical application of general principles, however rational or righteous, a more cautious and less arrogantly self-confident application of accepted, scientifically tested, general solutions to unexamined individual cases. (*L*, 92)

Berlin hints here at one of the strategies I shall later propose for reconciling pluralism and liberalism. Under pluralism not even liberal
values can be absolute, but the very moderation enjoined by
pluralism is cognate with a liberal sensibility. At the same time,
however, Berlin's remarks open up another problem. If basic human
values such as freedom and security are plural and incommensurable, then how can we choose rationally among them when
they conflict? His answer here, 'logically untidy, flexible and even
ambiguous compromise', may strike some as honest and realistic,
but others as vague and intellectually lazy. I shall return to this issue
in chapter 6.

A further question raised by 'Political Ideas' is that of the influence on totalitarianism of the Enlightenment and Counter-
Enlightenment respectively. When Berlin identifies the twentieth
century with 'irrationalism', it might seem that he is attributing contemporary totalitarianism as a whole to the rejection of reason he
associates with certain streams in the Counter-Enlightenment. Such
a view would seem to contradict the picture he presents in *Karl
Marx*, where he tends to see the totalitarian outlook as a corrupt
development of eighteenth-century rationalistic optimism: Marx is
portrayed there as inspired more by science (although this takes a
historicist form) than romanticism.

The contradiction is more apparent than real. To begin with, what
Berlin means by 'irrationalism' in 'Political Ideas' is not so much the
outright rejection of reason found in some Counter-Enlightenment
thinkers, but rather a narrowing of reason to a purely instrumental
function, the abandonment not of reason as such but of the reasoned
questioning of ends as well as means. In this sense 'irrationalism'
is a characteristic product not of the Counter-Enlightenment but
of the Enlightenment's scientistic stream with its tendency to
technocracy. In other words, 'Political Ideas' is consistent with what
was to become Berlin's usual emphasis on the surprising degree to
which the excesses of the twentieth century can be traced to the
Enlightenment, and the equally surprising potential of the Counter-
Enlightenment and romanticism to provide an antidote. This does
not mean, however, that Berlin neglects the role of irrationalism in
its more thoroughgoing sense, and thus the role of the Counter-
Enlightenment and romanticism, in the genesis of totalitarianism in
its Fascist form in particular. His general view might be roughly
summarized as follows: the Enlightenment is the chief source of
totalitarianism in its Communist variant, whereas the Counter-
Enlightenment and romanticism are the chief sources of fascism.

But this is a crude generalization that will need qualification in due course.

Berlin's most basic point in 'Political Ideas' is wholly in line with his emerging pluralist outlook: that fundamental value conflicts of the kind he identifies between freedom and security should be seen for what they are, with all the difficulty which that entails. Such conflicts should not be ignored or disguised by the rhetoric of national destiny or the end of history or gross national product. The silencing of the questions that would reveal these collisions is one of the principal marks of totalitarianism, but the evasion of those questions is a feature of contemporary forms of liberal and social democracy too.

In these essays of the early 1950s Berlin shows himself to be a committed and eloquent Cold Warrior, but not a one-dimensional one. A penetrating critic of Stalinism, he is also alert to the shortcomings of the democratic camp; indeed, he argues that the two sides have, to some extent, similar failings and intellectual roots. The search for those roots, beneath the play of surface phenomena, is his characteristic project. At this early stage he is able only to hint at the deepest levels. Beneath Stalin lies Lenin, and beneath Lenin, Marx. But the most dangerous ideas in Marx have roots in deeper soil still.

Determinism and history

One of the deeper patterns of thought underlying Marxism is a certain conception of history. Central to this is the notion of determinism, the idea that all historical change is determined by causes independent of the will of individual human beings. For Marx, the ultimate agency of historical change is not the actions of individuals, or even that of social classes, although the latter play a significant intermediate role. Rather, history is driven by impersonal mechanisms at work within the economic base of a society. These mechanisms operate according to regularities which can be observed and formulated as a set of laws: history, on the Marxist view, is a science on the model of the natural sciences. These two ideas, that history is 'determined', and that it can be treated as a 'science', are not unique to Marxism, but are essential supports for the Marxist outlook. Berlin takes issue with both of them.

He tackles determinism in an essay that was widely read in the 1950s and 1960s, 'Historical Inevitability' (1954). Determinism is defined as the view that historical events are caused ultimately by impersonal forces beyond the control of the individual. Different determinist accounts variously identify these impersonal forces as physical factors, or environment, or custom, or the evolution of 'some larger unit' such as 'a race, a nation, a class, a biological species . . . a "spiritual organism", a religion, a civilisation, a Hegelian (or Buddhist) World Spirit', and so forth (*L*, 98). This is not to say that human agency plays no role at all in the causation of events; rather, human agents are themselves made what they are by some such antecedent factor (*L*, 7).

Berlin does not argue directly that determinism is false, but rather that it is incompatible with some of our most basic moral categories. If we were really to keep faith with determinism in our lives, we would have to revise those categories drastically, indeed to an extent we can scarcely imagine. In particular, determinism is incompatible with our ordinary notion of freedom of choice, and therefore with our ordinary notion of moral responsibility. If our actions are determined by impersonal forces, then they are ulti- mately beyond our control, attributable to the impersonal forces and not to our own choice. If so, the idea of 'the individual's freedom of choice [in a causal sense] . . . is ultimately an illusion, [and] the notion that human beings could have chosen otherwise than they did rests upon ignorance of facts' (*L*, 110). Consequently, the notion that individuals can be held morally responsible for what they do must also be a mistake, since 'not individuals, but these larger entities, are ultimately "responsible"' (*L*, 115). 'The more we know, the farther the area of human freedom, and consequently of responsibility, is narrowed' (*L*, 110). Along with the notion of moral responsibility perishes any meaningful use of concepts such as praise or blame, at any rate as we now understand these ideas. 'For the omniscient being, who sees why nothing can be otherwise than it is, the notions of responsibility or guilt, of right and wrong, are necessarily empty; they are a mere measure of ignorance, of adolescent illusion; and the perception of this is the first sign of moral and intellectual maturity' (*L*, 110).

It follows that if we were really to live our lives as if determin- ism were true, we would have to change our moral language and thinking to a degree impossible for us. We would have to dispense with the notions of individual freedom of choice, moral responsi- bility, praise, blame and remorse, and with all the kinds and shades of description and judgement which employ these. This point does not demonstrate that determinism is false (*L*, 4, 122). However, the difficulties Berlin points to as standing in the way of such a revision are clearly such as to make it almost inconceivable.

> These categories permeate all that we think and feel so pervasively and universally that to think them away, and conceive what and how we should be thinking, feeling and talking without them, or in the framework of their opposites, psychologically greatly strains our capacity – is nearly, if not quite, as impracticable as, let us say, to pretend that we live in a world in which space, time or number in the normal sense no longer exist. (L, 121)

A world in which determinism was honoured in practice would be one in which blame would attach to a murderer no more than to his dagger; Samuel Butler's *Erewhon*, where crime is an illness and illness a crime, would be no less rational a society than our own (L, 15). The strong implication of Berlin's discussion is that determinism falls barely short of logical incoherence. At any rate, it is a psychological impossibility for anything recognizable as a human society.

In particular, Berlin is concerned with the implications of determinism for historians. Not even those historians who officially support determinism are able to write and think consistently with it. For one thing, they are often prominent among those who urge their colleagues 'to avoid bias' (L, 117). What can this mean other than to avoid subjecting historical actors to unjust judgements, a thought that implies the relevance, the rationality, of praise and blame? Berlin amplifies this point in his Introduction to the 1969 edition of the essay, while replying to E. H. Carr's objection that Berlin's position invites historians to moralize.[8] The point, Berlin replies, is not that historians should go out of their way to issue moral judgements, rather that such judgements cannot be avoided. 'The very use of normal language cannot avoid conveying what the author regards as commonplace or monstrous, decisive or trivial, exhilarating or depressing' (L, 22). This is true of the most even-handed of narratives. 'Detachment itself is a moral position. The use of neutral language ("Himmler caused many persons to be asphyxiated") conveys its own ethical tone' (L, 22–3).

A more effective objection brought by Carr is that Berlin, in opposing determinism to the extent that he does, seems to 'believe determinism to be false and reject the axiom that everything has a cause' (L, 20). Berlin denies that this is what he is doing, and repeats that his sole concern is to exhibit the conflict between determinism

and ordinary moral concepts. But this is a narrow defence in view
of the degree to which, on his view, determinism is literally unthink-
able. If determinism must be abandoned, that would seem to imply
a case for free will. Yet Berlin himself allows that the concept of free
will is also dubious: 'the notion of uncaused choice as something
out of the blue is certainly not satisfactory' (*L*, 29). Although he hints
that there may be some alternative position between free will and
determinism, he is not able to say what this is and retreats again to
his claim that he means only to draw attention to determinism's
radical implications.

On the issue of whether free will or determinism, or some further
alternative, comes closer to the truth, Berlin leaves us without guidance. But that is because he is less interested in the truth of such
matters for their own sake than in the moral and political implications of influential beliefs and their role in the history of ideas. More
central to Berlin's concerns is his discussion of why determinism
has become as influential as it has. One reason, he suggests, is that
its erosion of moral responsibility is, for some people, liberating.
They are liberated

> from all those moral burdens which men in less enlightened days
> used to carry with such labour and anguish . . . [L]ike soldiers in an
> army driven by forces too great to resist, we lose those neuroses
> which spring from the fear of having to choose among alternatives.
> Where there is no choice there is no anxiety, and a happy release from
> responsibility. (*L*, 160)

The irony is obvious: this is not liberation but dehumanization. The
view that Berlin presents here is that of the revolutionary commissar for whom anything is permitted, indeed required, by the logic
of history. History absolves from any crime those who act in its
name. The reference to choice generating 'neuroses' echoes one of
the themes of 'Political Ideas in the Twentieth Century', that of the
contemporary crushing or evasion of moral conflict. Determinism
releases the commissar (and the bureaucrat) from fretting about
such things, and enables him to continue the necessary work with
a clear conscience.

Another explanation for the influence of determinism is the effect
of scientism. The prestige of the natural sciences led the eighteenth-
century rationalists to believe that not only the natural but also the
social world could be comprehended through a set of law-like
propositions. And if human conduct is law-governed, then human

conduct must be determined, not free. From this followed the vogue for 'scientific' explanations of history, the ambition of which was to lay bare the laws that governed the development of entire civilizations and ultimately of humanity as a whole. One of the greatest of these projects was, of course, that of Marx. But the dream of scientific history, Berlin replies, is an illusion based on 'a false analogy' (*L*, 142). History and science are two very different things.

Berlin develops this point in 'The Concept of Scientific History' (1960). Posing the question, Can history be a science?, he answers emphatically, No. To demand of history that it become a science 'is to ask it to contradict its essence' (*CC*, 141). The key point is that historical explanations are profoundly different in kind from explanations in the natural sciences. The task of the natural sciences is to abstract from our observation of the natural world a set of laws that will infallibly and precisely predict and 'retrodict' (explain) events in that world. The perspective of natural scientists is that of observers of phenomena from the 'outside'. Their method is that of logical deduction or empirical induction, yielding propositions that can in principle be verified or falsified by those standards. The historian, on the other hand, whose task is to explain human conduct, necessarily does so from the 'inside', that is, from the perspective of the actors themselves. That is because the explanation must include an account not merely of physical behaviour but also of the meaning of that behaviour, its ends, motivations, underlying values and beliefs. This latter kind of explanation is too complex and perspective-dependent to be reduced to a set of neutral, abstract laws like those of the natural sciences. Rather, historical explanation requires *Verstehen*, 'understanding'.

This does not mean that the study of history is a poor or defective form of natural science; rather, that it has its own appropriate aims and methods, and calls forth its own set of skills and excellences. In addition to the capacity for the inside view, the good historian needs a certain 'grasp' or 'sense of reality', an intuitive appreciation of the general shape of lived human experience (*CC*, 141).[9] 'A man who lacks common intelligence [i.e. a sense of reality] can be a physicist of genius, but not even a mediocre historian' (*CC*, 141). In judging whether their explanation is a good one, historians cannot simply test their views against a set of abstract rules. Rather than deduction or induction, the historian's test must be a looser and more complex notion of 'coherence'. Historians must judge whether the accounts they offer, and the generalizations they hazard, fit with a background 'sense of the general texture of experience' or with 'the network of our most general assumptions, called commonsense knowledge' (*CC*, 114, 115). This background sense cannot be made fully explicit because 'the web is too complex': even our most straightforward claims about ourselves rest on a myriad of deep assumptions which we cannot question simultaneously. 'The true reason for accepting the propositions that I live on earth, and that an Emperor Napoleon I existed, is that to assert their contradictories is to destroy too much of what we take for granted about the present and the past' (*CC*, 114). Historical claims presuppose a vast network of assumptions that cannot be captured by simple law-like propositions, yet the network is an unavoidable touchstone for judging the adequacy of such claims (*CC*, 128).

Recall that elsewhere (in his work on Herzen) Berlin uses the expression 'sense of reality' to stand for a rather different notion: an awareness of the real-life consequences of ideas and actions for real people (*RT*, 111, 207). In 'The Concept of Scientific History' he hints at a connection between these two thoughts. The proponents of scientific history, by placing 'their faith in a given pattern' (*CC*, 142) ahead of their acknowledgement of concrete human complexity, have lost touch with reality in both senses. Once we have forced our understanding of human experience into conceptual boxes, it becomes easier to ignore the real effects of our actions and to force actual people into wooden boxes. The concept of scientific history, like that of its ally, determinism, can have real and terrible consequences for human freedom.

Enemies of liberty

From freedom in the sense of free will, or 'causal' freedom, Berlin turns to freedom in the social and political context. The modern fate of freedom in this latter sense is one of his principal themes in the Mary Flexner Lectures, 'Political Ideas in the Romantic Age', delivered at Bryn Mawr College, Pennsylvania, in 1952. The material for the Flexner Lectures was taken from a much longer typescript which Berlin thought of as the 'torso' of his work in the history of ideas.[10] The torso was the product of his massive reading for the Marx project, and constituted an intellectual quarry which Berlin then mined in much of his published work thereafter.

In the torso Berlin sketched the outlines of what would become his mature position in many areas, but three in particular: the complex political legacy of Enlightenment rationalism and its critics, the contrast between negative and positive liberty, and the vulnerability of positive liberty to corruption. The Enlightenment, inspired by Newtonian science, liberated humanity by dragging the received authority of religion, state and custom before the bar of reason. But it also threatened to create a new tyranny of scientists and bureaucrats through its ambition to reduce human conduct to a few laws of nature which would then determine the laws of the enlightened political society. The emphasis of critics like Vico and Herder on the limitations of scientific method for understanding human conduct, and on the cultural and historical particularity of human values, was therefore a salutary correction to Enlightenment scientism. But the romantic reaction to rationalism also brought its own problems, and prominent among these were the implications of the characteristic romantic understanding of the nature of freedom. We should distinguish between a pre-romantic, 'liberal' view of freedom as absence of interference with whatever a person might wish to do, and a 'romantic' conception of freedom as direction by the 'real' self within. This is Berlin's initial formulation of the distinction between 'negative' and 'positive' liberty. Here, too, he first sets out what I shall call his 'inversion thesis': his argument that the romantic conception of liberty is dangerous because susceptible to being twisted into the very opposite of what freedom ordinarily means. The positive liberty of the romantics, however noble or innocent its inspiration, provides a model by which the dictators of the twentieth century can justify their oppressive rule in the language of freedom itself.

By what steps precisely does this twisting of the idea of freedom occur? Berlin's best-known account of the process is the central narrative line of 'Two Concepts of Liberty'. Before turning to this, however, I shall consider the equally dramatic presentation of freedom's inversion in the BBC broadcasts Berlin gave in 1952, also based on the torso, now published as *Freedom and its Betrayal: Six Enemies of Human Liberty* (2002). The 'six enemies' of the subtitle are Helvétius, Rousseau, Fichte, Hegel, Saint-Simon and Maistre. Significantly, the list does not include Marx: Berlin's net is now cast wider and deeper – although Marx remains something of an unseen presence in several of these lectures. What the six thinkers have in common is that they all thought and wrote in the period that began about thirty years before and ended about thirty years after the French Revolution of 1789. For Berlin this means that 'these are the earliest thinkers to speak a language which is directly familiar to us', and that 'the kind of situation to which they seem relevant . . . is often characteristic not so much of the nineteenth century as of the twentieth' (*FIB*, 2, 3). These are thinkers engaging with a period of immense technological, social and political revolution, much like our own, in which rival visions of human nature and the good life contend violently. If we want to understand the central ideological conflict of our own time, Berlin is saying, we should examine its roots in the thinkers he discusses. In particular, we should study these thinkers if we want to understand the threat posed in the twentieth century to individual liberty – at any rate 'to what is normally meant' by individual liberty, namely the negative idea, 'the right freely to shape one's life as one wishes, the production of circumstances in which men can develop their natures as variously and richly, and, if need be, as eccentrically, as possible' (*FIB*, 5). Berlin's six thinkers are the intellectual ancestors of twentieth-century communism and fascism. All of them claim to be benefactors of humanity, and some to be champions of liberty; but all produce, in the end, doctrines highly destructive of liberty in its ordinary negative sense.

Berlin's enemies of freedom can be divided into three categories. First, there are those who openly oppose individual liberty, like Joseph de Maistre. For Maistre, liberty is positively dangerous, one of the shibboleths of the eighteenth-century Enlightenment which led to the French Revolution. The degeneration of the movement of 1789 into the Jacobin Terror shows the use that human beings typically make of liberty. Contrary to the ludicrous optimism of the *philosophes*, human nature is dark, vicious, bloody. Nature at large is a realm of violent competition and killing, and human beings, in their natural condition, merely follow these instincts in their own way. The only hope for a civilized existence consequently depends on the containment or restraint of human nature, not its liberation. This is achieved through the maintenance of a social order secured by 'the two anchors of society – religion and slavery' (Maistre, quoted in *FIB*, 144). Human beings must be enslaved by the coercive power of the state, memorably symbolized for Maistre by the public executioner. The executioner is commonly regarded with a peculiar horror, but that is the point. 'All greatness, all power, all social order depends upon the executioner; he is the terror of human society and the tie that holds it together. Take away this incomprehensible force from the world, and at that very moment order is superseded by chaos, thrones fall, society disappears' (Maistre, quoted in *FIB*, 149). That the force be 'incomprehensible' is vital:

sheer violence must be supplemented by mystification. The role of religion is to cloak the institutions of social control in an aura of mystery impenetrable to the questioning that would undermine them. Human reason is feeble and can be made to serve many masters, but when directed against the foundations of authority it is corrosive. Rational institutions are unstable because they can be as easily challenged as upheld by rational means; lasting institutions must be irrational, resting on antiquity, force and mystery. This, then, is Maistre's credo: liberty is the enemy; human beings need order, discipline, the priest and the executioner. Surely, someone might say, this whole outlook can be dismissed as a backward-looking relic of premodernity. Berlin disagrees. Maistre's open assault on liberty 'is really ultra-modern', anticipating 'the anti-democratic talk of our day' (*FIB*, 132). The grim view of human nature, the emphasis on struggle and death, the worship of the state and the cult of the irrational – all these themes identify Maistre as 'a kind of precursor and early preacher of Fascism' (*FIB*, 153).

In a second category are those thinkers who merely neglect, rather than openly attack, individual liberty. They may allow that liberty is something to be valued, but the effect of their thought is to promote other values as more important. Typical of this tendency are those who want to reconstruct human knowledge and society on scientific lines, and prominent representatives of this scientific (or scientistic) outlook include Helvétius and Saint-Simon. Claude-Adrien Helvétius is a classic representative of Enlightenment scientism, the father of modern utilitarianism who regards all human motivation as reducible to a single law: seek pleasure and avoid pain. Human happiness, understood in these terms, is limited at present, thanks to the malign influence of traditional rulers, who manipulate others for their own ends. The remedy is 'a kind of social hygiene' in which current vices are cleansed away and happiness made accessible to all (*FIB*, 14). This goal cannot, at least initially, be achieved by education or reasoned argument, since the reason of most human beings is at present corrupted by the irrational social environment in which it develops. Therefore, manipulation will still be necessary, but it will be manipulation for the ends, and using the means, made known by the new science of the hedonic springs of human conduct. Legislation will adroitly marshal pleasures and pains to guide behaviour: 'a system of sticks and carrots for the human donkey' (*FIB*, 16). What about 'the rights of man' and individual liberty? In the world of Helvétius, happiness is the goal, not liberty. Liberty, in its basic, negative sense, includes the liberty to make mistakes, even 'to do evil'; but liberty in this sense disappears from the utilitarian utopia, 'since everyone has now been conditioned to do only what is good' (*FIB*, 22–3). The world of Helvétius is 'a technocratic tyranny' which looks forward to the technocratic aspects of twentieth-century communism and fascism (*FIB*, 25–6).

In Henri de Saint-Simon Berlin finds another prophet of elitist technocracy. Saint-Simon anticipates Marx when he locates the driving force of history in technology and invention. Progress is achieved if those human needs current at any given time are maximally satisfied, if opportunities are available for the best talents, if a society exhibits unity and strength, and if innovation and discovery flourish. This will be possible only when a society is properly organized, its functions rationally planned in order to make the best possible use of its resources. The drafting and execution of the plan must be placed in the hands of a qualified elite. By 'elite' Saint-Simon does not mean the traditional aristocratic and military leaders; their day is done. Rather, he means those most capable of leading a society in the new industrial age: creative people like artists, researchers and checkers like scientists, and, at the top of the hierarchy, organizers like managers and bankers. These classes will take their allotted places within a centralized state that will direct the rest of society. What, once more, of liberty? Liberty is valuable for Saint-Simon to a degree, but only in an instrumental sense as 'a battering ram', useful in the eighteenth century for demolishing outmoded feudalism but incapable of building anew in the nineteenth (*FIB*, 126). Not freedom but planned efficiency is Saint-Simon's fundamental value. What ordinary people want is boots, not liberty. This slogan, common to both the bland welfarism of the American New Deal and European social democracy on the one hand, and to the brutal authoritarianism of the Fascists and Communists on the other, Berlin traces 'to the gentle, humanitarian, noble Saint-Simon' (*FIB*, 130).

Finally, a third category contains the most dangerous enemies of liberty because the most seductive. These are the writers who claim to be on the side of liberty, even to rank it above all other values, but who redefine it to mean its very opposite: the 'inversion thesis'. In this connection Berlin names Rousseau, Fichte and Hegel. Rousseau sets the pattern for the others. Liberty, for Rousseau, is an absolute value: it may never be legitimately surrendered or diminished because the possession of liberty is the essence of a person's humanity. But other values, such as social co-operation and consci-entious adherence to the moral law, are absolutes too. How can these various imperatives be reconciled? The standard view of the social contract tradition is that some measure of liberty must be traded for some measure of physical and moral security, but this is not possible for Rousseau given his reading of these goods as absolutes. His solution is to redefine liberty: liberty *is* social co-operation and right action. The vulgar idea of liberty as negative non-interference refers merely to an amoral, animal liberty, con-sistent with acting wrongly. But to act wrongly is to depart from the standards of the 'inner, better, more real self' which necessarily seeks the good (*FIB*, 46). Truly human liberty entails the libera-tion of that which is distinctively human, namely a person's capac-ity for self-direction in accordance with moral rules, the will of 'the true self'.

In political society the true self is to be identified with the state: 'the State is you, and others like you, all seeking your common good' (*FIB*, 44). Hence political freedom is obedience to 'the General Will', the will of the whole sovereign body for the common good. That is why someone can be 'forced to be free' in Rousseau's famous, and for Berlin notorious, phrase (*FIB*, 47). The state knows your true will better than you do. In forcing you to act in accor-dance with its laws, it merely liberates your authentic moral will from your appetites. Liberty is now effectively inverted so that it means nothing other than obedience to the state. Starting from Rousseau's 'deification of the notion of absolute liberty', Berlin writes, 'we gradually reach the notion of absolute despotism' (*FIB*, 47). The result is a licence for authoritarian and totalitarian leaders to defend oppression in the name of freedom: 'there is not a dicta-tor in the West who in the years after Rousseau did not use this monstrous paradox in order to justify his behaviour' (*FIB*, 47). Rousseau, Berlin concludes, 'claims to have been the most ardent and passionate lover of human liberty who ever lived'; but he was also, in fact, 'one of the most sinister and most formidable enemies of liberty in the whole history of human thought' (*FIB*, 49).

The perverse pattern set by Rousseau is reproduced and devel-oped by Fichte and Hegel in the context of German philosophy after Kant. Kant himself was influenced by Rousseau, taking from him the idea of true freedom as the freedom of the moral self in oppo-sition to the passions. Fichte, Berlin argues, takes up this idea and gives it a collectivist and ultimately nationalist twist. The impera-tives of the true self suggest the authority of something greater than ourselves. What can this be? One answer is Kant's: the universal moral law. Another is Fichte's: the voice of the nation – for Germans, the German nation. 'Then the great paean begins,' writes Berlin, 'the great nationalist, chauvinist cry. Individual self-determination now becomes collective self-determination, and the nation a community of unified wills in pursuit of moral truth' (*FIB*, 69). The lecture on Fichte ends with a series of quotations from Heine, who warns the French against underestimating the destructive potential of the ideas emerging in Germany. 'Armed Fichteans will come, whose fanatical wills neither fear nor self-interest can touch . . . A drama will be performed in Germany in contrast with which the French Revolution will seem a mere peaceful idyll' (*FIB*, 72). For Berlin, this is 'a genuine vision of the doom to come' (*FIB*, 72).

In Hegel the authentic self is identified still more grandiosely with 'the world spirit' progressively realizing itself through the process of human history. Freedom, on this view, becomes submission to the stream of history, the adjustment of will and appetite to the demands of the epoch. For Berlin, this is essentially a doctrine of 'might makes right'. The winners in history are right, of necessity. 'The only thing which is bad is to resist the world process. For the world process is the incarnation of reason' (*FIB*, 97). Whatever *is* must be justified because necessitated by history's deterministic pattern. Here, Berlin's attack on inverted freedom converges with his critique of Marxism and historical determinism. Behind Stalin stands Marx, and behind Marx, Hegel.

The lectures that make up *Freedom and its Betrayal* are remarkably powerful performances.[11] They may be open to objection at various points – Rousseau and Hegel, for example, are arguably more subtle thinkers than Berlin makes them appear – but these treatments are undeniably striking and vivid. Moreover, their basic point is well taken. In the modern age, since the French Revolution, human liberty has been subject to unprecedented celebration but also unprecedented assault – sometimes from the very people who speak most loudly in its name. The most dangerous, because most insidious, attack has come from those who define freedom as the liberation of the authentic self. Against this 'romantic' ideal, with its potential for inversion, Berlin asserts what he takes to be the ordinary or basic notion of liberty, the notion he wishes to defend:

> The essence of liberty has always lain in the ability to choose as you wish to choose, because you wish so to choose, uncoerced, unbullied, not swallowed up in some vast system; and in the right to resist, to

be unpopular, to stand up for your convictions merely because they are your convictions. That is true freedom, and without it there is neither freedom of any kind, nor even the illusion of it. (*FIB*, 103–4)

The contrast here between the liberty of the authentic self and that of the unqualified empirical self is the basis for Berlin's celebrated version of the distinction between negative and positive senses of liberty.

Summary

Throughout the early 1950s Berlin explores the vicissitudes undergone by the concept of freedom in modern times. Writing in the context of the Cold War, he searches for the origins of Stalinism in patterns of thought lying deep within the Western intellectual tradition. Since the French Revolution, Berlin believes, the ideal of liberty has achieved an unprecedented apotheosis, and has also been subjected to unparalleled dangers. The most obvious threat is posed by extreme Counter-Enlightenment thinkers like Maistre, for whom political liberty is simply a mistake – a view which anticipates twentieth-century fascism. But a greater threat comes from within the Enlightenment itself, in the scientistic strand according to which human conduct can be reduced to a set of laws to be formulated and enforced by experts. The historical determinism at the heart of Marxism is prefigured by the scientism and managerialism of optimistic and well-meaning Enlightenment thinkers like Helvétius and Saint-Simon. Finally, the unkindest cut is delivered by those writers, principally within the romantic reaction to the Enlightenment, who purport to be lovers of liberty, but who twist its meaning into obedience to the state: men such as Rousseau, Fichte and Hegel. This abuse of the idea of freedom is the theme that Berlin will develop in his most famous essay, 'Two Concepts of Liberty'.

4

Two Concepts of Liberty

In 1957 Berlin accepted the Chair of Social and Political Theory at Oxford, and the following year delivered his inaugural lecture, 'Two Concepts of Liberty'.[1] This is Berlin's masterpiece, the culmination of his thinking about freedom in the 1950s. Indeed, 'Two Concepts' is one of the most famous works of twentieth-century political thought. Berlin's seminal formulation of the distinction between negative and positive conceptions of liberty remains a standard point of departure for analyses of political freedom in contemporary political theory. His account of the historical and conceptual implications of the distinction, especially his suspicion of the positive conception, has been hugely influential. As is the nature of classics, however, Berlin's essay is also highly controversial. For all those who regard it as a leading authority on liberty, there are probably as many who see it as 'deeply flawed'.[2] In the face of such objections, one may fairly ask whether the significance and quality of Berlin's 'Two Concepts' has been overestimated.

I shall argue that, on the whole, Berlin's text does deserve its classic status. Many of the objections launched against 'Two Concepts' turn out to be based on misunderstandings which have accumulated through a kind of Chinese whispers effect, where each new misconception confirms and builds on the last. One of my central concerns will therefore be to identify several misreadings of the text which have been so persistent that they have achieved the status of myths. In a different category are those complaints which, although not mythic, are still mistaken or unpersuasive. This is not to say that my defence of Berlin will be unqualified or uncritical. Some of the critics' arrows hit their mark, if not scoring bull's-eyes then at least landing in the outer circles. I shall try to arrive at a balanced view that does justice to both Berlin and his critics.

More specifically I shall argue that both the strengths and the weaknesses of Berlin's case can be better understood if we consider his treatment of liberty in the light of his idea of value pluralism. This is Berlin's account of fundamental moral values as multiple, potentially conflicting and sometimes incommensurable. I have already mentioned certain intimations of this key notion in Berlin's earlier work, but the last section of 'Two Concepts' contains his first extended formulation and his first clear indication of the idea's significance for his political thought as a whole. While the negative–positive nexus was widely debated from the moment the essay appeared, there was little systematic discussion of Berlin's value pluralism until the 1990s. Even now, after considerable investigation of value pluralism and its implications for the foundations and nature of liberalism, the theme of pluralism is seldom brought together with that of negative and positive liberty in an adequately integrated view. The secondary goal of this chapter is to provide just such an integrated account. My treatment of pluralism here will be incomplete, because it raises many issues that I shall have to postpone until chapters 5, 6 and 7. Nevertheless, Berlin's understanding of liberty cannot be appreciated without some attempt to connect it with his pluralism. This is essential in order to clarify Berlin's meaning, to reveal the errors of some of his critics, and to show where he is mistaken.

I begin by setting out the main lines of Berlin's basic distinction between negative and positive senses of liberty, taking note of some common misinterpretations. In the second section I focus on Berlin's principal purpose in 'Two Concepts', his critique of the positive conception, following this through several different levels of analysis and criticism. Finally, I review and debate the major objections to Berlin's position, paying special attention to the bearing on these issues of value pluralism.

Negative and positive liberty

'Two Concepts' is a panoramic survey of the idea of freedom in the modern world. The immediate context of Berlin's inquiry is the Cold War: 'the open war that is being fought between two systems of ideas' (*L*, 168). The two rival systems are defined by the different answers they give to the question of the nature and extent of political authority, hence of the nature and extent of human freedom. Berlin thus begins his investigation by contrasting two views of freedom, 'negative' and 'positive', associated with the liberal-democratic and Communist worlds respectively, before proceeding to a critique of the positive idea.

Berlin did not invent the distinction between negative and positive liberty, but his formulation is more frequently cited than any other. For Berlin, negative liberty encompasses 'the area within which a man can act unobstructed by others' (*L*, 169). More fully, a person is free in the negative sense when he or she is not prevented, by human act or omission, from doing what he or she may wish to do.[3] The standard obstacle to freedom in this sense is coercion: force or the threat of force. Mere incapacity – for example, my inability 'to jump more than ten feet in the air' – is not an obstacle to freedom thus understood, since it involves no human act or omission (*L*, 169). Negative freedom is therefore to be distinguished from capacity or ability. Berlin concedes, though, that in some cases the line between freedom and capacity may be debatable. For example, negative liberty may or may not include freedom from poverty, depending on one's theory of the nature of a person's poverty: whether attributable to the agency of others or merely to the person's own incapacity (*L*, 169–70).

Berlin regards the negative idea as the 'normal' sense of the word 'liberty' (*L*, 169).[4] He associates it with 'the classical English political philosophers', instancing Hobbes, and more broadly with British and French liberals, including Locke, J. S. Mill, Constant and Tocqueville (*L*, 170, 171). These latter thinkers all hold that a substantial minimum area of negative liberty is essential to human well-being. Berlin never endorses this commitment explicitly, although it is clear enough that he is deeply sympathetic with it. There is no doubt that he associates negative liberty with the liberal outlook, and that it is negative liberty, on the whole, that he wants to defend. His own position must therefore be broadly liberal.

Positive liberty is the idea not of the absence of interference but of having control over one's life. It derives 'from the wish on the part of the individual to be his own master', to be genuinely the author of his own actions (*L*, 178). Crucially, the tendency in the positive idea is to allow that this kind of control can be diminished not only by the interference of other people, but also by obstacles within one's own personality. These may include factors such as ignorance, desires or emotions. Thus, the classic form taken by positive liberty is the traditional idea of 'self-mastery', of one's reason being in control of one's passions, which goes back at least to Plato.

With these basic points in place, two persistent misinterpretations of Berlin's negative–positive distinction, amounting to myths, can be cleared away immediately. Myth 1 is the belief, repeated by many commentators, that Berlin's two categories are intended to be exhaustive of all senses of freedom.[5] The objection follows that if every kind of freedom must be understood as either negative or positive, the result is that we lose important distinctions, nuances and possibilities. As a criticism of Berlin, this is clearly misdirected. Near the start of 'Two Concepts' he explicitly acknowledges that the word 'liberty' has 'more than two hundred senses' and that he proposes 'to examine no more than two of these', albeit important ones (*L*, 168). It may be that the critical attention attracted by Berlin's analysis has led some people to believe that the negative–positive division is meant to be exhaustive, or that negative and positive liberty are the only kinds of liberty that matter; but neither of these is Berlin's view. In general, what he is saying is that there are many valid conceptions of liberty, each capturing a particular aspect of that complex idea. (This reading is controversial, but I shall defend it later.) Of these, the negative and positive conceptions, or families of conceptions, are especially salient in the contemporary world.

Another tenacious misunderstanding, myth 2, has it that Berlin's discussion confusingly runs together under the 'positive' label several different ideas that ought to be kept separate.[6] Berlin defines positive liberty as having control over one's life (self-mastery or authentic self-direction), but some commentators allege that he sometimes confuses that idea with quite different concepts. Of these the two most common suspects are, first, 'effective' freedom or freedom as capacity to act, and secondly, freedom as political participation. But although it is surely useful to separate these different senses of freedom – autonomy, effective freedom and political participation – Berlin does not confuse them. It is true that his discussion is complex, nuanced and not always crystal clear. But it is not true that he at any stage presents the formal–effective distinction as a negative–positive distinction. The nearest equivalent to the formal–effective distinction in Berlin's discussion is a contrast between negative freedom and the conditions for its exercise – a contrast I shall return to later. Berlin nowhere presents effective freedom as 'positive'. The association of positive with effective freedom is widespread, but it has likelier sources elsewhere.[7]

As for the alleged confusion of positive liberty with political participation, Berlin never equates these ideas. It is true that in some parts of 'Two Concepts' he makes connections between positive liberty and collective self-government or sovereignty. But although this complicates the picture, it is not misleading, since there is an important overlap between positive freedom as individual autonomy and freedom as participation in collective autonomy.[8] To have control over one's life arguably requires having at least some control over the political system under which one lives. The notion of collective sovereignty sometimes goes further, as in Fichte's idea that the immediate subject or bearer of such freedom is not the individual person but the collective personality of the whole political society or nation. But this, too, can be understood as an extension of positive liberty, the collective person being substituted for the individual as the locus of the authentic self. There may be other, 'non-positive' versions of freedom as political participation, but Berlin's view does not rule these out; nor do they falsify his explanation of participatory freedom as an outgrowth of the positive idea. All things considered, Berlin's text is not misleading about positive liberty in the way suggested.

To sum up, Berlin's basic negative–positive distinction is between negative non-interference and positive self-mastery or autonomy. He does not claim that these terms exhaust all conceptions of liberty, he does not confuse positive liberty with effective freedom, and although he does associate positive liberty with political participation, his account of this connection is not misleading. Let us now see what Berlin does with the negative–positive distinction.

The critique of positive liberty

Berlin's central purpose in 'Two Concepts' is to mount a critique of positive liberty. This is not to say that he is either completely hostile to the positive idea or exclusively dedicated to its negative counterpart, but there is no doubt that he is more suspicious of the positive notion. His critique is prosecuted through three different phases or levels, which can be thought of as progressively deepening his investigation.

1. The inversion thesis

At the first level, the one most often discussed, positive liberty is criticized as tending, at least in some forms, to support political authoritarianism. This is Berlin's 'inversion thesis', introduced in the previous chapter: the positive conception allows 'liberty' to be inverted into its very opposite. But Berlin's argument has been frequently misunderstood. Many commentators have supposed that he rejects positive liberty absolutely and in any form, and consequently that he regards the negative idea as the only valid or desirable concept of liberty.[9] This interpretation is far too simple, and should be identified as myth 3.

In fact, Berlin acknowledges that there are many different versions or interpretations of the basic positive idea, and he is careful to note that some of the most famous of these are distinctly and powerfully individualistic. These include the self-mastery ideal of the ancient Stoics, according to which liberty consists in freeing ourselves from the worldly ambitions that make us hostages to fortune. Stoic freedom is a 'retreat to the inner citadel' of control over one's own desires and emotions (*L*, 181). Berlin does not really approve of the Stoic ideal, describing it elsewhere as an abandonment of the genuinely social and political dimensions of freedom, and essentially 'a very grand form of sour grapes' (*RR*, 37). But Stoic freedom, however deficient in that respect, is not authoritarian: the Stoics try to cope with political oppression; they do not justify it. Similarly, Kant's ideal is that of an inner freedom, consisting in the control of the appetitive part of the self by the rational part. Genuine freedom is genuine self-control, and this is possible only if the contingent, changeable desires are mastered by that element of us which is law-governed (*L*, 181–3). Thus far, positive conceptions of liberty are strongly individualistic in tendency. Their political implications are at worst quietist, and may even, as in the case of Kant, suggest an ideal of personal autonomy that any legitimate political system should respect.

However, it is also too simple to say merely that Berlin defends some versions of positive liberty and attacks others.[10] Rather, there is a strong undercurrent in his account – never completely explicit but evident none the less – to the effect that the logic of positive liberty as such ought to make us wary. From their individualistic or liberal beginnings, Berlin argues, positive conceptions of liberty have developed in modern times in illiberal and ultimately totalitarian directions. The process by which this has occurred is historically contingent – it could have been otherwise – but it is not merely accidental.[11] The positive idea itself, even in the Stoics and Kant, contains a feature, not found in the negative concept, that lays it open to authoritarian corruption. This is the idea that the human personality is divided between two selves: on the one hand, the 'higher' or 'true' or authentic self, usually (although not always) associated with reason; on the other, the 'lower' or 'empirical' self, usually associated with the desires and emotions. Once this distinction is drawn, Berlin argues, the way is open to advocating the suppression of people's actual desires and wishes in the name of their 'true' or 'real' self. Moreover, this suppression of the empirical self can then be described as being not merely for the victim's own good but as liberating, since only then is the person – that is, the 'true' self – really in control (*L*, 179–80).

This slide down the slippery slope is helped along by the addition of either of two assumptions. First, it helps dictators if we (or they) suppose that they know the requirements of the true self better than the individual concerned. This, of course, could be denied, but may be harder to deny if we add a second assumption. Fichte, for example, supposes that the true self is to be identified with a collective self: the nation or some universal entity in which the individual person merely participates as an integral part. On this view it becomes harder for individuals, as no more than parts of a greater whole, to back their own judgement as to the demands of authenticity. This too could logically be denied, and the individual reasserted as the sole authority regarding the contents of his or her authentic identity. But Berlin insists that the very idea of the 'true' self, distinguishable from the merely empirical or contingent desires, is what opens the door to freedom's betrayal. The very idea of the true self raises the logical possibility that a person's actual desires can be mistaken and, if so, ought to be suppressed. The doctrine of the divided self does not guarantee authoritarianism, but it offers authoritarianism aid and comfort.

Negative liberty is not so vulnerable to such a move, since it implies that fulfilment of a person's empirical wishes is the proper goal of free action. Liberty in the negative sense is merely non-interference with whatever the agent may wish to do, whatever other people may think of it, a space in which one can 'go to the good or the bad in one's own way' (*POI*, 182). The positive idea, with its doctrine of the true self, is more open to moralistic interpretations, where the true self is identified with one particular account of morality and the good life. If to be free is to act morally, and if others know better than we do what is morally required, then the way is open to the redefinition of freedom as obedience to the commands of others. At this point the positive conception leaves behind its individualist origins, and becomes twisted into 'a monstrous impersonation' of liberty (L, 180). Liberty is inverted into obedience.

2. The confusion thesis

The inversion thesis is actually only one instance, albeit the most spectacular, of a more general problem that exercises Berlin. This is the tendency in modern political discourse to cheapen the ideal of liberty by blurring its boundaries with other values. I shall call this second level of Berlin's case the 'confusion thesis'. Because liberty is universally accepted in the modern world as unquestionably desirable, regimes of all ideological stripes claim that their policies are liberating. But Berlin cautions against stretching the meaning of liberty to a point where it becomes empty and therefore worthless. 'Liberty is liberty, not equality or fairness or justice or culture, or human happiness or a quiet conscience' (L, 172).

It is again the positive rather than the negative conception that tends more easily to be stretched in this way. Berlin points to several examples, of which the elision of liberty with obedience is merely the most egregious. Another case is the confusion of liberty with knowledge or understanding, a confusion encouraged by the traditional self-mastery notion of freedom as being governed by the rational part of the self.[12] This line is given a historicist twist by Hegel and Marx (L, 187–91). If to be free is to be rational, and to be rational is to understand and accept the laws of historical necessity, then to be free becomes synonymous with adaptation to whatever wave of history is currently in force. Berlin insists that all these slippery equivalences be rejected. Liberty is liberty, not knowledge or submission to history.

Berlin is sometimes criticized for insisting too rigidly on conceptual clarity, requiring the strict maintenance of definitional boundaries at the expense of broader and more generous views.[13] But he is by no means as pedantic as he is often made out to be. A case in point is his discussion of the line between freedom and the recognition of 'status' or identity. To achieve 'recognition' in this sense is to be respected as possessing a certain dignity, including a capacity for self-government, either as an individual or as a member of a group (L, 203). Writing against a background of 1950s decolonization, Berlin observes that formerly colonized peoples, for example, can experience such recognition as liberating: a liberation from paternalism and disrespect. But is this quite the same thing as liberty, properly understood?

Berlin is caught in two minds. At first he is inclined to insist that recognition, although unquestionably an important value, is not quite the same thing as liberty. To be ruled by one's own nationals is not liberating if that rule is oppressive. Consequently, recognition is 'akin to, but not itself, freedom . . . [It is] more closely related to solidarity, fraternity, mutual understanding' (*L*, 204). But on reflection he finds the precise line hard to draw: 'We cannot simply dismiss this case as a mere confusion of the notion of freedom with that of status or solidarity, or fraternity, or equality, or some combination of these. For the craving for status is, in certain respects, very close to the desire to be an independent agent' (*L*, 205). Recognition combines elements of both negative and positive liberty: a sphere of non-interference and the capacity for authentic self-direction. In the end, Berlin concedes, it is not unreasonable to regard recognition as 'a hybrid form of freedom' (*L*, 206). Moreover, recognition shades into the idea of popular sovereignty, which Berlin explicitly allows as a legitimate species of positive freedom: collective rather than individual self-direction (*L*, 208–12).

Still, even if recognition and popular sovereignty are genuine types of freedom, Berlin stresses that we should be clear about the contrast between these and negative liberty. Indeed, these various senses of freedom are not only distinct but also potentially conflicting. Popular sovereignty alone does not make a genuinely 'free society', since, as Mill and other nineteenth-century liberals pointed out, 'the sovereignty of the people could easily destroy that of individuals' (*L*, 208). Freedom for the individual depends on the liberal doctrine of guaranteed 'frontiers' of freedom, maintained even against democratic governments, within which people are negatively free to do as they please (*L*, 211).

3. Monism and pluralism

Up to this point, positive liberty has been associated by Berlin with authoritarianism (the inversion thesis) and muddled political thinking in general (the confusion thesis). In a brief but highly significant final section, 'The One and the Many', Berlin reaches the third and final level of his critique of the positive idea: positive conceptions of liberty tend to rest on metaphysical assumptions of a 'monist' nature. For Berlin, the defining mark of positive liberty is its constitutive notion of the 'true' or 'real' self. Each person (or nation, etc.) is supposed to have one true identity, which in the free agent is liberated or realized. The true self is defined as that which wills the one way of life, or pattern of self-development, appropriate to it. This in turn presupposes the notion of a single moral order which mandates that pattern. Positive liberty presupposes moral monism.

So far as modern systems of authoritarianism depend on positive conceptions of liberty, therefore, they depend at a deeper level on the moral monism that positive liberty implies. Positive liberty is no more than the tip of the authoritarian iceberg; the concealed base is usually moral monism.

> One belief, more than any other, is responsible for the slaughter of individuals on the altars of the great historical ideals – justice or progress or the happiness of future generations, or the sacred mission or emancipation of a nation or race or class, or even liberty itself, which demands the sacrifice of individuals for the freedom of society. This is the belief that somewhere, in the past or in the future, in divine revelation or in the mind of an individual thinker, in the pronouncements of history or science, or in the simple heart of an uncorrupted good man, there is a final solution. This ancient faith rests on the conviction that all the positive values in which men have believed must, in the end, be compatible, and perhaps even entail one another. (L, 212)

Moral monism is typically the ultimate premiss of the authoritarian outlook.

Moral monism and its opposite, pluralism, are not straightforward ideas, and I shall look more closely at them in subsequent chapters. For the present it is enough to make the following basic points. According to Berlin, the dominant Western view of morality has always been monistic (*CTH*, 7). Moral monism, at its broadest, is the idea that all ethical questions have a single correct answer, at least in principle, which can be read off from a single, universally valid moral law. If there is a single, universally valid moral law, providing correct answers to all ethical questions, then there is a single, universally valid conception of the good life or of human well-being, which gives effect to that law. This single conception of the good is uniquely superior to all alternatives. If there is a uniquely superior good life, then it is possible, again in principle, to arrive at a blueprint, 'a final solution', for the perfect political society, the society which realizes the single best way of life.

This vision of 'a final harmony in which all riddles are solved, all contradictions reconciled' has been the dream of authoritarian thinkers 'from Plato to the last disciples of Hegel or Marx' (*L*, 213). The utopianism encouraged by the monist faith suggests that in order to realize the goal of the perfect society, literally no sacrifice, whether of liberty or other values, can be too great. The monist goal, since it is overriding, justifies by definition its enforcement at any cost. This remains true even when the monist ideal is freedom itself. Here it is usually positive liberty that is being commended, because it is the positive idea that lends itself more easily to identification with the *true* self, hence the uniquely desirable form of life, and political utopia. Utopianism, authoritarianism and positive liberty are all significantly linked, and the key to the linkage is monism.

Moral monism, however, is false, Berlin argues. Human goods are deeply plural rather than unitary. 'The world that we encounter in ordinary experience is one in which we are faced with choices between ends equally ultimate, and claims equally absolute, the realisation of some of which must inevitably involve the sacrifice of others' (*L*, 213–14). Our experience of persistent and often intractable moral conflict should tell us that such conflicts arise because the basic goods of humanity – goods such as liberty, equality and justice – do not fit together in a single perfect harmony or hierarchy. Rather, many of these goods are 'in perpetual rivalry with one another', so that to realize one is often necessarily to diminish another (*L*, 216). Moreover, they are 'not all of them commensurable' (*L*, 216). That is, when they do conflict there is no common measure by which they can be weighed against each other. Rather, each is its own measure, an intrinsic good possessing its own distinctive weight and force. Liberty is liberty, equality is equality; no amount of one wholly compensates for the loss of the other. The practical consequence is that when such values collide we are faced with choices that are hard, perhaps agonizing and even tragic. Such choices will be hard in two senses: first, something of value will necessarily be sacrificed; secondly, there can be no single, neat, universal formula that will decide such questions for us. How we should best respond to these choices is a difficult question. For Berlin, there is no easy answer to 'the agony of choice' of this kind (*L*, 214). The best we can do, he suggests, is to be guided by 'the general pattern of life in which we believe' (*L*, 47). I shall return to this problem in chapters 6 and 7.

What, if anything, are the political implications of value pluralism? Berlin believes that pluralism invites us to eschew utopianism and authoritarianism in favour of moderation in general and liberalism in particular. If pluralism is true, then many different ways of ranking incommensurable goods, in particular cases or in general, may be equally reasonable: there is no uniquely correct formula when it comes to evaluating rival rankings of goods, or ways of life. The monist belief that there must be such a formula if only we could discover it is mistaken. Consequently the dreams of the utopians must be recognized as illusions, and dangerous illusions so far as they encourage political extremism. Moreover, given the unavoidability of choice among conflicting incommensurables, choice itself moves to centre-stage in the human condition, becoming a meta-value that must be accommodated. Implicit in these considerations is a case for liberalism as the political system that will maximally accommodate freedom of choice and reasonable disagreement among rival ways of life. I shall return to the details and merits of that case in chapter 6.

In this context the negative and positive ideals of liberty are surely examples of the distinct, potentially conflicting and incommensurable values that Berlin believes human beings live by. Liberty as a whole is a fundamental good that ought to be distinguished as incommensurable with other such goods, like equality. But liberty is also a complex good containing different components or aspects which are themselves incommensurable and may be incompatible with one another. The negative and positive ideas represent two key aspects of liberty – non-interference and autonomy – which stand in just such a pluralist relationship. In this light both the inversion and confusion theses serve to illustrate the deeper theme of value pluralism and the errors of monism. Monism encourages the confusion of distinct values by holding out the promise that they can all be embraced by a single seamless system. Consequently, monism abets liberty's inversion by allowing it to be identified with obedience to the demands of the true self or the nation's historical mission, and so forth.

Note that if negative and positive liberty are basic, although incommensurable, human goods, then we have a further reason to reject myth 3, the belief that Berlin simply dismisses positive liberty in favour of negative. In fact, he explicitly acknowledges positive liberty to be 'a valid universal goal' (L, 39). He is clear that some versions of positive liberty capture real and important aspects of human well-being not present in the negative idea, such as liberation from internal or psychological constraints, or liberation from alien political rule. Berlin urges us to be wary of ways in which the positive idea can be abused, even inverted, but not to reject the concept as incoherent or lacking value.

However, it is also true that for Berlin a liberal political order is associated with special attention to negative liberty. Positive liberty is a legitimate good from a pluralist point of view, but negative liberty should be accorded a more central role in the context of politics. 'Pluralism', Berlin concludes, 'with the measure of "negative" liberty it entails, seems to me a truer and more humane ideal than the goals of those who seek in the great disciplined, authoritarian structures the ideal of "positive" self-mastery by classes, or peoples, or the whole of mankind' (L, 216). The reasons for this emphasis have already been given. On the one hand, Berlin associates the positive idea with a tendency to utopianism and authoritarianism by way of the false and dangerous doctrine of moral monism. On the other hand, he links negative liberty with the clearing of a space for choice, a goal in keeping with pluralism. How far these associations can rightly be maintained is a further question, but I shall return to this in chapters 6 and 7.

To summarize the trajectory of Berlin's argument in 'Two Concepts', his initial distinction between negative non-interference and positive self-mastery yields political implications which can be traced through three progressively deepening levels of thought. First, Berlin applies the distinction specifically to the Cold War context: negative liberty is the guiding ideal of the liberal-democratic West, positive liberty that of the authoritarian Communist states. In the hands of the Communists and others, the positive idea has become twisted into the opposite of genuine liberty: the inversion thesis. Secondly, the inversion of positive liberty is an instance of a wider problem, that of allowing liberty, especially positive liberty, to be run together with other goods that ought to be kept distinct: the confusion thesis. This point suggests a critique not only of communism but also of post-colonial nationalism and other political positions. Finally, both inversion and confusion are cases of a deeper problem still, namely the denial of value pluralism, which is endemic in Western political thought as a whole. It is the tendency to moral monism that has opened the door to the totalitarian inversion of liberty in the modern age, and to the confusion of values more generally.

The critics

'Two Concepts' has generated an immense critical literature, and I can select only the most prominent lines of argument to discuss here.[14] These criticisms can be roughly aligned with the following theoretical or political perspectives: analytical philosophy, socialism, liberalism, republicanism, feminism and postmodernism. In evaluating these critiques, I shall pay special attention to the value-pluralist dimension of Berlin's argument. This often clarifies Berlin's purpose, and defuses some objections while enhancing others.

1. Is the negative–positive distinction invalid?

Some philosophers have questioned whether the negative–positive distinction drawn by Berlin, or any such distinction, is valid or useful. The best-known argument along these lines is that of Gerald MacCallum, Jr., who sees Berlin as claiming that there are just 'two fundamentally different kinds of freedom'.[15] In one passage he seems to attribute to Berlin the view that these two concepts are, respectively, 'freedom from' and 'freedom to'.[16] Rather, says MacCallum, freedom is always both from and to. There is just one valid concept of freedom, which always takes a 'triadic' form such that an *agent* is said to be free *from* some constraint *to* act or refrain from acting in some way. Disputes about the nature of freedom should be understood as disputes about the proper content of the three variables. This is a more fruitful model for understanding freedom than Berlin's, MacCallum thinks, because it enables us to account for many different views rather than forcing all views into just two camps.

To this Berlin could reply, first, that MacCallum is a victim or perpetuator of myth 1, the assumption that Berlin's distinction is intended to be exhaustive. It is MacCallum, not Berlin, who claims his analysis is exhaustive, and who might be accused of forcing all conceptions of freedom into a structure that does not apply in all cases.[17] Thus Berlin, in his later reply to MacCallum, argues briefly that freedom can be 'from' without being 'to': that we can seek release from constraints without conceiving of any particular goal which that release would make possible (*L*, 36 n. 1). But this may not be Berlin's best response. Among other things, it unnecessarily encourages another frequent misunderstanding of Berlin's analysis, namely that his negative–positive distinction can be understood simply as marking off 'freedom from' and 'freedom to'. Call this myth 4. Berlin does use the 'from/to' formulation in passing (*L*, 36 n. 1, 178), but it is clearly no more than a sketchy shorthand for the more complex distinction he has in mind between non-interference and self-mastery.

A more effective reply to MacCallum may be that Berlin's distinction is actually consistent with the triadic analysis. On this view the negative and positive ideas could be seen as two broad schools of opinion on how we should give content to MacCallum's three variables. Negative liberty could be understood as the absence of human interference with the purposes, whatever they may be, of the 'empirical' self; positive liberty as the mastering of obstacles preventing the realization of the 'true' or authentic self. Indeed MacCallum seems to allow this.[18] A problem with this reading is that Berlin suggests, in both the original essay and the later Introduction to *Four Essays on Liberty* (1969), that the subject of negative liberty could be either empirical or authentic (*L*, 37, 181). I think this should be treated as a mistake on Berlin's part, since it fits so badly with his central argument, the inversion thesis. Throughout most of 'Two Concepts' the notion of the dual self is presented as peculiar to positive liberty, as that which distinguishes it from negative liberty, and that which makes the positive idea susceptible to inversion in a way that negative liberty is not.

To say that the negative and positive ideas can be seen as rival accounts of the content of MacCallum's triad is to present them as alternative *conceptions* of liberty within a single overarching *concept*.[19] This is a controversial reading of Berlin, because some critics have followed MacCallum in supposing that Berlin insists on the negative and positive ideas as wholly distinct concepts with nothing in common.[20] Here is another point at which the pluralist dimension of Berlin's argument should be borne in mind. If we approach the concept/conceptions issue in isolation from Berlin's pluralism, his position is simply inconsistent, since the text contains clear evidence of both views (compare *L*, 204 and 212). But if we recall the pluralist background, we can see why Berlin seems to be insisting on two concepts: non-interference and self-mastery are incommensurable values. At the same time, we can see that the distinctness that Berlin wants to stress here need not exclude the notion of common ground between the two ideas (an overarching concept of liberty) altogether. Incommensurability can obtain not only between different goods (e.g. liberty and equality) but also within a single good, if it is a complex one like liberty, among its component parts or aspects.[21] That, I suggest, is the case here. Negative and positive liberty are forms or aspects of liberty, although forms which invoke incommensurable goods. What they have in common is not necessarily a single 'essence' but perhaps a looser 'family resemblance'.[22] This is a quite plausible way of reading Berlin consistently with MacCallum. If so, Berlin's negative–positive distinction holds.[23]

2. Is Berlin's definition of negative liberty too narrow?

The next issue concerns the boundaries and politics of the negative idea. Berlin is sometimes accused of taking an excessively narrow view of what counts as a constraint on negative liberty, and therefore of what it is to be free in the negative sense. In particular, some critics have complained that on Berlin's view a person's negative liberty can be obstructed only by the deliberate interference of other people. This seems to ignore two other potent constraints on freedom: first, obstacles internal to the person, including ignorance, fear and other psychological states; secondly, external obstacles not caused deliberately, such as poverty.

The first of these disputed areas has been prominently explored by Charles Taylor.[24] Taylor accuses Berlin of accepting an 'extreme' or 'crude' version of negative liberty as exclusively the absence of external obstacles (physical or legal) to an agent's potential actions. This crude view, held previously by Hobbes and Bentham, rejects more complex conceptions of liberty as self-realization, which involve the absence of internal, psychological constraints. In Berlin's case, negative liberty is confined to the absence of external constraints in order to foreclose the sort of argument, based on the possibility of internal divisions within the self, that leads to liberty's inversion. But the crude negative idea is indefensible, Taylor argues. If it were true, I would be less free in Britain, where ubiquitous traffic lights represent many external obstacles to my potential actions, than in Albania, where religious worship is prohibited but there are many fewer traffic lights. The truth is that my freedom is genuinely diminished by laws that prevent me from worshipping as I choose, but not by my having to obey traffic signals. Genuine freedom therefore involves not merely the absence of obstacles but the absence of obstacles to my 'significant' purposes, and these may as easily be internal as external to my personality.

Taylor's critique is less convincing than it may at first appear. First, it should be recalled that Berlin, unlike Hobbes and Bentham, does not reject the idea of freedom as involving liberation from internal constraints. He allows the notion of internal constraints as part of his conception of positive liberty. Also, since the negative and positive categories are not exhaustive, he leaves open the possibility of other conceptions of liberty that recognize internal constraints. Within the idea of negative liberty, though, it is true that Berlin seems to deny the possibility of internal constraints. Is this view not unduly narrow? Ignorance, illusion, fear, mental illness – all these can prevent us not only from acting authentically (positive liberty), but also, more simply, from doing what we might otherwise do (negative liberty). Why should Berlin not expand negative liberty to include relief from internal constraints?

The problem is that to do so he would need to invoke the idea of the true or authentic self, thereby collapsing negative liberty into positive and abandoning what is distinctive in the negative idea. Suppose that fear prevents me from sky-diving. Does my fear make me unfree? It does so only if my fear is properly seen as a *constraint*. But does my fear constrain my wish to sky-dive, or would it be truer to say that my sky-diving ambitions constrain my usual prudence? Which of these possibilities is true will depend on whether I can be identified more fully with the fearful or prudent part of my personality, or with the adventurous sky-diving part. In other words, to speak of freedom from constraints internal to the personality is inevitably to be involved in judgements of authenticity – that is, to enter the territory of positive liberty. Taylor's argument threatens, in effect, to interpret all freedom as positive freedom, the freedom of the authentic self. That would be a mistake, Berlin could rightly reply, since it would exclude the genuine sense of liberty captured by the negative idea, the notion of the freedom to do whatever we might want to do, whether it is authentic to us or not.

A similar point can be made against another aspect of Taylor's view. Even if we accept his claim that negative liberty should include the absence of internal constraints, it is a further question whether these (or external obstacles) must be thought of as constraints on 'significant' purposes. To think this is to write 'significance' into the definition of liberty: to be free is then to be unimpeded in pursuing only what is 'significant'; to be prevented from pursuing purposes deemed (by whom?) insignificant is no diminution of freedom at all. Berlin resists such moves, rightly. The freedom to pursue trivial or 'insignificant' purposes is still freedom. Genuine liberty must include the liberty to 'go to the good or the bad in one's own way', to 'commit blunders', even 'to do evil' (*POI*, 182; *L*, 91; *FIB*, 22). Such freedom may not be as valuable as other kinds in some or even most situations; there may often be good reason to trade it for some other value. But that does not disqualify it as freedom. Moreover, the freedom to act as one pleases, for good or ill, has its own value, which is incommensurate with that of the freedom to act significantly or authentically. The negative idea remains necessary to capture this dimension of freedom and its value, and Berlin is correct to insist on it.

A final question raised by Taylor's discussion is whether, and if so how, freedom can be *measured*. Taylor argues that the narrowness of Berlinian negative liberty prevents us from judging accurately whether we are more or less free under alternative political systems. On Berlin's negative view, where what matters is the absence of external constraints on whatever one might wish to do, we may be forced to the counter-intuitive conclusion that Britain is on the whole less free than Albania because many more potential actions are obstructed by British traffic lights than by Albanian proscription of religion. But Berlin's negative conception implies no such conclusion. 'The extent of my [negative] freedom' depends not only on 'how many possibilities are open to me' but also on other factors, including 'how important' those possibilities are, either in my own life plan or according to 'the general sentiment of society' (*L*, 177n.; see also 211). That is, Berlin can agree with Taylor that the extent of freedom is in part a matter of the importance of the freedom concerned, but disagree, for the reasons already given, that judgements of importance should be written into the definition of negative freedom itself. The incidence of negative liberty is one thing, the value or weight it should be accorded is another.[25]

A second set of issues concerning the boundaries of negative liberty has been raised by critics sympathetic to socialism. They have complained that since only deliberate acts of interference count as obstacles to negative liberty on Berlin's view, he thereby rules out poverty as an obstacle, and so rules out a conception of negative liberty as involving relief from poverty.[26] The objection connects with the formal–effective distinction introduced earlier. Berlin's narrow view of negative liberty, it is said, amounts to a merely formal freedom. This contrasts with those effective conceptions according to which liberty is a capacity to act on one's desires, a capacity made possible by the possession of any necessary resources. If freedom is merely negative or formal, then policies aiming at the relief of poverty cannot be justified in terms of freedom. Rather, freedom is strictly a matter of non-interfer-ence with people's lives, and this suggests a policy of minimal government intervention as advocated by *laissez-faire* or classical liberals such as Herbert Spencer, Hayek and Robert Nozick.[27] Such a view, it is said, rests on an artificially narrow understanding of freedom, since freedom can surely be diminished as effectively by poverty as by force or coercion.

On the question of whether poverty can obstruct liberty Berlin's comments are ambiguous, but in the light of the value-pluralist thesis his answer is probably, no. The ambiguity of Berlin's text is illustrated by his concession that poverty could count as a constraint on negative liberty if it were the result of deliberate human agency, coupled with his silence as to whether this is in fact the best understanding of poverty (*L*, 169–70). The pluralist thesis, however, suggests strongly that he intends to keep negative liberty separate from relief from poverty, since for Berlin pluralism supports the practice of maintaining distinctions among different goods in general, and between liberty and other goods in particular.

However, it is one thing to clarify Berlin's position, another to endorse it. If his view is that negative liberty excludes relief from poverty, then there is justice in the complaint that Berlin's position is arbitrarily narrow. He admits that those who argue for the inclusion of poverty among the constraints on negative liberty do so 'very plausibly' (*L*, 169). One such plausible argument is the case made by David Miller that negative liberty properly includes the absence of any constraint on a person for which other human beings can be held morally responsible.[28] Indeed, Berlin himself seems to go even further in one place, apparently admitting as legitimate obstacles to negative liberty constraints that are the unintended consequences of human 'arrangements' (*L*, 170). One can appreciate Berlin's motives in wanting to respect the deep plurality of goods and prevent the undue inflation of talk about liberty, but still conclude that he goes too far when he tries to draw a clear line between liberty and relief from poverty.

Even if Berlin has too narrow a conception of negative liberty, however, such a conception does not commit him to support for *laissez-faire*; nor does Berlin intend that it should. The belief among socialist writers that his view of freedom makes him an adherent of 'classical' or *laissez-faire* liberalism could be called myth 5. Berlin's concern for negative liberty does not imply *laissez-faire* for two reasons. First, supposing that the relief of poverty is not a species of liberty, it is still an important good, and one that justifies the sacrifice of some liberty (*L*, 172–3). This again is in keeping with Berlin's value pluralism: liberty is not the only good, and it does not always override others. An excessive exaltation of negative liberty is precisely what is wrong with the 'unrestrained capitalist competition' championed by *laissez-faire* (*L*, 38). Secondly, the possession of resources, if not identical with liberty itself, is surely among the most important 'conditions' for the exercise of liberty (*L*, 38). Berlin recognizes that sheer absence of interference may be of little value to people without the means to take advantage of it. Moreover, he is quite clear that *laissez-faire* is actually destructive of negative liberty itself, since unrestrained capitalist competition has led historically to 'brutal violations of . . . basic human rights', such as rights to free speech and association (*L*, 38).

Berlin's political point here is not at all that negative liberty implies *laissez-faire*. Rather, it is that if justice requires that we trade off some degree of liberty in exchange for increased security or capacity to act, then we should be clear that this is what we are doing, and not pretend that we are increasing freedom without cost. Berlin can perhaps be faulted for pedantry in insisting on too sharp a distinction between freedom and capacity, but not for lack of balance or compassion in failing to condemn 'the bloodstained story of economic individualism' (*L*, 38), nor for political blindness in failing to see a role for the state in tackling poverty. I shall say more about Berlin's commitment to economic redistribution in chapter 8.

3. Is Berlin too hostile to positive liberty?

More than Berlin's version of the negative–positive distinction itself, and more than his policing of the boundaries of negative liberty, the heart of his argument in 'Two Concepts' is his critique of the positive idea. Another widespread objection to Berlin's discussion is that this critique is misplaced or at least exaggerated. In its strongest form the objection is that Berlin mistakenly rejects positive liberty altogether, or that he holds the negative idea to be the only valid conception of liberty. These interpretations of Berlin's position I have already rejected under the heading of myth 3. It is true, however, that the overall effect of Berlin's discussion is to convey a wariness of positive liberty, a wariness that is not apparent in anything like the same degree with respect to its negative cousin. The implicit message seems to be that we had better avoid positive notions of liberty where possible, especially as a political ideal. The reason is that Berlin tends to associate positive liberty, unlike negative liberty, with authoritarianism, with the confusion of distinct ideas, and with moral monism. How far do these associations hold true? Could it be that Berlin, even if he does not dismiss positive liberty, still sells it short?

Many commentators, including many who share Berlin's liberal convictions, have pointed out that positive liberty is not always authoritarian in its implications, either historically or conceptually.[29] The classical anarchists of the nineteenth century, for example, usually uphold a positive ideal of liberty, yet combine this with a complete rejection of political authority.[30] Berlin himself concedes that some positive conceptions have taken distinctly individualist or liberal forms: the inner self-mastery of the Stoics, and the notions of rational and moral self-direction found in liberal thinkers including Locke, Kant, J. S. Mill and T. H. Green. Common to these non-authoritarian interpretations of the positive idea is an insistence that the final authority on the content of the authentic self is the individual person rather than any external authority or 'greater' self of which the individual is a part. Berlin's rejoinder is that this insistence is 'a counsel of perfection' (*L*, 199). It is too easy for the dictator to reply that his subjects are not yet fully rational and that he cannot wait for them to discipline themselves. Once we concede a gap between the actual will and the 'real' will, the door is open to the totalitarian temptation.

Berlin's view here is surely too narrow. Even though he does not dismiss all positive liberty, he tends to exaggerate the ease with which its more individualist versions can be collapsed into its more collectivist and authoritarian forms. Having conceded that the steps by which this occurs are 'not always . . . logically reputable' (*L*, 179), he ought to be more willing to allow that individualist readings of positive liberty are stable enough. The passage from Stoic self-mastery to Stalinist submission is in fact broken by several logical pot-holes. Berlin is inclined to minimize these obstacles by switching, when they appear, from conceptual argument to historical observation: for whatever reason, it is the positive rather than the negative conception that has 'in fact, and as matter of history' been more frequently abused (*L*, 181). But the sheer fact that an idea has been abused does not warrant its condemnation. The historical incidence of certain distorted forms of positive liberty does not justify Berlin's suspicion of positive liberty as such. Nor is the notion of the divided self sinister enough, on its own, to bear the weight of concern that Berlin places on it. The idea of the true or authentic personality does not always lead to political oppression; indeed, sometimes, as with the Stoics, it is a site of resistance. On the whole,

Berlin's position on positive liberty is too pessimistic, like someone who proposes the abolition of motor vehicles because they may be used for the wrong ends.

Moreover, Berlin sells positive liberty short from a specifically *liberal* point of view. He does not fully appreciate the importance to liberal thought of one species of positive liberty in particular, namely personal autonomy. Liberals disagree among themselves about which values are most fundamental to the liberal tradition, but it is at least arguable that the most important of all liberal goods is personal autonomy rather than negative liberty or toleration.[31] For many liberals, negative liberty, although indispensable, does not capture the whole of individual freedom. To be negatively free is to be unimpeded in acting on whatever desires one might happen to have. But those desires may well be the product of external influences, whether deliberate conditioning or routine socialization. In either case, it is important to see that for a person's life to be truly free, her actions must be 'her own' in a stronger sense than that allowed by negative liberty. She must be prepared to take a critical view of her own desires, acting only on those she truly owns. This is the ideal of personal autonomy. J. S. Mill, for example, sees freedom in its fullest sense as including the capacity of individuals to make their own plan of life, requiring not just the absence of interference but also critical reflection on the claims of custom.[32] Even if personal autonomy is not *the* fundamental liberal commitment, it is surely at the heart of much modern liberalism, and indeed of what makes liberalism attractive.[33]

Personal autonomy belongs to the positive rather than the negative family of freedoms, but it does not have authoritarian implications. It counts as a positive conception of liberty because it appeals to a notion of the authentic rather than merely 'empirical' self. The autonomous agent is prepared to question her own desires rather than act on them uncritically. But the notion of authenticity invoked here is not that of the 'true' self, the single pattern – that of a human essence or national mission – to which the person must conform in order to count as fully realized. Rather, liberal positive liberty or autonomy consists in an open-ended process of authentication consistent with the validity of many different life plans.[34] The autonomous person on this view is one who stands back from her beliefs, values and projects to subject them to critical scrutiny as worthy or unworthy of endorsement. The beliefs or values which she endorses at this level are those with which she is prepared to identify. On this account, authentic identity has no fixed content, but is created through a process of critical reflection and negotiation.

If liberal positive liberty is open-ended in this way, then it is not susceptible to the sort of inversion and confusion that concern Berlin, and it is not monistic. There will be no fixed conception of the true self for the dictator to hold up as a justification for coercion, only a process which is necessarily internal to the individual. Nor, for the same reason, will this kind of autonomy be easily confused with other goods, since it does not take the pursuit of any particular good as its goal. Liberal autonomy may be assisted by relief from poverty or by active political participation, but it is not necessarily to be identified with either of these. Finally, in the absence of any notion of the 'true' self, the link is broken between this species of positive liberty and moral monism. Liberal autonomy is consistent with Berlin's value pluralism because it assumes no uniquely valid conception of the good life – hence no single correct ranking of incommensurable values independently of the individual's own contextual judgement. Rather, the autonomous person on the liberal view is one who negotiates her authentic identity among many different, incommensurable options. Indeed, the existence of such options has been argued by Joseph Raz to be implied by the valuing of personal autonomy: if autonomy is valuable, then there must be 'an adequate range' of distinct options from which the autonomous agent can choose.[35] Further, it might be argued that a higher valuation of positive liberty as autonomy is not only consistent with Berlin's value pluralism but actually required by it. I shall develop this point in chapter 7.[36]

To sum up, Berlin is indeed too critical of positive liberty. He does not simply dismiss the idea, and he is right to draw attention to the authoritarian potential in certain versions of it, but he exaggerates the slipperiness of the slope that leads from the Stoics to Stalin. However, although this is a significant flaw in his account, it is understandable in the political context he was addressing. Also, it is not fatal to his general view. To say that Berlin ought to be more enthusiastic than he is about personal autonomy is not to take issue with his deepest commitments. Indeed, in chapter 7 I shall argue that a case for personal autonomy as central to liberalism follows from Berlin's deepest commitments, in particular his commitment to pluralism.

4. Does Berlin exclude or undervalue freedom as non-domination?

Another line of criticism comes from the 'republican' tradition of political thought, which emphasizes the centrality to human well-being of active participation in the public sphere in service of the common good. Against this background, two writers in particular, Quentin Skinner and Philip Pettit, have argued that Berlin's analysis of liberty unduly neglects a distinctively republican conception of freedom. On this conception, liberty is constrained not only, as on the negative view, by actual interference or coercion, but also by the potential for interference.[37] A slave remains a slave even when his master does not interfere with him. What makes him a slave is the fact that his master always has the power to interfere, even if that power is not exercised. We are unfree not only when others coerce us but also when we are dependent on others, living in their power, at their mercy. Consequently, to be free is not only to be uncoerced but to be free from the domination or power of others. I shall call this the idea of freedom as 'non-domination', following Pettit.[38] Pettit alleges that the effect of Berlin's focus on the negative–positive distinction is to 'conceal from view' or to 'foreclose' non-domination as a legitimate third option.[39] Skinner's complaint is harder to pin down. In his earlier work he accused Berlin of uncritically accepting a modern orthodoxy to the effect that negative non-interference is the only valid conception of liberty, thereby ruling out by definition the older republican or 'neo-roman' tradition.[40] More recently, Skinner qualifies this criticism somewhat. He now credits Berlin with being aware of the republican tradition, but still sees him as insisting that 'the essence of liberty' is non-interference, and thus as contributing to a modern tendency that has 'contrived to ignore' freedom as non-domination.[41]

Non-domination should be acknowledged as an important dimension of freedom, but the republican attack on Berlin is misdirected. Pettit's claim that Berlin's focus on negative and positive liberty 'forecloses' other possibilities is, once again, evidence of the persistence of myth 1. Berlin does not rule out the possibility of freedom as non-domination. Skinner's earlier position, and to some extent his current view, seem to rely on myth 3, contrary to which Berlin does not claim that the only legitimate conception of liberty is the negative one. Berlin describes the negative idea as the 'ordinary' meaning of liberty and tells us to be wary of the positive

notion. But it should be clear by now that he sees the positive conception as a genuine expression of liberty, albeit susceptible to
abuse. Thus he does not insist that interference or force or coercion
are the only constraints on freedom.

Indeed, Berlin could consistently acknowledge the validity of
freedom as non-domination. He actually comes close to doing so
when he writes that negative liberty involves not just the absence
of coercion but '*security* from coercion' (*L*, 201; my emphasis), and
that 'the extent of my social or political freedom consists in the
absence of obstacles not merely to my actual, but to my potential,
choices' (*L*, 32). According to Skinner, Berlin denies that dependence
can be a constraint on liberty when he 'confidently' separates liberty
from 'status' or 'recognition'.[42] But status and recognition in Berlin's
sense are not the same as non-dependence in the republican sense.
A person or group could be respected and recognized as possessing the capacity for self-government, yet still be in the *de facto*
power of other persons or groups. This is Berlin's point when he
says that decolonization does not always wholly liberate. And even
if non-domination were equivalent to recognition, Berlin does not
'confidently' distinguish recognition from liberty. On the contrary,
he allows that recognition overlaps both negative and positive
senses of liberty, so as to constitute 'a hybrid form of freedom' (*L*,
205, 206), as I noted earlier in connection with the confusion thesis.

The upshot is that these lines of republican attack on Berlin fail,
but also, more positively, that there is plenty of room in Berlin's
position to acknowledge republican non-domination as a legitimate
dimension of freedom. This can be done either by extending negative liberty to include the absence of dependence, or by interpreting the positive idea to embrace non-domination as an aspect of
authentic self-direction, or by conceiving of non-domination as a
different kind of freedom altogether. Berlin's view leaves all these
options open.

Pettit goes further, however, alleging that non-domination is not
only valid but superior to negative liberty as a political ideal. The
principal advantage of non-domination is that it brings a greater
degree of certainty or security.[43] The person who is free only in
the negative sense always stands in danger of interference from
more powerful people, but those who possess freedom as non-
domination are by definition relieved of that possibility.

Various lines of reply are possible. First, Berlin might remind the
republicans that although non-domination is valuable, so too is
negative liberty. Or, to put it another way, although dependence is

a threat to freedom, so too are force and coercion.[44] The emancipated slave is no longer in the legal power of his master, but may still be assaulted by the lynch mob. Whether we can say that either of these concerns is more important than the other, all things considered, is doubtful. Sometimes coercion is more of a problem, sometimes dependence. Negative non-interference is sometimes more pressing, whereas non-domination is more urgent at other times. This view is reinforced by Berlin's value pluralism. If non-interference and non-domination are distinct values, then they may properly be regarded as incommensurable. In that case they cannot be subjected to any absolute ranking, at least in the abstract. Later (in chapter 6) I shall argue that particular circumstances may generate reasons to rank one incommensurable good above the other, but even then different circumstances will justify different rankings. Before we can judge that non-domination always or generally trumps non-interference, we shall have to review a substantial range of cases. In the absence of such a case-by-case review, the most we can safely say is that if value pluralism is true, then in some circumstances non-domination will outrank non-interference, whereas in other cases the reverse will be true.

I conclude that Pettit's insistence on the superiority of freedom as non-domination over negative liberty is at least not proved. On the whole, the republican case for non-domination need not be presented as a criticism of Berlin, since he could agree with the essentials of that case. He could accept that non-domination captures a valid and important aspect of freedom, and that freedom from dependence is in general no less valuable than freedom from coercion. He does not hold up negative liberty as an absolute or overriding ideal; it is at most the safer political option in comparison with positive liberty. He acknowledges that there are many cases where rival values and principles will justify the sacrifice or restriction of negative liberty. There is nothing in Berlin to say that such countervailing values could not include non-domination, whether conceived as a species of freedom or as a good independent of freedom. That is, there is nothing to prevent Berlin from accepting that non-domination outranks or qualifies negative liberty across some substantial range of cases. He would only add, rightly, that (1) non-domination does not always outrank non-interference; (2) when it does, we should be clear about the precise terms of the trade-off involved; and (3) there must always be at least some minimal area of non-interference, some impassable 'frontiers of freedom', if a society is to count as 'free' (*L*, 171, 173, 209–11). These requirements need not, and probably would not, be disputed by the republicans.[45]

5. Are Berlin's conceptions of liberty biased against women and other groups?

A further line of criticism stems from feminist and poststructuralist or postmodernist perspectives. Feminists have found in Berlin's analysis material for both agreement and dispute. Some have been happy to appeal to either negative or positive liberty, or both, as worthy ideals.[46] Liberal feminists, for example, have sought the expansion of negative liberties when they have called for the liberation of women from discriminatory legal and social constraints. Radical feminists have sometimes argued for the strengthening of women's positive liberty by promoting what they see as the claims of an authentically female identity hitherto marginalized by patriarchy. Another view is that positive liberty is preferable to negative from a feminist perspective, because positive liberty identifies the self with community, thereby connecting with a distinctively female ethic of 'care' based on values of relationship-maintenance, community and negotiation.[47]

A more hostile feminist response is that both negative and positive conceptions of liberty ought to be rejected, because both contain an inherently masculine bias. Diana Coole, for example, offers two main reasons for this. First, to emphasize negative non-interference is to promote the standard liberal commitment to a private realm of society in which public intervention is forbidden or discouraged. Yet it is this private realm, including the family and perhaps civil society more broadly, that has been a traditional site of women's oppression.[48] To this Berlin could reply that any free society must maintain *some* boundary between public and private, in that any such society must place some limits on what the state may legitimately do to people. The absence of any such limits is precisely the definition of totalitarianism. Consistently with constitutional restraints, a state may justly intervene in civil society and the family where necessary in order to secure the well-being of any person. The pluralist outlook is again relevant here to remind us that negative liberty is not the only good. But in any case, negative liberty requires non-interference with individuals, not non-interference with families or civil society. State intervention in these areas may be justified, obviously enough, in the name of negative liberty, in order to secure individuals, including women, from coercion and other relevant forms of constraint (including poverty, as I have argued).

The second reason Coole offers for regarding Berlin's negative and positive conceptions of liberty as inherently gender-biased draws on the claims of poststructuralists and postmodernists. The argument is that the negative and positive ideas presuppose particular views of the self or subject of freedom that are essentially oppressive to women and others because they privilege certain (male, white) values or conceptions of the good, these in turn reinforcing the traditional exclusion and down-valuing of vulnerable social groups such as women. In particular, Berlin's negative liberty depends upon 'a rather specific, liberal, Enlightenment view of the self' as actually or potentially rational.[49] Positive liberty, despite its contrasts with negative liberty, shares with it the ideal of the rational self as the proper subject of liberty, in this case asserting itself against not only external constraints but also internal, psychological obstacles such as the passions.[50] Both conceptions of liberty thereby celebrate reason and exclude or downgrade those aspects of the human self associated with the non-rational: 'its passions, emotions, body and dreams; its madness, instincts, emotions and fantasies'.[51] Along with these various shadows of reason, this outlook excludes and disvalues those groups traditionally associated with them: the mad, the sexually 'deviant' and women. The negative and positive conceptions of liberty, far from pointing the way to human liberation, are complicit in our continuing unfreedom.

This objection reads into Berlin a series of assumptions that are not only absent from his view but actually antithetical to it. Berlin's idea of negative liberty does not presuppose a 'rational' but rather an 'empirical' self, defined by a contingent set of beliefs, values and desires, any of which may be non-rational. It is precisely the identification of freedom with rationality (and virtue) that Berlin finds objectionable in some of those versions of positive liberty to which he is most clearly opposed. The idea of freedom, he believes, must leave room for our acting in ways that are not rational or even desirable (*POI*, 182; *L*, 91; *FIB*, 22) – although how such freedoms should be evaluated in particular cases is another matter. The same basic point applies to positive liberty. The idea of rational self-mastery is only one version of the broad positive category, which includes the kind of open-ended autonomy I discussed earlier in connection with the liberal critique.

Once more, these points are reinforced by the value-pluralist dimension of Berlin's thought, which stresses the multiplicity and incommensurability of the options facing both the person choosing in a space of negative liberty and the person seeking to be autonomous. In neither case does 'reason' or 'morality' in the abstract point to a single *telos* at which the free person must aim. Berlin's pluralism does imply certain limits to the legitimate range of options, limits defined by a common 'human horizon' and by a 'central core' of goods acknowledged to be universal, as I shall show in chapter 6. But those universal limits and goods are very broadly defined. In general, the idea of value pluralism ought to be attractive to many of those who have been drawn to postmodernism. Berlin himself exhibits certain tendencies that postmodernists may find sympathetic: notably his intense suspicion of the scientistic strain within the Enlightenment, and his notion of the incommensurability of goods and the distinctness of cultures and historical epochs. Value pluralism, in short, may satisfy much of the postmodernists' sense of the legitimate multiplicity of moral experience, but without the extreme relativism that logically cuts the ground from beneath any postmodernist attempt to argue for a coherent political programme.[52]

6. Is Berlin's analysis outdated?

A final objection is that Berlin's treatment of freedom is now largely irrelevant, because it was directed against a totalitarian threat that has now receded.[53] This objection has an air of futility about it, since Berlin's essay manifestly continues to fascinate many readers, including some quite hostile to its conclusions. The distinction between negative and positive liberty is still applied to topics as varied as free speech and pornography, Northern Ireland and Africa.[54] As for the critique of positive liberty, the objection betrays both an unwarranted complacency about our current political environment and a one-dimensional understanding of Berlin's multi-dimensional text.

Recall the three levels of Berlin's argument. First, the inversion thesis continues to resonate. As contemporary international terrorism has made all too clear, the idea that liberation can be sought through total identification with an ideal which is greater than the individual, and which is believed to be legitimately enforceable by massive use of violence, is alive and flourishing in our world.

However, it is the second and third levels of 'Two Concepts' that are, perhaps, the most important for us now, namely the confusion thesis and the related theme of value pluralism. Berlin's separation of the two freedoms, and of freedom under any definition from other goods, is a master-class on the subject of the radical plurality of values and the political implications of that plurality. The first step in appreciating the incommensurability of human goods is to see them as fully distinct. Once that is achieved, we can begin to see the true nature of the hard choices that politics generates, the consequent need for trade-offs and compromises, and the shallowness of those views which deny the reality of uncompensated moral and political loss, whether the wishful utopianism of those on the left for whom all good causes coalesce, or the narrow cost–benefit analysis favoured by some on the right. This remains an invaluable lesson for the politics of the twenty-first century.

Summary

In 'Two Concepts of Liberty', Berlin presents a classic formulation of the distinction between negative and positive liberty, and proceeds to a subtle, multi-layered critique of the positive idea. All things considered, his argument has stood up remarkably well to the waves of criticism to which it has been subjected, especially when reconsidered in the light of his value pluralism. Some of that criticism, it is true, reveals real shortcomings in Berlin's position. These include his excessively narrow definition of negative liberty, with its apparent exclusion of poverty as a genuine restraint on freedom, and his undervaluing, from a liberal perspective, of positive liberty conceived as personal autonomy. Many other objections, however, have been less well founded. Among these are some that, through their persistent misreading of the text, deserve the status of myths: (1) the assumption that the negative and positive categories are intended to be exhaustive of the idea of liberty; (2) the claim that Berlin confuses positive liberty as autonomy with effective freedom and with political participation; (3) the allegation that Berlin's critique of positive liberty amounts to outright rejection and that he thinks negative liberty is the only legitimate conception; (4) the belief that his negative–positive distinction is merely between freedom 'from' and 'to'; (5) the assertion that Berlin's endorsement of negative liberty implies a case for *laissez-faire*. Further critical arguments, although not based on myths concerning the text, are also mistaken. These include the rejection of the negative–positive distinction by MacCallum; Taylor's argument that negative liberty must acknowledge internal as well as external constraints and must be directed only to 'significant' ends; the republican claim that Berlin rules out freedom as non-domination, and Pettit's further argument that non-domination is not only distinct from negative liberty but superior to it; the feminist and postmodernist arguments that both negative and positive conceptions involve exclusive and oppressive notions of the subject. All these objections fail.

Moreover, the positive achievement of 'Two Concepts' is immense. To interpret the essay merely as an exercise in Cold War rhetoric, or even as an important contribution to the analysis of freedom, is to underestimate its depth, force and subtlety. Most fundamentally, 'Two Concepts' is an exploration of the power, the irony and the historicity of ideas. The power of ideas is implicit in the way Berlin sets out the problem: the two rival conceptions of liberty influence the fate of millions. The dark irony of much human thought is exemplified by the way the positive idea of liberty, which began as a genuine and important expression of human freedom, is gradually subverted to become a tool of authoritarian politics. Finally, 'Two Concepts' demonstrates the centrality of the historical dimension in any proper understanding of ideas. The corruption of positive liberty can be grasped only by tracing the stages of its development in distant and sometimes obscure recesses of moral and political thought. Ultimately, Berlin believes, the roots of modern authoritarianism lie very deep indeed, in the monist foundations of mainstream Western thought as a whole.

5

The Enlightenment and its Critics

Berlin's account of the modern betrayal of freedom, traced in the previous two chapters, is only the first layer of his archaeology of twentieth-century totalitarianism. In 'Two Concepts of Liberty' he suggests that the foundations of modern tyranny lie in still lower strata of European thought, ultimately in the moral monism that he believes is central to the Western philosophical tradition. To this he opposes his value pluralism. Before exploring Berlin's pluralism, however, I should first consider an intermediate level of Berlin's excavation, namely the role of the Enlightenment and its opponents, the Counter-Enlightenment and romanticism. This theme became central to his work in the 1960s and 1970s, and is important for two reasons. First, it provides a further illustration of Berlin's characteristic method in the history of ideas, the practice of imaginative empathy – indeed, not only an illustration but also a theoretical defence. Secondly, and more importantly, it deepens and illuminates the links between Berlin's analysis of authoritarianism and freedom, on one side, and his understanding of value pluralism and monism, on the other.

Berlin's attitude to the Enlightenment and its opponents is complex. Although committed to the moral and political ideals of the French *philosophes*, he is hostile to what he sees as their characteristic scientism, which he links with Marx and ultimately with Soviet totalitarianism. The Counter-Enlightenment and romanticism, on the other hand, lead to another kind of totalitarianism, namely fascism, through the rejection by thinkers like Maistre and Hamann of the ideals of reason and humanism. Yet Berlin also sees their antiscientistic approach as a weapon against the dangerous utopian strain in the Enlightenment. Moreover, he believes that other important figures of the Counter-Enlightenment, Vico and Herder, anticipate his key notion of value pluralism. But there is a further twist. By developing his value pluralism through the historical and cultural particularism of Vico and Herder, Berlin also invites the question of whether pluralism can be distinguished from a relativist view. If this distinction cannot be maintained, then Berlin's pluralism threatens to undermine his liberal commitment to the universal ideals of the Enlightenment. I argue that Berlin does succeed in separating pluralism from relativism, but the larger issue of the relation between pluralism and liberalism remains open and will be pursued in chapter 6.

My discussion proceeds as follows. I begin by sketching the general shape of Berlin's contrast between the Enlightenment and certain of its leading critics: Vico, Hamann and Herder. Next I come to the account Berlin gives of the romantic successors to the Counter-Enlightenment, and of their principal political legacy, nationalism. In the final section I look again at Berlin's treatment of Vico and Herder, focusing on his claim that they anticipated his idea of pluralism, and on the issue of whether pluralism can be distinguished from relativism.

Enlightenment and Counter-Enlightenment

Berlin regards the interplay between the eighteenth-century Enlightenment and the subsequent reaction against it as the key historical passage in the making of the contemporary world.

> It appears to me that a radical shift of values occurred in the latter half of the eighteenth century – before what is properly called the romantic movement – which has affected thought, feeling and action in the Western world. This shift is most vividly expressed in what seems to be most characteristically romantic in the romantics ... I hope to show that this revolution is the deepest and most lasting of all changes in the life of the West, no less far-reaching than the three great revolutions whose impact is not questioned – the industrial in England, the political in France, and the social and economic in Russia – with which, indeed, the movement with which I am concerned is connected at every level. (*RR*, pp. xii–xiii)

This revolution of values began with what Berlin calls 'the Counter-Enlightenment', both the bridge and the point of disruption between the Enlightenment and romanticism.

Berlin recognizes that there are 'many divisions' within the Enlightenment, but he emphasizes what he sees as a mainstream view within the dominant school of the French *philosophes* and their followers in the German *Aufklärung* (*TCE*, 276–7; *RR*, 24–5). This he describes as resting on three 'pillars' (*TCE*, 278). First, there is a massive faith in the powers of human reason. Whether on the mathematical model of Galileo and Descartes or the mechanical model of Newton, the heroes of the scientific revolution of the seventeenth and early eighteenth centuries showed how far it was possible to advance in the quest to understand the workings of the natural world. Secondly, there is the belief that this new understanding is possible because the natural world possesses an underlying structure which is itself rational in the sense that it can be understood by human beings. Moreover, this general principle must apply to the human world: human nature is part of the structure of nature in general, and similarly exhibits regularities that are universal and permanent. The universality of human nature in turn implies a set of universal human ends or purposes or goals. What exactly these are is disputed – candidates include happiness, pleasure, liberty – but all supporters of the Enlightenment agree that there is some such set of universal values.

The third pillar of the French Enlightenment is for Berlin the most significant of all: scientism. The same modern scientific methods that have laid bare the hidden patterns of the natural world must produce the same results in the social world. From a secure basis either in self-evident axioms or in empirical observation, we can formulate, by way of logical deduction or induction respectively, the laws of nature. Surely the same procedure can identify the laws of human nature. Once we have a properly scientific understanding of how human beings function, individually and collectively, we can use that knowledge to change human life for the better. We can then shape our institutions in accordance with what human beings truly want and need, in contrast with current standards, which express only ignorance, superstition and the self-interest of political and religious elites. This is what makes the supporters of the Enlightenment 'the party of progress and civilisation' (*TCE*, 277). Indeed, some of these thinkers, like Condorcet, look forward not merely to progress and improvement but to the perfectibility of human nature and society.

One might have expected Berlin, as a liberal, to be fully aligned with the Enlightenment and to reject the Counter-Enlightenment whole-heartedly. But this is not so. It is true that, as he says, 'fundamentally I am a liberal rationalist. The values of the Enlightenment, what people like Voltaire, Helvétius, Holbach, Condorcet, preached, are deeply sympathetic to me' (*Conv.*, 70). Berlin applauds and identifies with their dedication to reason and individual liberty, and their opposition to cruelty, ignorance, obscurantism and oppression. Conversely, his condemnation of those thinkers, like Maistre, who are violently opposed to Enlightenment ideals is no less clear, despite his capacity to illuminate their ideas as if they were his own. In addition, Berlin links some of the authoritarian forms of positive liberty, like that of Fichte, with notions of the true self as will rather than reason, and with the will not of the individual but of collective entities like the nation or state. These notions are typical of the anti-Enlightenment mind, and Berlin draws attention to the dangers in them.

However, Berlin is also critical of certain tendencies in the Enlightenment, and deeply sympathetic to some of the responses of its critics. In key respects the heroes of the Enlightenment 'are dogmatic and too simplistic' (*Conv.*, 70). In particular, Berlin takes aim at Enlightenment scientism. Berlin's opposition to scientism has its origins in his rejection of logical positivism and in his book on Marx, but it is his work on the Enlightenment and its critics that enables him to develop his critique in detail. While he accepts the authority of modern science in explaining the natural world, when it comes to the human world he insists that the methods of the natural sciences have serious limitations. They can describe the outward behaviour of human beings, but they cannot account for the inner purposes which make that behaviour human; for that we need the 'inside view' of the historical and cultural imagination. Further, scientism is not merely misguided but potentially authoritarian. If in morality, as in physics, there is a single mutually consistent set of rules that can be known and demonstrated by experts – the dream of Saint-Simon, for example – then expertise has a just title to political authority at the expense of democracy and liberty. Again there is a link with authoritarian positive liberty. Even if my true self is the rational self, scientism implies that people other than me, experts and leaders advised by experts, may know better than I do what my rational self requires. Thus the Enlightenment, despite its mission of liberation, is also a source of totalitarianism: the ideal of the unrestrained rule of scientists culminates in Soviet communism.

Hence Berlin's obvious fascination with those early critics of the mainstream Enlightenment whom he groups under the collective title of the 'Counter-Enlightenment'. He mentions many thinkers under this heading, but spends most time on four in particular. I have already discussed Berlin's treatment of one of these. Joseph de Maistre's visceral rejection of human reason as an adequate guide, his belief in the natural vice and aggression of human beings, and his insistence on the consequent need for absolute and unquestioned political and religious authority backed by mystery and force – all these qualify him, in Berlin's account, as one of the most profound enemies of the Enlightenment and liberty. But in addition to Maistre, three other writers are central to Berlin's notion of the Counter-Enlightenment: Vico, Hamann and Herder. His main work on these thinkers is now collected in *Three Critics of the Enlightenment* (2000).

Giambattista Vico is described by Berlin as 'born before his time', destined in his own day and afterwards to be 'widely misrepresented and misinterpreted', yet also 'a man of original genius' (*TCE*, 21). Initially a follower of the scientistic 'new philosophy' of Descartes, Vico became a ground-breaking critic of the Enlightenment faith in natural science. Two aspects of this are Vico's particular targets. The first is the scientistic ideal of objectivity in observation and measurement as a model for all fields of knowledge. In *The New Science* (1725), Vico draws a distinction between two different kinds of knowledge, 'external' and 'internal'. The kind of knowledge made possible by the natural sciences is valuable, but also limited in the sense that it can only describe and explain phenomena 'from the outside'. As Berlin puts it, 'we observe, we learn facts about, but we cannot understand, stones or the death-watch beetle' (*TCE*, 48). When it comes to human behaviour, however, a different, 'internal' kind of knowledge is possible, indeed essential, because human conduct is not merely mechanical or instinctual but purposive. We can and must understand our own purposes, and by extension those of other people, in a way in which we cannot understand stones or beetles. For Vico, human actions are what they are because they express the actors' view of the world. Therefore, human behaviour cannot be adequately understood by external observation alone, recording the movement of bodies in space; rather, it involves 'entering into' the purposes which the behaviour is intended to serve. 'The way to understand such men and their worlds is by trying to enter their minds, by finding out what they are at, by learning the rules and significance of their methods of expression – their myths, their songs, their dances, the form and idioms of their language, their marriage and funerary rites' (*TCE*, 11).

How is this possible? Vico's answer is that human beings possess a capacity for 'imaginative reconstruction' (*fantasia*), the ability to place oneself, in imagination, in someone else's shoes (*TCE*, 49). He concedes that in the case of people remote from us in time or place this is difficult and requires 'great effort', but he insists that the effort is practicable, subject to realistic limitations, none the less. Even in such remote cases we have, through our common humanity, a capacity for 'conceiving the *modificazioni* of the human mind, for knowing what human beings could, and what they could not, have done or thought' (*TCE*, 50). Indeed, compared with the knowledge produced by the natural sciences, that of the 'humane studies' is not merely equally valuable in its own distinct way, but for Vico positively superior. As Berlin writes, 'because I, or other men, are not mere passive spectators but actors, and understand, "enter into", the purposes, states of mind or will, of which actions are the expression, such knowledge . . . is more "transparent" . . . than mere contemplation of the successions and compresences of things in nature can ever be' (*TCE*, 48). Descartes' natural-scientific model of knowledge is neither the only nor the most secure form that knowledge may take.

The second feature of Enlightenment scientism attacked by Vico is its static, ahistorical approach. The *philosophes*, like mathematicians and physicists, search for universal and unchanging principles in human conduct and values: a natural law, based on a universal and eternal human nature. Vico rejects the notion of a permanent and universal human nature and natural law (*TCE*, 54, 59, 106–9). The human world is not static or fixed or ready-made, but the product, at every moment, of an unceasing process of change and development, crucially including change and development of people's inner purposes and values. Corresponding to these changes, societies pass through successive historical phases, each of which is marked by its own cultural style, with its own legal, political, ethical and aesthetic standards. Human beings think and act differently from one historical stage to the next. To understand human affairs is consequently to understand how they have developed in the way they have, that is, to seek a 'genetic' or historical explanation (*TCE*, 55). History, far from being a collection of entertaining but inconsequential tales, as the Cartesians had claimed, becomes on this view 'the queen of all the studies' (*TCE*, 47). Vico thus anticipates the historicist approach to the humanities that will later bloom in the work of Hegel and Marx.[1]

Vico is chronologically the first of Berlin's Counter-Enlightenment figures, but his work was little known outside his native Naples and exerted little direct influence on the thinkers to follow (*TCE*, 112–18, 170). In the writing of Johann Georg Hamann the Counter-Enlightenment makes a new beginning. Hamann's background is that of East Prussian pietism, a Protestant sect distinguished by its introspective, emotional approach to God and its emphasis on sincerity of faith. In Hamann's time this attitude to life seems increasingly out of tune with the Enlightenment-based social and political reforms of Frederick the Great with his legion of French advisers. In this respect, Berlin writes, Hamann voices 'the cry from the heart of human beings pushed against the wall by Frederick's great new broom' (*TCE*, 350).

Hamann is, for Berlin, 'the first out-and-out opponent of the French Enlightenment' (*TCE*, 254). While Vico had pointed to the limitations and flat-footedness of scientism, Hamann condemns every aspect of the Enlightenment, describing it as 'an insult to the forces of life and nature', 'a blasphemy against the nature of man and his creator', 'an inversion of natural values' (*TCE*, 271, 272–3, 290). The pretensions of the *philosophes* to objective and comprehensive knowledge are impertinent, destructive and pathetic: impertinent because they amount to a usurpation of the place of the Deity; destructive because their abstract laws rob God's world of its irreducible variety, colour and mystery; pathetic because such systems in any case provide no real knowledge. Truth, for human beings, is intensely particular, accessible through concrete experience alone (*TCE*, 283). Like Vico, Hamann emphasizes that real understanding requires the inside view. Genuine knowledge is possible only by way of 'intuitive understanding' rather than calculation and demonstration (*AC*, 7; *TCE*, 295, 299). If anything, Hamann goes further than Vico, applying the inside view not only to human conduct but to nature itself. For Hamann, there are purposes in nature too, the purposes of God. The world is a message from God to humanity, but there are better and worse ways of reading the message. The philosophers of the Enlightenment employ methods that are bound to fail, since they address only the outer surface of things, not their inner meaning. For Hamann, not only the Bible but also 'stones and rocks speak the Lord', but we must be prepared to listen (*TCE*, 253).

Particularism of another kind is the central theme of the last of Berlin's Counter-Enlightenment masters, Hamann's disciple Johann Gottfried Herder. Like Vico and Hamann, Herder rejects what he sees as the scientism and heavy-handed moral universalism of the Enlightenment, and celebrates the variety of human experience. Above all, Herder stresses the fact and desirability of *cultural* variety. Each human culture possesses a unique identity, a 'collective individuality' which expresses the distinctive experience and outlook of its people (*TCE*, 225, 238). Indeed, according to Berlin, Herder sees human cultures as not merely different from one another but radically so: they are 'incommensurable', so different that there is no common standard by which they can be critically compared (*TCE*, 176, 206, 213–18, 233–9). ' "Every nation has its own inner centre of happiness, as every sphere its own centre of gravity" ' (Herder, cited at *TCE*, 211; *RR*, 63). Hence each culture possesses its own validity, its own norms of judgement. 'Each collective individuality is unique', writes Berlin,

> and has its own aims and standards, which will themselves inevitably be superseded by other goals and values – ethical, social and aesthetic. Each of these systems is objectively valid in its own day, in the course of 'Nature's long year' which brings all things to pass. All cultures are equal in the sight of God, each in its time and place. (*TCE*, 238)

For Herder, on Berlin's account, all cultures are equally valid, and none may be judged appropriately except on its own terms. To understand a culture, once again, is to take the inside view, to ' "feel oneself into everything" ' (*sich hineinfühlen*, or, in Berlin's usage, *Einfühlen* or *Einfühlung*: *TCE*, 211, 197, 236). Only those who have themselves experienced the storms of the North Sea, or who can at least transport themselves there in imagination, can truly understand the songs of the Viking skalds (*TCE*, 195–6, 236; *AC*, 11).

It follows that Herder rejects the Enlightenment tendency to grade whole cultures against one another and to award past civilizations positions on a ladder of progress which reaches up to the present day. Rather, each society has its own unique merits. The Middle Ages, condemned by Voltaire for its ' "abominations, errors and absurdities" ' . . . also possess "something solid, cohesive, noble and majestic" which our age, with its "enervated coldness . . . and human misery", can scarcely understand' (*TCE*, 216). For Herder there is no linear progress from one civilization to the next, only the incommensurable outlooks of distinct civilizations, each with its own indefeasible set of beliefs and values. It is this view in particular that Berlin singles out as anticipating his own value pluralism. It is easy to see how such a move raises the problem of relativism, but I shall return to that issue later.

To summarize the main themes of the Counter-Enlightenment according to Berlin, these emerge principally in reaction to Enlightenment scientism. Against that view, Vico, Hamann and Herder are united by two main tendencies. First, in contrast with the ideal of scientific, God's-eye *objectivity* in human affairs, the three thinkers all stress the value and necessity of the inside view, the need to place ourselves imaginatively in the shoes of those individuals and societies we are trying to understand. This method is, of course, Berlin's own. Secondly, Vico, Hamann and Herder are united in their hostility to the *universality* of scientism, and consequently in their embracing of various dimensions of particularism. The inside view shows that human purposes and values vary in many significant ways. The most radical account of this variation of concrete experience is given by Hamann, for whom any generalization at all is suspect. Berlin rightly observes that a particularism so extreme becomes absurd, since 'without some generalisation there can be no symbols, no words, no thought' (*TCE*, 352). He is happier with the more moderate senses of particularity developed by Vico and Herder, who emphasize historical and cultural discontinuity respectively.

Berlin's interpretations of the Enlightenment and its critics have not gone unchallenged. A frequent complaint has been that his account of the universalist and scientistic thrust of 'the Enlightenment' is too monolithic, since it fails to acknowledge the interest taken by many Enlightenment thinkers in the role of the emotions and in human diversity.[2] Similarly, the notion of a unitary 'Counter-Enlightenment' has been criticized for not distinguishing between mere 'critics' and outright 'enemies' of the Enlightenment, the former accepting the basic framework of rational inquiry, the latter rejecting it.[3] Again, Berlin's fellow liberals have sometimes wondered whether his empathetic treatments of the Counter-Enlightenment figures have not been too friendly, bending over backwards to be tolerant when the more appropriate response would be stout resistance.[4]

While some of the critics may score hits on Berlin concerning points of detail, the general shape of his view remains plausible and engaging. An important point to bear in mind is that he typically presents himself not as offering a comprehensive account of a thinker or a period, but rather as selecting particular lines of thought among others because of their significance for our current beliefs and situation. Introducing his work on Vico and Herder, for example, he writes that 'these studies are not intended as an exami-nation of the entire oeuvre of either Vico or Herder: only of those among their theses which seemed to me the most arresting, impor-tant and suggestive' (*TCE*, 6). He is well aware that the Enlighten-ment contains 'many divisions' (*TCE*, 276), but focuses on the scientistic stream within the Enlightenment as especially significant. Similarly, his emphasis on those features that are common to the Counter-Enlightenment does not prevent him seeing that Maistre, for example, is a very much more extreme thinker than someone like Vico. As for his allegedly excessive generosity towards extrem-ists like Maistre, it is true that when Berlin puts on their intellectual clothes he sometimes seems to be enjoying his fancy dress a little too much. But of course his point is not that we should agree with such thinkers; rather, we should try to understand them, the better to know the enemy. Like a method actor, Berlin needs to identify with his role, but he identifies with Maistre only in the sense that Marlon Brando identifies with Colonel Kurtz in *Apocalypse Now*. For Berlin, as for Brando, genuine understanding of human thought and conduct requires imaginative empathy, and this remains true of the thought and conduct we condemn. Understanding does not exclude adverse judgement; on the contrary, any judgement, whether positive or negative, depends on prior understanding. I shall return to this point in the last section of this chapter.

Supposing that we accept the general outlines of Berlin's account of the contest between Enlightenment and Counter-Enlightenment, the next question is: what are its moral and political implications? I pursue this question in the following sections. In the first two of these I examine the political message of the Enlightenment's critics, tracing Berlin's account of their influence on nationalism by way of romanticism. In the final section I look at Berlin's interpretation of Vico and Herder in particular as proto-pluralists.

Romanticism

The revolt against the Enlightenment that began with Vico, Hamann and Herder continues, Berlin argues, with their romantic successors.[5] In a series of lectures he delivered in 1965, now published as *The Roots of Romanticism* (1999), he describes the emergence of the romantic movement out of the Counter-Enlightenment, noting its various streams but emphasizing its unifying features. These latter include the anti-scientism and particularism inherited from forerunners like Hamann and Herder, to which the romantics add their own distinctive stress on the power of human will and creative genius. In turn, romanticism gives rise to nationalism.

According to Berlin, both the Counter-Enlightenment and romanticism emerge principally out of the same cultural matrix, namely late-eighteenth-century Germany. Berlin stresses two socio-historical factors. First, the Germans of this period suffered from a massive inferiority complex in relation to the French. By comparison with France, Germany seemed like 'a somewhat backward province', politically and culturally divided, and humiliated militarily in the Thirty Years War and the Napoleonic Wars (*RR*, 34). Hamann and Herder detest what they see as the artificial manners and bloodless science of the Parisian *philosophes*. Similarly, their romantic successors are motivated in part by resentment of French intellectual and cultural hegemony, contrasting the shallow cleverness of France with the deeper, more authentic, spiritual sensibility of the Germans.

Secondly, Berlin draws attention to the fact that so many key figures in both the Counter-Enlightenment and romanticism come not merely from Germany but from a particular part of Germany, namely East Prussia. This is significant because of the pietist influence there, as already noted in connection with Hamann. This is also the religious background of Herder and Kant. For Berlin, the characteristic pietist emphasis on the authenticity of the inner life, by contrast with political and social engagement, is a good example of the 'retreat to the inner citadel' he had discussed in 'Two Concepts of Liberty' (*RR*, 36-7; compare *L*, 181-2). There is a link here with the Germans' wounded self-esteem. People retreat to their inner citadels when they feel they cannot act or express themselves in more public ways: 'this was a very grand form of sour grapes ... You gradually hedge yourself round with a kind of tight wall by which you seek to reduce your vulnerable surface – you want to be as little wounded as possible' (*RR*, 37). In due course, however, this originally defensive strategy was transformed into a doctrine of aggression, the ideal of the vigorous collective expression of the authentic will in the nation-state.

The notion that the fullest development of humanity requires the fullest assertion of the will is one of two doctrines that Berlin identifies as 'the heart of romanticism' (*RR*, 118). The other is the related idea that the will creates reality. According to Berlin, the romantics hold that there is no independently existing structure of things that we can take as an object of knowledge. Reality is, for human beings, not objective but the active creation of their minds, a dynamic process or flow, 'a perpetual forward self-thrusting, perpetual self-creation of life' (*RR*, 119–20). Reality, including moral reality, the values we live by, is not discovered but invented. The agency of this invention is 'the free untrammelled will' (*RR*, 117).[6]

Berlin narrates the emergence of this dual doctrine of romanticism through successive stages, each represented by characteristic thinkers. The first of these is Immanuel Kant. This may seem surprising because of Kant's orthodox reputation as the classic representative of the Enlightenment, the writer who associates reason and toleration with human maturity. Berlin does not claim that Kant is himself a romantic, rather that he is a crucial influence on certain aspects of romanticism and a pivotal figure in some respects between the romantics and their predecessors in the Counter-Enlightenment. The pietist background is again significant. In Kant's case this is expressed through his attachment to the idea of the free will as an essential attribute of humanity. To be governed by the passions is, for Kant, to be governed by that which is external and alien to what makes us human, namely our will to act in accordance with self-imposed rules of reason and morality. Kant is no opponent of modern science, but his view contains an anti-scientistic element with which Hamann would have agreed: that human beings are not merely objects in nature to be understood with the tools of natural science alone. To understand human beings is to understand the central role of the will in human conduct. Indeed, for Kant the free will is the only intrinsic good, and the truly human being is the autonomous being.

Kant, however, is no more than a proto-romantic at best, because his idea of the free will is so closely identified with the acceptance of rational and moral rules found as pre-existing structures in the human mind. The ideal of the indomitable will is taken a step further by the playwright, poet and philosopher Friedrich Schiller, whom Berlin sees as one of the first genuine romantics. Schiller shares Kant's basic view of will and autonomy as the marks of humanity because they enable us to rise above servitude to nature (*RR*, 78). Genuine tragedy is generated by human attempts, whether successful or not, to resist such external forces. But Schiller goes further. Liberation consists in the successful assertion of the will in resistance even to the obligations of conventional morality (*RR*, 81–2). Schiller's drama introduces a new kind of hero, the person whose authentic self-expression puts him at odds with ordinary life and normal social standards. Berlin finds in this another aspect of Turgenev's idea of the 'superfluous man' for whom society has no place, but whose loss is also society's loss. Schiller's hero may act in ways that by conventional standards are mistaken or even immoral, but the suggestion is that the genuinely free will is itself an ethical standard, either tragically at war with ordinary social rules or even superior to them.

Schiller and other romantic writers thus introduce into European thought and literature an ethic of authenticity. In previous times what counted was how far one's conduct measured up to standards that are true or valid independently of our will or desires. For romantics like Schiller, according to Berlin, ideals are not discovered, either by reason or feeling, because there are no ideals, pre-existent in nature, to discover. Rather, ideals are actively created by the will. The mark of ethical action is not correctness but sincerity or authenticity. Genuine liberation will occur, the potential of humanity realized, when we get beyond Kant's sense of morality as obligation, even self-imposed, and reconceive morality as our own, wholly free invention (*RR*, 87).

Even Schiller, however, is counted by Berlin as only a moderate or 'restrained' romantic (*RR*, 68). Beyond Schiller and writers like him is a further category or phase of extreme or 'unbridled' romantics, among whom the leading figure is Fichte (*RR*, 93). Berlin's discussion here connects with his earlier treatment of Fichte in *Freedom and its Betrayal*. Fichte takes over the Kantian stress on the ideal of personal autonomy, which he identifies in the romantic manner with the untrammelled, creative will. What he adds of his own are two further moves. First, there is a heightened emphasis, beyond that in Schiller, on the will as authentically expressing itself through sheer action, faith and self-creation, rather than reason or norms (*RR*, 88–9, 93). Secondly – a still greater contrast with Schiller – Fichte sees the will as not merely the will of the individual, but the collective will of some super-personal entity. This collective entity takes several forms in his thought, but the most influential of these is the nation, in particular the German nation (*RR*, 90–1, 95–6). Here we arrive at nationalism, which for Berlin is essentially an 'offshoot of the romantic revolt' (*AC*, 355).

Nationalism

In nationalism the romantic will is collectivized, identified with the nation, and enforced by the state. At the extreme this leads to fascism, but in Berlin's later work in the 1970s he argues that nationalism also expresses the fundamental human need for belonging. The failure of the great social prophets of the nineteenth century to predict the continued strength of nationalism is a symptom of the weaknesses of the Enlightenment: its excessive abstraction and universalism. Once again, the Enlightenment and its critics have left us with a mixed inheritance.

Like romanticism as a whole, nationalism is a creation of the Germans, according to Berlin, in part an expression of their wounded pride. In German nationalism we also see romanticism's Counter-Enlightenment origins, for the attributes of German-ness turn out to be precisely the reverse of those associated by Hamann and Herder with the *philosophes*. The Germans, who are capable of 'creative and original activity' and 'believe in spiritual reality', are contrasted with 'those who believe in inanimate nature, and who put her at the helm of the world' (Fichte, cited at *RR*, 96). Berlin is careful to note that Fichte is referring here not to Germany alone but to a broader category of 'Germanic' nations. Nevertheless, he believes that thinking like this sows the seeds of nationalism, and in particular of the extreme nationalism of the twentieth century.

The emergence of nationalism is a point of contrast between the romantics and their Counter-Enlightenment predecessors. The pre-romantic Counter-Enlightenment may produce some of the inspiration for specifically German nationalism, but its representative thinkers are not themselves nationalists. There is no sign of nationalism in Vico, who speaks in terms of civilizations and historical epochs, or in Hamann, usually preoccupied with the inner experience of the individual. Herder, although often credited with being the father of nationalism, is not a genuine nationalist on Berlin's reading (*TCE*, 205–6). There is certainly a powerful sense in Herder of the 'nation', meaning a people conceived as a cultural and moral unit with its own personality. What is missing from Herder as a nationalist is any commitment to a political dimension of the nation, that is, the idea of the nation-state. Indeed, Herder tends to regard the state as a force for uniformity and restriction, a dead hand on the living culture (*TCE*, 181–2). Herder is, at most, a cultural rather than a political nationalist.

It is romanticism that creates 'full-blown' or extreme nationalism (*AC*, 343). The old emotions of national belonging, or patriotism, or xenophobia, all found in premodern times, are not enough. More salient (although not universal) is the phenomenon Berlin describes as 'the bent twig' (*CTH*, 246).[7] Wounds to a people's pride tend to provoke a reaction, as in the case of the Germans responding to the hegemony of the French. Another factor may be the dislocating effects of modernization, under which the nation becomes a new 'focus for loyalty or self-identification, or perhaps a base for power' for various groups and classes (*AC*, 346). But the key condition for nationalism on Berlin's account is that a society possess 'an image of itself as a nation', at least in the minds of an intelligentsia who are willing and able to promote it (*AC*, 347). This national image must appeal to 'some general unifying factor or factors', the standard list including language, ethnic origins, a shared history and a homeland. What the romantics crucially supply here is the idea of a shared national will, a collective goal or destiny. This is the contribution of Fichte in particular, but his notion of the collective will and its moral force is made possible by the general 'apotheosis of the romantic will' that characterizes the whole movement (*CTH*, 207).

Berlin develops his understanding of nationalism by distinguishing it from mere 'national consciousness' (*AC*, 338). Consciousness of belonging to a national group dates back to the ancient world, but the exaltation of this kind of belonging as the focus of a conscious political doctrine is distinctly modern. In this modern sense Berlin defines nationalism (he still has its more extreme forms in mind) as 'the elevation of the unity and self-determination of the nation to the status of the supreme value before which all other considerations must, if need be, yield at all times' (*AC*, 338). He sees nationalism in this sense as possessing four central characteristics. First, it takes the nation as the primary focus of identification and belonging. Secondly, the nation is conceived organically, that is, as a living whole with its own needs, goals and personality. A crucial implication of this is that the goals of the nation override those of subordinate units, on the model of the needs of the body as a whole overriding those of particular parts. The nation is 'the essential human unit in which man's nature is fully realised' (*AC*, 341). Thirdly, the nation's goals become the basis of moral justification: 'they are to be followed because these values are those of *my* group – for the nationalist, of *my* nation' (*AC*, 342). Finally, when the nation's values are thwarted, they may legitimately be promoted by force if necessary. This connects with the overriding value of the nation: 'Nothing which obstructs that which I recognise as my – that is, my nation's – supreme goal, can be allowed to have equal value with it' (*AC*, 343).

Berlin's analysis here comes close to identifying nationalism with fascism, and indeed in his discussions of both romanticism and the Counter-Enlightenment he highlights several anticipations of characteristically Fascist ideas. The basic theme in this regard is irrationalism. The Fascists' rejection of free speech, toleration and representative democracy is based in part on a rejection of reason as the arbiter of public policy and of human conduct in general. This general anti-rationalism seems to be endorsed by the critics of the Enlightenment in their more extreme statements. Berlin's strongest example in this connection is Maistre, whom he links with Fascist thought explicitly, although without demonstrating any direct causal influence.[8] But Hamann, too, is described in the subtitle of Berlin's principal essay on him as one of the founders of 'modern irrationalism' (*TCE*, 243). For Hamann, real human understanding is intuitive, even mystical, rather than objective and analytical, as the *philosophes* would have it. Moreover, the Enlightenment project is not merely mistaken but dangerous, because it saps the raw energies that are the real driving force of human existence. 'The tree of knowledge has robbed us of the tree of life' (*CTH*, 229, 232). The true centre of human life is not contemplation but action (*TCE*, 335). The same thought is echoed by the romantic poet Lenz – 'Action, action is the soul of the world' (*RR*, 55) – and in Fichte's 'glorification of the active, dynamic and imaginative self' (*RR*, 93).

The valuing of action over reason is one of the staples of fascism.[9] So too is the romantic account of the legitimate ends of action, namely that these have no ethical limits; authenticity is all. Again there is a hint of that already in Hamann: 'Every creature has a natural right to appropriate all that surrounds it to the limits of its power' (*TCE*, 336). Similarly for Fichte, 'civilised nations are free, free to live in peace, but no less free to fight and make war: "culture is not a deterrent of violence but its tool"' (*CTH*, 227). Behind this, again, is the romantic 'notion of the unpredictable will either of a man or of a group, which forges forward in some fashion that is impossible to organise, impossible to predict, impossible to rationalise. That is the whole heart of Fascism: what the leader will say tomorrow, how the spirit will move us, where we shall go, what we shall do – that cannot be foretold' (*RR*, 145). The romantic idea of the artist as the creative genius, the supreme representative of the unlimited will, is a source of the Fascist cult of the leader who is entitled to mould human materials as he pleases (*RR*, 145–6). The Fascist contempt for ethical limits, either universal or conventional, is an inheritance from the romantic conception of life as art.

Not all nationalism is fascism, however, and Berlin by no means condemns nationalism outright; nor does he consistently describe it in the terms he assigns to the 'full-blown' variety. In his essay 'Nationalism: Past Neglect and Present Power' (1978), he argues that no realistic view of politics can wholly ignore nationalism as a powerful, and in all likelihood permanent, feature of the human condition. Nationalism is an unavoidable fact about the world as we know it. The great liberal and socialist prophets of the nine-teenth century saw nationalism as a passing phase, destined to vanish along with the conditions that had sustained it: ignorance and intolerance or capitalism and imperialism as the case may be (*AC*, 339–40). But of course the prophets were wrong; nationalism has not gone away, nor indeed is it likely to. The reason is that nationalism, whatever else it may be, answers to a fundamental aspect of human nature, the need to belong. Berlin uses this point to reinforce one of his familiar themes, the one-sidedness of the Enlightenment. The liberals and socialists of the nineteenth century were blind to the continuing force of nationalism because of their shared prejudice in favour of universals and against particulars. 'The claims and ideals of mere national groups' would be swept away by 'the victory of reason or of material progress or of both' (*AC*, 340). Berlin might equally have seen the neglect of nationalism as a failure on the Enlightenment's own terms, since on his account the need for national belonging is itself a universal.

At any rate, Berlin argues that Enlightenment ideologies like lib-eralism and socialism must acknowledge the continued reality of nationalism and must accommodate themselves to it. Exactly what form that accommodation should take he does not say explicitly, but the general tenor of his remarks in 'Nationalism' and elsewhere suggests a need at least for wariness of the latent power in nation-alist movements, especially in countries with no tradition of liberal-democratic institutions. The outbreak of violent ethnic nationalisms after the fall of communism in 1989 is surely a powerful endorse-ment of Berlin's view. Once more the 'new world order' of global liberal democracy so confidently predicted by the cosmopolitans has proved to be illusory.[10]

However, there is also implicit in Berlin's remarks a more affir-mative view of nationalism. At least in some less than 'full-blown' forms, nationalism should be seen as not merely a brutal reality but as possessing positive value, because it satisfies people's need to belong. In 'Two Concepts of Liberty' Berlin develops the idea of 'belonging' as intimately connected with the experience of being 'understood', and so with achieving 'recognition'. My own people, he writes, 'understand me, as I understand them; and this understanding creates within me the sense of being somebody in the world' (*L*, 203). This 'reciprocal recognition', he continues, can be so important to people that they are willing to trade much of their personal liberty for it, accepting the legitimacy of authoritarian regimes as long as these are dominated by their own nationals. The stress on the value of mutual understanding explains the weight that nationalist movements often place on the defence of a local language, because this is the necessary framework for the particular cultural understanding they wish to promote.[11] Suppress my language, and you suppress my whole world-view. (The significance of language for culture is a theme Berlin notes in all the Counter-Enlightenment writers.) In turn, the link between culture, mutual understanding and language helps explain why, among the various ways people might identify themselves, specifically *national* identity has such a strong hold. It is at the level of the nation or people, rather than the family, church or private association, that language develops and is sustained, thereby shaping our understanding of self and other. If national identity is an especially important form of belonging, and if belonging is an essential part of human well-being, then nationality becomes an essential human good. Nationalism, the conscious promotion of nationality as a political goal, is, then, not merely ineradicable but desirable, at least in some forms.

The possibility for Berlin of desirable forms of nationalism is confirmed in a later interview, published as 'Two Concepts of Nationalism' (1991), where he divides nationalist movements into two categories. On one side is the aggressive, bent-twig variety exemplified by the Germans and Eastern Europeans, motivated by resentments born of humiliations, and intensified by notions of racial identity and superiority. On the other side, 'nonaggressive nationalism is another story entirely' (*TCN*, 19). This is the purely 'cultural' or non-political nationalism Berlin attributes to Herder, according to which each culture has a right to its own 'place in the sun', unmolested by others and not interfering with them. Overall, Berlin's vision is of 'a world which is a reasonably peaceful coat of many colours, each portion of which develops its own distinct cultural identity and is tolerant of others' (*TCN*, 21).

Berlin's vision suggests that nationalism and liberalism, each appropriately understood, need not be at loggerheads after all. Berlin himself does not speak in these precise terms, but a distinctive school of 'liberal nationalists' has emerged in recent years, several of them closely associated with Berlin and claiming his influence in this respect. For Berlin's student Yael Tamir, for example, the liberal and nationalist traditions, 'although generally seen as mutually exclusive, can indeed accommodate one another'.[12] Nationalism can be shorn of the ideas of race, resentment and superiority that have marred it in the past. Liberals, on the other hand, can be made to appreciate the value of nationalism, suitably qualified, as a precondition for liberalism, since it provides interpersonal bonds of identity, trust, security and co-operation without which liberal concerns for individual liberty and social justice are moot.[13]

Liberal nationalism has attracted some vigorous criticism, however, and some of this strikes expressly at Berlin.[14] One might question, for example, Berlin's vision of a world of independent and autonomous cultures. How far does this depend on an untenable notion of cultures as discrete wholes, internally univocal and externally independent? Again, how sharp is the line between 'aggressive' and 'non-aggressive' nationalisms? Berlin himself excels in showing how apparently benign ideas can be transformed into dangerous ones, as in the case of the slide from the defence of the individual will by Kant to the aggressive assertion of the collective will by Fichte. Similarly, a slippery slope from Herder's defensive cultural nationalism to Fichte's chauvinist political nationalism seems a definite possibility on Berlin's own account of these ideas in *Roots of Romanticism*. If all forms of positive liberty contain the seeds of authoritarianism, can the same not be said of all nationalisms?

More fundamentally still, how far is Berlin's anticipation of liberal nationalism, his picture of some nationalist aspirations as purely cultural or non-aggressive, consistent with his own value pluralism? On the one hand, the individual liberty emphasized by liberals, and on the other, the group belonging celebrated by nationalists, seem to count as incommensurable values on Berlin's own view. In 'Two Concepts' he observes that belonging, recognition and status are sometimes identified with freedom, but that if they do amount to a kind of freedom, this should be seen as a 'hybrid' that borrows from, but is not identical with, negative or positive liberty (*L*, 200–8). These values are distinct, and if so they may conflict.

National independence, for example, is consistent with oppression of the individual citizen. If liberty and belonging are distinct and incommensurable, calling for hard choices when they collide, then does the same not hold for the two ideologies by which they are respectively privileged? Are liberalism and nationalism not strict alternatives, and liberal nationalism an oxymoron?

This last objection looks especially troubling, since it goes to the heart of Berlin's thought, the nexus between his liberalism and his pluralism. Whether the problem can be solved depends on how one interprets pluralism, and in particular the notion of incommensurability. The objection makes a large assumption on this point: if values are incommensurable, then the stand-off between them is permanent and cannot be settled rationally. But is this true? My answer will have to wait upon further discussion of the nature of value pluralism in the next section and the ensuing chapters. I shall return to liberal nationalism specifically in chapter 8.

Pluralism and relativism

On Berlin's account, the legacy of the Counter-Enlightenment and romanticism includes irrationalism and fascism, but also many valuable ideas. Two broad lines of thought are especially important. The first is the role of belonging and recognition, especially at the national level, as I have just discussed. The second is the idea of value pluralism: that basic human values are irreducibly multiple, and that they may be conflicting and incommensurable. Pluralism is, for Berlin, a powerful weapon against authoritarian political thought, much of which rests on moral monism. In modern times the dominant intellectual and cultural expression of monism has been the French Enlightenment, especially in its scientistic strain. Consequently, Berlin looks for the pluralist antidote to monism among the Enlightenment's critics. But the question arises as to whether the 'pluralism' he finds in these thinkers is really a species of relativism. If so, this would have disturbing implications for Berlin's liberalism.

Recall that the notion of value pluralism was introduced by Berlin, after several hints in his earlier work, in 'Two Concepts of Liberty'. Pluralism is thus immediately associated with the struggle against political authoritarianism. Authoritarian justifications typically rest on some form of moral monism, the view that one or a few values override all others. If there is an overriding good, then

of necessity anything done in its name is justified; this is the doctrine that lies behind the worst brutality of the twentieth century.
Moral monism is directly opposed by value pluralism. If fundamental human values are plural and incommensurable, then no
single value or narrow range of values can be absolutely or universally overriding. Different goods will have strong claims in different circumstances. By contrast with the single-mindedness and
fanaticism allowed or encouraged by monism, Berlin argues, pluralism suggests a politics of compromise and moderation, the politics of liberalism.

The mainstream of the French Enlightenment, according to
Berlin, is monistic in character. At its broadest, monism is the basis
of the whole Western tradition of utopianism that reaches back to
Plato, indeed of the mainstream of Western philosophy, the 'perennial philosophy' (*philosophia perennis*) according to which all questions, including moral questions, have a single correct answer and
all correct answers fit together like a jigsaw puzzle (*RR*, 21–3; *CTH*,
5–7; *PSM*, 5–6; *POI*, 5–7). More specific expressions of monism
include those aggressive manifestations of nationalism which rank
the goals of the nation above all others. Above all, however, Berlin
emphasizes the dominant role played in modernity by the distinctively science-based monism of the Enlightenment. For Saint-
Simon, Marx and others, scientific investigation of the human
world, as of the natural world, will yield a harmonious set of laws
which can be formulated by experts. We shall then look forward to
the perfect realization of all human goods within a single moral and
political system which those same experts will authorize and
enforce. This, for Berlin, is one of the remote origins of Stalinism.

If Enlightenment scientism expresses the monist world-view,
then a likely place to look for arguments against monism is among
the Enlightenment's critics. Intimations of the rejection of monism
can be found, Berlin believes, as far back as Machiavelli.[15] But it is
the pivotal struggle between the Enlightenment and its opponents
that stimulates the emergence of the idea more clearly and influen-
tially. At any rate, Berlin attributes his own notion of pluralism to
these latter sources: 'My political pluralism is a product of reading
Vico and Herder, and of understanding the roots of romanticism'
(*POI*, 13; also *CTH*, 8–10, or *PSM*, 7–9). This statement is surely too
simple, since Berlin's pluralism probably has many roots. We have
already seen suggestions of the pluralist view surfacing in his
writing as early as *Karl Marx* in 1939. Nevertheless, there is no doubt
that Berlin thinks of Vico, Herder and the romantics as especially

significant forerunners of his own position, and that he attaches considerable importance to the project of finding signs of pluralism in these thinkers. Thus, in the closing pages of *Roots of Romanticism* he points to what he sees as an ironic twist in the romantics' influence. The most extreme romantics aimed to exalt unqualified self-expression, to reject all convention and all compromise, and 'to destroy ordinary tolerant life' (*RR*, 146). But by breaking with

> the classical ideal, of the single answer to all questions . . . they have given prominence to and laid emphasis upon the incompatibility of human ideals. But if these ideals are incompatible, then human beings sooner or later realise that they must make do, they must make compromises, because if they seek to destroy others, others will seek to destroy them; and so, as a result of this passionate, fanatical, half-mad doctrine [of the unrestricted will], we arrive at an appreciation of the necessity of tolerating others, the necessity of preserving an imperfect equilibrium in human affairs . . . The result of romanticism, then, is liberalism, toleration, decency and the appreciation of the imperfections of life; some degree of increased rational self-understanding. (*RR*, 147)

By opposing scientism, the romantics also oppose monism and hint at value pluralism, thereby opening the door to liberal moderation. Berlin makes the same claim for Vico and Herder, as I shall show in a moment.

Berlin's tracing of pluralism in the Counter-Enlightenment and romanticism adds historical depth to his account of the pluralist idea and strongly influences the way he formulates it. But his use of these sources also creates a major problem for his thought as a whole: what he calls 'pluralism' in these movements is sometimes hard to distinguish from the more familiar idea of ethical relativism.[16] If Berlin's value pluralism is really just a form of relativism, that damages his position in two ways. First, it means that the centre-piece of his moral thought is not a distinctive idea after all. More seriously still, a merely relativist starting point would undermine his liberalism. If pluralism collapses into relativism, then Berlin's resistance to totalitarianism collapses too, since Nazi Germany and the Soviet Union could be defended as authentic moral cultures, distinct from Enlightenment cultures but equally valid, and unimpeachable except on their own terms.[17]

Ethical relativism, at its broadest, is the view that there are no objective or universal moral principles or values, only particular moral judgements made from particular standpoints. In one version, 'subjectivism', the standpoint is that of the individual agent. On this view, what is morally right is whatever the individual feels or judges to be right. In the other main version, 'cultural relativism', the relevant standpoint is that of a particular culture or way of life. Here, what is morally right is whatever is judged to be right by the standards of the culture. For both subjectivism and cultural relativism the relevant standpoint is indefeasibly authoritative: there is no external point of view from which the judgement of the individual, or the norms of the culture, can be second-guessed. On either view, liberalism can be no more than the political expression of a particular individual or cultural perspective, one that happens to place a high value on individual liberty and toleration. The standard liberal claim, for example, that certain fundamental 'human' rights are valid not only locally but universally will be true only for liberals. Soviet or Nazi culture and its priorities will be no less legitimate. In short, if Berlin's pluralism is equivalent to relativism (as either subjectivism or cultural relativism), then the twin supports of his political thought, his liberal universalism and his value pluralism, threaten to pull apart.

Is the 'pluralism' that Berlin claims to find in the Counter-Enlightenment and romanticism distinguishable from relativism? In the case of Hamann and the romantics, the positions Berlin describes seem more akin to forms of subjectivism than anything else. Hamann is presented as holding that human knowledge consists wholly in the concrete immediacy of raw experience, which is distorted by any reasoned generalization or abstraction. 'This is in effect modern existentialism in embryo,' writes Berlin (TCE, 283). Similarly, when Berlin identifies 'the heart of romanticism' with the notion of the unrestricted will inventing moral and other reality, he explicitly aligns the romantics with radically subjectivist, existentialist and proto-existentialist thinkers like Sartre, Stirner and Nietzsche (RR, 142–5). So far, then, we have only subjectivism, not any distinctive 'pluralist' position.

It is Vico and Herder, however, whom Berlin would regard as the most significant precursors of value pluralism. Yet in their case too, much of Berlin's account points strongly in the direction of relativism, this time cultural relativism. Vico is presented as primarily a historicist thinker who rejects any notion of a permanent human nature or natural law, and who argues that each stage in the evolution of a culture or civilization has its own distinctive character and outlook. That outlook includes its own set of values, and these are the only appropriate measures of its achievement. Thus Berlin writes that for Vico human values 'belong to, and are effective and intelligible at, only their specific stage in human history' (*TCE*, 61). Again, 'each phase is incommensurable with the others, since each lives by its own light and can be understood only on its own terms' (*CTH*, 75). Comments like these look like strong statements of a relativist acceptance of the indefeasible moral authority of cultures.

The appearance of cultural relativism is even stronger in Berlin's interpretation of Herder, for whom cultures or nations, rather than civilizations or historical phases, are 'incommensurable'. Each culture possesses its own unique 'centre of gravity' such that there is no shared measure by which different cultures can be ranked or even compared critically. One can see why Berlin is attracted to this view of Herder. If there are no overarching standards for comparing different cultures critically, then there are no objective grounds from which to assert that one culture is morally superior to another. There can be no *Favoritvolk*, as Berlin puts it (*TCE*, 186). This helps to separate Herder's doctrine of the value of cultural belonging from the aggressive nationalism with which it is sometimes associated. However, in his anxiety to separate Herderian belonging from doctrines of national superiority, Berlin seems to have attached it to cultural relativism. Thus he draws attention to Herder's view that 'all these forms of life are intelligible each in its own terms (the only terms there are)' (*TCE*, 235). Each culture realizes 'an ideal of indefeasible validity' such that 'we are forbidden to make judgements of comparative values, for that is measuring the incommensurable' (*TCE*, 234, 233). If this view is indeed Herder's, how can he be other than a cultural relativist?

Berlin does acknowledge certain non-relative themes in Vico and Herder, but he promptly dismisses these as the least persuasive parts of their work. Vico, for example, sees the phases of social development as fitting into a universal pattern, 'the ideal history of mankind' (*storia ideale eterna*), which is ultimately progressive. The end at which this process aims, but never wholly achieves, is what Vico calls *humanitas*, the full realization of human capacities (*TCE*, 91). It seems that Vico has a conception of human nature after all, although conceived dynamically, rather than statically as by the *philosophes*. This does appear to distinguish him from the relativists, since the notion of a human *telos*, or end, suggests grounds for ranking cultures or their practices. The trouble is that Vico's teleology is the very part of his thought which Berlin finds least persuasive, regarding it as pure speculation (*TCE*, 137; also 87). Similarly, Berlin acknowledges that Herder possesses a notion of

Humanität, which stands for those 'universally valid goals', including freedom, toleration, mutual love and so forth, towards which all 'immortal souls' strive (*TCE*, 218). But again, Berlin dismisses this notion as 'notoriously vague', a commonplace of the German Enlightenment, and not as distinctive of Herder as 'his more frequent and characteristic pluralism and relativism [*sic*]' (*TCE*, 240).[18]

Berlin's rejection of the universalist components in Vico and Herder is well founded. Their notions of 'humanity' are indeed vague, selective and speculative. But dispensing with these leaves Berlin with the problem of relativism. Sometimes in the essays on these thinkers, as in the last passage quoted, he seems to concede that what he finds in them is historical or cultural relativism. At other times he insists on the term 'pluralism' as distinct from 'relativism', but does little to show where the difference lies (*TCE*, 198n.). On the contrary, the discussion of Herder in particular confuses the issue by very strongly assimilating pluralism to cultural relativism, in substance if not in name. The effect of this, as suggested earlier, is to eviscerate value pluralism as a distinctive position and to let in arguments which reduce Berlin's liberalism to no more than one cultural expression among others. To avoid this result, Berlin needs to develop an account of value pluralism which separates it more sharply from cultural relativism. More specifically, he needs grounds from which to evaluate cultural practices critically, rather than accepting cultures as morally authoritative and unassailable.

Berlin is sensitive to this objection, and replies to it in the later essay, 'Alleged Relativism in Eighteenth-Century European Thought' (1980). There he insists that Vico and Herder are not relativists but pluralists, and in the course of his argument he gives his most substantial account of the general distinction between value pluralism and relativism. Ethical relativism he defines as the view that the moral 'ideas and attitudes of individuals and groups are inescapably determined by varying conditioning factors', including culture and class (*CTH*, 77). According to cultural relativism, therefore, values are wholly conditioned by culture. If this were true, Berlin argues, then people would see things only from the point of view of their own culture. They would be 'insulated', occupying 'windowless boxes' or 'impenetrable bubble[s]' that would constitute their entire world (*CTH*, 85, 11). Consequently, they would be unable to appreciate or even understand the values of other cultures – at least as values in any way comparable with their own. In a relativist world we may be able to acknowledge the values of other cultures as externally observable behavioural goals on a level with those of other species, like ants. But we would be quite unable to understand or empathize with those values as in any way human goals like our own, because to do so would require 'entering into' them as purposes comparable to our own.

Yet of course, Berlin argues, the world is not like this. Much of the importance of Vico and Herder lies in their insistence – an insistence which separates them from the relativists – that we can understand and appreciate the values of other cultures (*CTH*, 82). We do this precisely by imaginatively entering into the cultural and moral world-view of those we are seeking to understand. What makes this possible is that, contrary to relativism (at least in its stronger forms), there is sufficient universality of human experience to make other cultures comprehensible to us, and through that comprehension to allow us to appreciate their norms as genuine values that we could imagine ourselves living by. Thus, our undoubted capacity to understand and empathize with the values of other cultures and historical periods presupposes certain 'limits of humanity', a common 'human horizon' or shared field of moral experience (*CTH*, 80, 11). Our ability to understand other cultures implies a set of universal values.

Several critics have objected that to understand the values of other cultures is not necessarily to share them.[19] Berlin himself allows this point when he says that we can simultaneously understand and condemn the practices of the Nazis (*POI*, 12–13; *Conv.*, 38). The actions of the Nazis are morally abhorrent, but they fall, regrettably, within the horizon of the humanly comprehensible – that is, we can understand these as the actions, however appalling, of human beings. But in that case the human horizon seems to amount to a commonality only of understanding, not of moral value. It embraces all those actions which we can comprehend as human, but that alone does not show us which of these actions all human beings should endorse. Within the horizon many different and deeply opposed moral codes would appear to be equally 'human', including both liberalism and Nazism. Consequently, the human horizon seems to rule out only a radical relativism of understanding (cognitive relativism), not ethical relativism. Moreover, Berlin's view appears to leave us with a paradox. How can we empathize with a practice and vehemently condemn it at the same time?

I suggest that these objections can be met by drawing a distinction, not present in Berlin but in keeping with his general position, between two senses or levels of 'value'. First, a 'value' might mean a specific action or practice, such as the Nazi practice of aggressive international expansionism. My 'understanding' this practice does not, of course, commit me to endorsing it. However, if my understanding is a genuine, internal understanding in Berlin's sense, then I necessarily appreciate the deeper purposes or goals which the practice serves – the 'values' which stand behind the practice or which the practice expresses. It is these deeper values that I may then share, even if I strongly reject the particular way they are expressed in the practice confronting me. Even though I am repelled by Nazi expansionism, I can understand the practice as a twisted, 'bent-twig' expression of the deeper goal of national or cultural belonging. It is this underlying value that I can identify with, and that implies a common horizon not only of understanding but also of values. Such values express 'the real needs and aspirations of normal human beings', and while specific expressions vary along with specific circumstances and beliefs, resulting in the cultural variety that we know (for good or ill), the underlying pattern of fundamental human needs and interests is universal (*CTH*, 84).

The important point that emerges from Berlin's discussion is therefore that while relativism divides moral experience into discrete, non-communicating compartments or perspectives, pluralism implies the existence of a significant moral horizon shared by all human beings. It is this that explains, as relativism cannot, why 'members of one culture can understand and enter the minds of, and sympathise with, those of another' (*CTH*, 84). The corollary is that the common horizon also provides, at least in principle, a basis for cross-cultural criticism, where fundamental human goods are denied or inadequately realized or distorted by a particular culture or ideology. Thus the military expansionism practised by the Nazis might be condemned on the ground that, although ostensibly serving the valid goal of cultural belonging, its claim to do so rests on grossly false beliefs concerning cultural and racial superiority and wilful blindness to the legitimate claims of other cultural groups. The underlying values are identifiably human and genuine, but the practice is misguided even when judged by those same basic terms.

Pluralism, therefore, unlike relativism, strikes a balance between respect for cultural difference and recognition that some cultural practices warrant criticism. While strong cultural relativism commits us to the uncritical acceptance of any conduct that has cultural backing, pluralism acknowledges grounds on which such conduct can be questioned. The questioning must be sensitive, but it can also be quite radical. It must be sensitive to the legitimate variety of human goods, and of the ways in which those goods may be interpreted and pursued in different times and places. Thus Berlin shows sympathy with the opposition of Vico and Herder to what they see as the characteristic Enlightenment habit of dismissing whole cultures as 'merely imperfections to be transcended' on the road to the world-view of the *philosophes* (*TCE*, 93). For Berlin, as for Vico and Herder, 'one culture is never a mere means to another', contrary to the attitude, for example, of Voltaire towards the Middle Ages (*TCE*, 214). Rather, each culture has its own distinctive strengths as well as weaknesses. This is because, on the pluralist view, there are many more goods and virtues, and legitimate interpretations of these, than can be expressed within the life of any one human society. All cultures emphasize some goods at the expense of others; strengths in certain areas come at the price of deficiencies elsewhere. Berlin's pluralist view is that we should acknowledge both strengths and weaknesses. Whole cultures should be neither idealized nor dismissed as worthless.

Does this mean that we can never judge one culture to be superior to another, all things considered? The general tenor of Berlin's remarks is that we should be wary of making this more radical kind of judgement, because it must take into account an immense range of human goods and interpretations, and must consequently balance many particular strengths and weaknesses. Nevertheless, the overall comparative evaluation of different cultures is not entirely ruled out, either by Berlin himself or by the logic of his position. We should indeed be careful in making such overall judgements, for the reasons he gives. But consistently with recognizing that all cultures have their strong and weak points, in terms of the fundamental human values, it may still be that one culture exhibits a more favourable balance of strengths over weaknesses than another. Thus it would not be out of the question to argue, consistently with pluralism, that liberal cultures are superior to others overall. I shall explore such arguments in the ensuing chapters.[20]

A good example of the pluralist balance between cross-cultural appreciation and criticism is provided in Berlin's account of Vico. Vico regards his own 'magnificent times' as superior to earlier phases of history, because *humanitas* is now more fully developed (*TCE*, 86). But that should not prevent us from seeing that we have paid a real and absolute price for our improvements. Homeric society was barbaric by comparison with eighteenth-century

Naples, but only such a society could have produced a masterpiece like the *Iliad* (TCE, 93). A world without the *Iliad* may be a better world overall because it embodies the most fundamental human values more fully. But it is still a world without the *Iliad*, which also expresses deep human values in a unique way. Vico's judgement is a classic illustration of what distinguishes the pluralist outlook from relativism. A cultural relativist would have to say that Homeric culture generates its own morality, which is necessarily valid on its own terms and unassailable in any other. Our moral criticisms of that society are irrelevant, since they merely express our own cultural perspective, the only one of which we are capable. Value pluralism, by contrast, invites us to 'transcend' our culture in order to understand, appreciate and evaluate the practices of other cultures (CTH, 85). We are able to do so because of humanity's common moral horizon, which provides a ground for both understanding and judgement. Unlike relativists, pluralists do not have to accept existing cultures as morally indefeasible.

I conclude that Berlin does succeed in showing that Vico and Herder are pluralists, not relativists, and in distinguishing value pluralism from cultural relativism more generally. The distinction turns on the pluralist commitment to a common moral framework, which is rejected by relativists. This addresses the first of the two problems listed earlier as arising for Berlin if pluralism and relativism cannot be separated. Value pluralism is established at this point as a distinctive moral point of view. But what about the second problem, that of the relation between Berlin's pluralism and his liberalism? So far we have seen Berlin argue that there must be a common moral framework (because this is presupposed by cross-cultural understanding), but we have not seen the actual shape or limits of the framework. What exactly does the common framework require of human beings, and what does it rule out? More specifically, how does the framework bear on the justification of Berlin's liberal politics? Do the human needs Berlin points to suggest a case in favour of liberalism, or are they consistent with non-liberal forms of politics? Are they even compatible with liberal ideals? I pursue these questions in the next chapter.

Summary

For Berlin, the late eighteenth and early nineteenth centuries saw an intellectual revolution which rivalled the French and industrial revolutions for significance in forming the modern world. This was the intellectual rebellion against the Enlightenment. We are the children of both the Enlightenment and its critics, and our patrimony is mixed in both cases. The Enlightenment has given us freedom and toleration, but also scientism, technocracy and ultimately, through faith in technocratic utopianism, Soviet totalitarianism. From the Counter-Enlightenment and romanticism we have inherited irrationalism and aggressive forms of nationalism, culminating in the totalitarianism of the twentieth-century Fascists. But Berlin believes that the Enlightenment's critics have also bequeathed to us the intellectual antidote to totalitarianism in all its forms, namely the notion of value pluralism. This claim threatens to unravel when pluralism seems to shade into cultural relativism, although Berlin succeeds in separating these ideas in the end. But does he separate them sufficiently to justify his liberalism? That question remains open.

6

Pluralism and Liberalism

Berlin's archaeology of totalitarianism, having begun with the
modern betrayal of freedom and continued with the scientism of
the Enlightenment and the Counter-Enlightenment rejection of
reason, reaches its deepest level with his analysis of moral monism.
According to Berlin, the roots of the worst horrors of the twentieth
century lie not merely in positive notions of liberty, or in Enlightenment dreams of technocratic perfectionism, or in the irrationalism of thinkers like Maistre and Hamann, but in the mainstream
belief of Western philosophy that all questions have a single answer,
and that all answers fit together in a single systematic account of
reality. Berlin is happy to allow that this monist picture is true of
the world of nature, the proper domain of the natural sciences.
When it comes to the world of human values, however, he is con-
vinced that the traditional picture is false. The ends of human
beings are multiple, they often conflict, and they cannot be combined in any single, specific conception of the human good. This is
Berlin's concept of value pluralism. There are hints of this in his
work at many points, going back to his pre-War book on Marx and
leading up to his first explicit statement of the idea in 'Two Concepts of Liberty'. By the end of his life pluralism emerges as one of
his two principal moral themes, to set beside his liberal commitment to individual freedom.

Yet the nexus between pluralism and liberalism also presents the
central problem in Berlin's thought. He seems generally to believe
that the two go together. But do they? On the one hand, the traditional liberal project is universalist, claiming validity for liberal

values such as individual liberty and toleration for all places at all times. On the other hand, pluralism, at least as presented so far, might be taken to suggest that there are many equally valid sets of values or ways of life, and that liberalism is no more than the political expression of one (or some) of these, with no justifiable claims to superiority over others. As I shall show, the claim that pluralism undermines liberal universalism often trades on the confusion between pluralism and relativism discussed in the previous chapter. But even when pluralism is distinguished from relativism, the issue of its relation with liberalism remains open. At the heart of pluralism lies the notion of the incommensurability of values. Even universal values may be incommensurable, and if they are, then we may be faced by hard choices when they conflict. The question then is why our response to those choices should be a liberal one. Where values are radically plural, what reason do we have to choose a characteristically liberal solution rather than some other?

I shall argue that Berlin does not wholly succeed in explaining why pluralists should be liberals. The shortcomings of his arguments in this regard open the door to anti-liberal interpretations of his notion of pluralism that go very much against the spirit of his overall view. This is not the end of the matter, because I shall eventually show that even though Berlin's own arguments in this connection are not adequate as he states them, some of them can be revived and improved as part of a more rigorous pluralist case for liberalism. But I shall take up that line of argument in the next chapter. For the present I review Berlin's critique of monism and the elements and basic implications of his concept of value pluralism, and then examine the account he gives of the relation between pluralism and liberalism.

The problem of monism

The idea of value pluralism sits at the very centre of Berlin's thought. Some readers may be inclined to dispute this claim, since he never offers any systematic or careful analysis of the concept. Typically he allows it to emerge from discussions of other ideas, as in the final section of 'Two Concepts of Liberty', or from studies of particular thinkers like Vico and Herder. This may give the impression that pluralism is a significant side-issue for Berlin, but no more than that. Such an interpretation would be mistaken. First, it ignores the fact that the pluralist theme, although often muted, persists throughout Berlin's writing. Hints and intimations appear, as I have indicated, in the study of Marx, in the essays on the Russian thinkers, and in the broadcasts on the 'enemies of human liberty'. More explicit statements are prominent in Cold War texts like 'Political Ideals in the Twentieth Century', in 'Two Concepts', and in the later work on the Enlightenment and Counter-Enlightenment. Secondly, Berlin himself confirms pluralism as one of his central concerns when he comes to reflect on his life's work in his last essays and interviews, for example in 'The Pursuit of the Ideal' (1988) and 'My Intellectual Path' (1998). There he makes it clear that pluralism is the antidote he prescribes for the moral monism that forms the deepest foundation of twentieth-century totalitarianism. This opposition between monism and pluralism is a theme I have touched on at several points in preceding chapters, but I shall draw together the main strands of these accounts before looking more closely at pluralism and its ethical and political implications.

First, value pluralism must be understood in contrast to moral monism. Berlin defines moral monism, at its broadest, as the view that all ethical questions have a single correct answer, and that all these answers can be derived from a single, coherent moral system (*L*, 212–13; *CTH*, 5–6; *PSM*, 5–6; *POI*, 5–7). The coherence of the monist system might be explained in different ways. Berlin sometimes identifies moral monism with the notion of the ultimate compatibility of all values and claims properly understood. On this view, what appear to be moral conflicts are really just illusions created by our imperfect understanding of morality. If we had a better grasp of the true contours of moral goods, we would see that they never really collide but fit together like a 'cosmic jigsaw puzzle' (*CTH*, 6; *PSM*, 5; *RR*, 23).

This is not an entirely satisfactory account of monism, because monists need not insist on the ultimate compatibility of values or the unreality of moral conflict. A monist could concede that values are deeply incompatible, and conflicts among them real and unavoidable, but still argue that all such conflicts have a single correct resolution. There are at least three forms this resolution might take. First, the monist might argue that all goods can be commensurated as units of a common currency which the best decision would then maximize. The classic example of this kind of monism is utilitarianism (in its various versions), according to which all human goods can be reduced to units of the super-value, 'utility', variously defined. The correct action is simply that which produces the most utility. Secondly, the monist might propose that even if goods cannot be commensurated they can still be ranked, so that the superior good always overrides the subordinate. It might be claimed, for example, that liberty always outranks equality or efficiency.[1] Thirdly, the monist might argue that there is a single, rationally defensible procedural rule that can be used to resolve value conflicts without recourse either to a common currency or to a ranking. Here an example may be provided by Kant's categorical imperative.[2]

There are, then, several ways in which monism might be asserted in the face of the incompatibility of values. Consequently, monism is better conceived as requiring not that values be compatible, but that conflicts among them have a single correct resolution indicated by a single correct formula, which in turn has recourse either to a common currency or to a rank order or to a procedural rule. Berlin does not draw these distinctions, but they are consistent with what he does say, and he hints at them in his references to pluralism as involving not only the incompatibility but also the incommensurability of values.

According to Berlin, monist thinking is the deepest basis for political authoritarianism, and ultimately the totalitarianism of the twentieth century. We have already seen some of the links between totalitarianism and monism in previous chapters. One such link is by way of positive liberty. Positive conceptions of liberty become dangerous when they subordinate the actual individual to some notion of an ideal or true self. What makes that possible, Berlin suggests, is the idea of the authentic person as one who lives in accordance with a single, correct conception of the human good. The positive liberty beloved of twentieth-century dictators is thus underwritten by moral monism. Similarly, monism supports the scientistic strain in the Enlightenment, from which derive the authoritarian technocratic visions of Saint-Simon and Marx. It is only if morality is conceived as a single coherent system of rules on the model of the physical world that it makes sense to expect a final objective science of human conduct which will generate laws to be administered by experts.

More generally, monism underpins totalitarianism by way of utopianism. The attraction of monism is the prospect it offers of our formulating a system from which we can then derive a single correct answer to any moral problem. The true moral system, once known, will enable us to iron out all political conflicts and make possible a perfected society in which there will be universal agreement on a single way of life. This is the belief that unites Plato,

Rousseau, Hegel and Marx. That list, Berlin suggests, should immediately give us pause, for these are among the principal intellectual
sources of modern totalitarianism.

It might be objected that Berlin's linking of totalitarianism with
monism in 'Two Concepts' does not fit with his analysis of the
Enlightenment and its critics. The general tendency of that analysis, as I argued in the last chapter, is to associate monism with the
Enlightenment by way of scientism, and so with totalitarianism in
its Communist form. Fascism, on the other hand, seems on Berlin's
account to owe more to the Counter-Enlightenment, which he
presents as significantly anti-scientistic, anti-monist and proto-
pluralist. But if fascism emerges from the pluralist Counter-
Enlightenment, then how can Berlin, in 'Two Concepts', present
monism as underpinning twentieth-century totalitarianism in
general?

Berlin could answer that the lines of influence he traces should
not be seen as mutually exclusive or rigidly one-dimensional. He
does present Soviet communism as primarily, through Saint-Simon
and Marx, a product of Enlightenment scientism and therefore of
monism. But he also notes the debt owed by Marx, through Hegel,
to the historicism of the Counter-Enlightenment (*KM*, ch. 3).
Further, Berlin need not, and does not, deny that communism is
influenced by the romantic movement, with its emphasis on the
force of the will and on the possibility that the will may be collective. Similarly, while he would probably maintain that the influence
of the irrationalist component of the Counter-Enlightenment is
uppermost in the make-up of fascism, he says nothing to discount
the modernizing, industrial and bureaucratic aspect of the Fascist
outlook and its appeal to scientific expertise.[3] More importantly, the
view is compelling that fascism, no less than communism, depends
on the monist faith in a single right answer to all questions – Berlin's
phrase, 'a final solution', has obvious resonance here (*L*, 212). The
chief difference is that while under communism the answer is dictated by the impersonal scientific laws of history, the Fascists look
to the authority of the *Volksgeist* as mediated by a charismatic leader.
The Fascist *Volksgeist* is not merely the spirit of one culture among
others, as on Herder's cultural-pluralist view, but the wisdom of a
superior people.[4] This is an expression not of pluralist incommensurability but of monist hierarchy.

A more serious objection to Berlin's linking of monism with totalitarianism is that the connection is not a logical one. Clearly, there
are monist thinkers like Locke and J. S. Mill who do not argue for

an authoritarian state. Here Berlin could reply that this shows only that monism is not sufficient for authoritarianism. He understands the relation between monism and authoritarianism in much the same way as he pictures the relation between positive liberty and authoritarianism. Monists are not necessarily political authoritarians, but most political authoritarians are in fact monists. Monism leads in the direction of authoritarianism down a slippery slope. To suppose that morality is monistic is to suppose that there is a single correct answer in all cases, mandated by a single moral formula. To suppose that there is a single formula is to hold out the hope that all moral and political questions will be answered eventually, that moral and political systems can thereby be perfected. To believe that moral and political perfection is possible, even in principle, is to invite the thought that its realization justifies the employment of any means. Along this slippery slope, Berlin argues, there is a distinct, historically detectable association between moral monism and political totalitarianism.

This reply is not entirely convincing. As with the parallel critique of positive liberty, the slipperiness of the slope from monism to totalitarianism can be questioned. Again, the key steps are all possibilities, rather than logical requirements. A monist thinker could, with good reason, stop short of supposing that the true formula will ever be known with certainty, or that its content would allow the use of oppressive means to its realization. These reservations would be insisted upon by J. S. Mill, for example.

But even if moral monism is not always dangerous, Berlin would respond that it is in any case false. Monism does not do justice to the depth and persistence of conflict in the moral experience of human beings. Rather, 'the world that we encounter in ordinary experience is one in which we are faced with choices between ends equally ultimate, and claims equally absolute, the realization of some of which must inevitably involve the sacrifice of others' (L, 213–14). The moral world we know is better captured by the idea of value pluralism. According to pluralism, basic human goods are not always compatible, rankable or commensurable, but rather irreducibly multiple, frequently conflicting, and sometimes incommensurable with one another. This is a world of disagreement and dilemma. If goods are ultimately incompatible, then there is no possibility, even in principle, that all of them can be realized simultaneously. If goods are unrankable or incommensurable, then when they conflict there is no single way of deciding between them that will be uniquely correct in all cases. Each incommensurable good is its own measure; depending on the circumstances, there will be many reasonable ways of resolving conflicts among them. Consequently, there is no possibility in a pluralist world of moral or political perfection, or 'a final solution' to all moral and political problems. Along with monist utopianism falls the standard justification of totalitarian dictatorship, the idea that one goal overrides all others and justifies any sacrifice. No single value or narrow set of values can carry that moral weight.

At this point it might be said that 'ordinary experience' alone is insufficient to demonstrate the falsity of moral monism and the truth of value pluralism. Yes, a moral monist could reply, the moral world as we currently know it is riven by dispute and indecision, but that is only because the underlying monist structure of morality is not yet fully understood. We may yet come to understand that structure and get the answers we want, but even if we do not, that does not prove that the answers are not there in principle. And if ordinary experience is not enough to show that monism is false, then it cannot show that pluralism is true.

Berlin does not discuss this objection; indeed, he nowhere provides any extended defence of pluralism's truth. Nevertheless, he could reply that although the objection has logical force, there is also something rather hollow about it. For one thing, the claim that the discovery of the monist truth may still lie in the future seems to be on a level with the Marxist claim that the end of history is just around the corner: the predicted event remains a logical possibility, but given centuries of fruitless waiting it is deeply improbable. More specifically, Berlin draws attention to the evident failure of the most promising of all routes to the monist truth, namely the scientism of the Enlightenment (*CC*, 7, 162; *SR*, 42).

A defender of Berlin might also argue that pluralism is better able than monism to explain the phenomenon of rational regret for lost value. If monism were true, then all genuine values would fit together so that to act rightly could never involve any absolute loss which it would make sense to regret. So, for example, an action justified on utilitarian grounds would maximize the human good (in terms of happiness or preference satisfaction), to the effect that whatever the costs of the action, these would necessarily be outweighed by the commensurate benefits. But experience teaches that we are frequently confronted by regrettable loss even when we are acting rightly. Vico, for example, can argue that the modern age is an improvement, all things considered, on the Homeric world, yet coherently regret the loss of the distinctive values that produced the

Iliad (*TCE*, 93). On the monist view such losses would be only apparent, not real, because they would be outweighed by commensurable gains. Only on the pluralist view are these losses real, in line with experience, because our most fundamental values are plural, potentially conflicting and 'equally ultimate'. The case for value pluralism may not be conclusive, but it is strong.[5]

Pluralism analysed

Berlin's pluralism may be said to contain four constitutive elements: (1) the idea of universal values; (2) an emphasis on the irreducible plurality of values; (3) a stress on the pervasiveness and intensity of conflict among values; and (4) the crucial claim that many human values are incommensurable with one another. I shall consider these elements in turn.

1. Universal values

Berlin argues that at least some goods are universal, either valuable for, or actually valued by, all human beings. I showed in the last chapter why Berlin thinks this must be true: otherwise our evident capacity to transcend our own culture and understand others would not make sense. I also showed that he needs some such notion of universal values in order to separate pluralism from relativism, and consequently to defend liberal universalism. As to the precise content of these universals, however, Berlin gives no systematic account. In one essay he seems to identify the universal goods with the 'habits and outlook of the western world' (*CTH*, 205), while in another he criticizes the liberal and socialist prophets of the nineteenth century as 'Europocentric' (*AC*, 353–5). From time to time he mentions particular basic goods that may be universal, one example being courage, which 'has been admired in every society known to us' (*Conv.*, 37). His most frequent candidates for universality are liberty, equality and social welfare (*L*, 172; *CTH*, 12). Within the broad notion of 'liberty', it may be that negative non-interference and positive self-mastery are also universals.

If Berlin says relatively little about the content or substance of the universal goods, he says rather more about their general nature or form. Again, however, his remarks are unsystematic and often inconsistent. One notable inconsistency is between his two favourite images of value universality, which convey rather different ideas. Sometimes he refers to the common 'limits of humanity' or 'human horizon' beyond which behaviour is no longer recognizably human and understanding is impossible (*CTH*, 11, 80; *PSM*, 10). I introduced this idea in the last chapter. Elsewhere Berlin speaks of a 'central core' of values which all human beings share (*PSM*, 243; *TCE*, 277). The notion of the core is distinctly narrower and more demanding than that of the horizon. The horizon excludes only what is not recognizably human, and consequently permits almost anything. Someone who sees no difference between kicking a pebble and killing his family is beyond the human pale, because his values or purposes are literally incomprehensible (*CC*, 166). But the actions of the Nazis, although morally detestable to most people, are not incomprehensible in this way. Rather, those actions are performed in pursuit of more remote ends that we can understand and so acknowledge to be human, no matter how misguidedly expressed in the case at hand. On this view, therefore, not even Nazi society would be excluded by Berlin's common moral horizon – he is quite explicit about this (*POI*, 12–13; *Conv.*, 38). The core, on the other hand, is concerned less with moral limits than with requirements, namely those values which all or most people have accepted historically. This is bound to be a subset of the merely 'human' values and practices, since not all goals that are recognizably human have been widely pursued. The practices of the Nazis fall within the horizon but are somewhat less likely to satisfy the core.

Whether we are speaking of the horizon or the core, Berlin's account of value universality contains further inconsistencies. In one place he writes that 'the multiple values are objective, part of the essence of humanity rather than arbitrary creations of men's subjective fancies' (*POI*, 12). But his more characteristic view is that universal values should be conceived empirically, as what people happen to want rather than as components of a human essence or *telos*: 'there are values that a great many human beings in the vast majority of places and situations, at almost all times, do in fact hold in common' (*Conv.*, 37; similarly *CTH*, 18; *PSM*, 15).[6] In another passage this empirical view is qualified as '*quasi*-empirical, because concepts and categories that dominate life over a large portion (even if not the whole) of recorded history are difficult, and in practice impossible, to think away' (*L*, 45). Again, Berlin sometimes claims that the universal goods add up to 'a minimum without which societies could scarcely survive' (*CTH*, 18; *PSM*, 15), while elsewhere they are presented as requirements not just for survival but for 'a minimally decent society' (*Conv.*, 114).

All of these competing formulations have one thing in common: in every case Berlin's universal values are extremely 'thin' or generic. They are so general or abstract that most human societies would satisfy them, including many highly illiberal societies. This is most obvious in the case of the human horizon, which is consistent with anything identifiably 'human', including the Nazis. But the core, too, is unlikely to be substantial, especially when coupled with Berlin's empirical or 'quasi-empirical' account of universals, according to which values are universal when they are in fact universally desired over long periods of history. The historical record provides little evidence of anything actually desired or admired by all, or even most, human societies except goods or virtues described at the very highest level of generality. Among the examples proposed by Berlin, courage is a plausible candidate (although what particular actions count as courageous is likely to vary across cultures), but liberty and equality, not to mention social welfare, are highly dubious.

The thinness of Berlin's notion of universality is significant because it revives the issue of the relation between his pluralism and his liberalism. In the last chapter I argued that Berlin's liberalism would be threatened if his pluralism turned out to be equivalent to relativism, since relativism would undermine the universality of his liberal ideals. That threat receded when Berlin was able to separate his pluralism from relativism, the crucial move being the pluralist commitment to a common moral horizon. But it now turns out that Berlin's common horizon is so broad, its contents so general, that it excludes virtually nothing. Berlin's distinction between pluralism and relativism now looks more formal than substantial. His universals are likely to be consistent with a huge range of deeply illiberal values and ways of life. A local commitment to liberal values may be consistent with value pluralism, but so is much else. On this view liberalism is on a moral par with many other moral and political systems. And if that is true, then pluralism would seem to rule out liberal universalism, the claim that liberal values are not merely equal to others but superior. On Berlin's view so far, liberalism can be no more than one legitimate encampment within the common moral horizon among others.

2. The plurality of values

The second element of Berlin's value pluralism is the idea that human values, including universals, are irreducibly plural. There are many intrinsic goods, that is, goods desirable for their own sake and not reducible or subservient to any others. The precise range of this plurality Berlin leaves open, although he says it has limits. 'The number of human values, of values which I can pursue while maintaining my human semblance, my human character, is finite – let us say 74, or perhaps 122, or 26, but finite, whatever it may be' (*POI*, 12). This finitude connects with the possibility of cross-cultural understanding, and so with the common moral horizon. It is because the range of values is bounded by 'the limits of humanity' (*CTH*, 80), that I can enter imaginatively into the practices and goods experienced by others, even if I do not live by them myself.

An important question to ask here is: 'plurality of what?' The phrase 'plurality of values' is ambiguous because the term 'values' can be understood in different ways. According to John Gray, there are three different 'levels' of value plurality in Berlin: first, *among* goods, like liberty and equality; secondly, *within* goods, for example, between the negative and positive species of liberty; and thirdly, among 'cultural forms' or ways of life which represent bundles or packages of goods.[7] It is this last level, that of cultural pluralism, which Gray emphasizes as the basis of his anti-liberal interpretation of pluralism, as I shall show. If cultures are plural in Berlin's sense, involving incommensurability, then liberalism can be exhibited as one incommensurable cultural view among others, with no valid claim to superiority.

I shall return to the details of Gray's argument later, but it is worth pointing out straight away that there is a problem with his culture-based reading of Berlinian plurality. The idea that not only goods and sub-goods but cultures are incommensurable is one that, as I have conceded, does appear in Berlin's texts, especially in his treatment of Vico and Herder. But how can this be squared with his notion of the common moral horizon? If there are universal values, even if these are highly generic, then it cannot be true that cultures are wholly incommensurable. Within the common horizon cultures must overlap, sharing at least something of the same human outlook. Despite what Berlin himself sometimes says, his better view is that it is primarily *goods* (and sub-goods) that are plural in his sense, rather than cultures. No doubt the plurality of goods will also lead to considerable valid cultural variation, since it will be reasonable for different groups of people to pursue distinct packages of goods, and to pursue these in divergent ways. But that legitimate cultural variation will be parasitic on the more fundamental plurality of goods. If this were not true, and value pluralism involved an acceptance of cultural pluralism on a level with the plurality of goods, then there would be nothing to separate pluralism from cultural relativism. If value pluralism is to be a distinctive idea, then it must refer primarily to the plurality of goods, not cultures. Moreover, the claim that goods are more radically plural than cultures is persuasive, given the force of Berlin's argument for the common moral horizon. The possibility of cross-cultural understanding shows that, despite great differences among cultures, there are also points of commonality at the level of generic human purposes and interests. The priority of goods over cultures within the idea of pluralism has important implications for the defence of liberalism, as I have already suggested, but I shall return to these when I come to Gray's case in chapter 7.

3. Conflicts among values

The third element of Berlin's value pluralism is his emphasis on the potential for conflict among goods, again including universals. Obviously goods do not always conflict, but often they do, and then we have to make a choice. We must 'allow that Great Goods can collide, that some of them cannot live together, even though others can – in short that one cannot have everything, in principle as well as in practice' (CTH, 17; PSM, 14). Such collisions and the choices they generate can occur within a society or 'within the breast of a single individual' (CTH, 12; PSM, 10). It is hard to believe that Berlin's own experience of personal value conflict – for example, in the division of his loyalties between Britain and Zionism, and more generally in his position between the Enlightenment and Counter-Enlightenment – did not influence his sense of pluralism as much as his reading of Vico and Herder.

'[O]ne cannot have everything, in principle as well as in practice': this is one of Berlin's most fundamental themes, driven home on many occasions in many different ways. It is important to see that the kind of value conflict Berlin is talking about is not merely circumstantial but conceptual. There are various ways in which values can collide.[8] In some cases conflicts are caused simply by circumstances, as when I have time to go either to the swimming pool or to the library, but not both. Berlin, however, has in mind conflicts among values 'in principle', so that to realize one such value is necessarily to neglect or destroy another: 'total liberty for wolves is death to the lambs' (*CTH*, 12). Again, this can be true at both the individual and the social level. A person who chooses the satisfactions of single life cannot also enjoy the benefits of having her own family. The Homeric society that produced the *Iliad*, with its celebration of the heroic virtues, cannot also enjoy the goods characteristic of Christianity. The range of human values is finite, limited by recognizably human purposes. Nevertheless, the range is great and its elements are often incompatible. No single life, whether of an individual person or even of a whole society, can fully realize all human values.

The inference Berlin draws from this kind of incompatibility of goods is of course his rejection of 'the ideal', the utopian vision of moral and political perfection.

> The notion of the perfect whole, the ultimate solution, in which all good things coexist, seems to me to be not merely unattainable – that is a truism – but conceptually incoherent; I do not know what is meant by a harmony of this kind. Some among the Great Goods cannot live together. That is a conceptual truth. (*CTH*, 13; *PSM*, 11)

For Berlin, political perfection is impossible, not merely in the sense that it is beset with practical difficulties, but 'in principle', because so many fundamental human goods are conceptually incompatible.

But the incompatibility of goods, even at a conceptual level, does not wholly explain Berlin's rejection of political utopianism. This is the corollary of a point made earlier: that to accept the deep incompatibility of values is not necessarily to abandon moral monism. Even if certain goods are conceptually incompatible and have to be traded off or ranked against each other in practice, it might still be argued that there is a single correct way of doing this in all cases. It might be argued, for example, that utility is the common currency for all goods, or that liberty always overrides everything else, or that we should always follow a procedural rule like the categorical imperative. In other words, there is a form of perfectionism that is not defeated by the idea of conceptual incompatibility alone. This kind of utopian system would not suppose that all good things could be fully realized simultaneously, but it would nevertheless claim that there is a single correct formula for answering all moral and political questions. This, too, Berlin would regard as a false and dangerous view; but to justify his position he would need to appeal to the final element of his pluralist idea.

4. Incommensurability

This last component of Berlin's pluralism is its most distinctive. Once again, he never analyses it very carefully, but a reasonably coherent picture can be teased out of what he does say, as follows. The basic idea is that some goods are so distinct from each other that they share no common measure. Each is 'equally ultimate', possessing its own intrinsic value and independent moral force (*L*, 213). For example, if liberty and equality are incommensurable values, then each makes an independent claim on us. Neither can be translated into terms other than its own, and no amount of one will wholly compensate for any amount of the other.

The immediate implication is that when incommensurable values collide, we are faced with difficult choices. First, in choosing one good we may necessarily forgo another, and so suffer a loss that cannot be wholly compensated. Secondly, if each incommensurable good is its own measure, then we will not be able to determine choices among such goods by applying simple monist rules such as utilitarianism. On the pluralist view, utility is merely one value among others. Values in conflict have to be weighed against one another without the help of any such convenient measure. This removes the possibility of moral or political perfectibility in the second sense mentioned in the last section, where the need to trade off or rank goods is accepted but it is maintained that there is only one correct way of doing so in all cases. If values are incommensurable, then it will be equally rational to privilege many different values, and no single currency or ranking or decision procedure will always be valid.

Beyond this general picture, Berlin's account of incommensurability, and consequently of what is involved in choosing among conflicting values, is vague and inconsistent. Sometimes he seems to endorse a very strong conception of incommensurability under which values are wholly incomparable and choices among them non-rational. For example, in his essay on Machiavelli Berlin writes that 'Entire systems of value may come into collision without possibility of rational arbitration' (*PSM*, 320). In a broadcast talk he insists that 'You cannot say love is inferior to honour, and you do not want to say honour is inferior to love. Both these are ultimate values, and there is no way of settling the issue: you must just plump in some sort of way.'[9] If this is his view, then his commitment to liberal solutions to moral and political questions looks arbitrary. Indeed, on this strong reading of incommensurability, no political position is rationally justifiable, since any such position rests ultimately on a non-rational plumping for one set of values rather than another.

However, the strong interpretation of incommensurability is neither Berlin's only view nor his best. He repudiates it explicitly in a later article, where he says that reasoned choice among incommensurable goods is possible, if not in the abstract then at least in (some) particular cases.[10] He offers no examples, but it may help to consider the following conflict between impartial fairness and personal attachment. The utilitarian William Godwin believed that 'political justice', understood as the impersonal maximizing of human happiness, should always come before anything else. In his notorious example, if there is a fire and I have to choose between rescuing my father or Archbishop Fénelon, a benefactor of humanity, Godwin claims that I should choose the archbishop.[11] Most people would say that this judgement is mistaken, because it ignores the special bond between parents and children. There are indeed cases where we should give priority to impartial justice over our personal affiliations, as where a judge is presiding over a trial or an official is awarding a public contract. But humanity-wide impartiality does not always come first, as the Fénelon example shows almost everyone except Godwin. Whether partiality or impartiality should take priority depends not on any absolute monist ranking or decision procedure, but on the particular context in which the conflict occurs. Incommensurables such as these cannot be ranked in the abstract, but there may be good reason to rank them in particular cases.

Consequently, Berlin's better view of incommensurability, and therefore of value pluralism, is a more moderate one that allows at least some room for rational choice. Although incommensurability may place problems in the way of reasoned decision making, it does not rule out reasoned choice within a particular context. Choosing among incommensurables is always hard in the two senses mentioned above: it cannot be guided adequately by any simple monist standard, and it always involves regrettable loss. Moreover, *some* cases may present genuine dilemmas in which there is no decisive reason to favour one option over another. But in other cases, choosing among incommensurables, although difficult, need not be irrational or arbitrary. Rather, decisive reasons to choose in one direction rather than another will be generated by context. As Berlin puts it, 'the concrete situation is almost everything' (*CTH*, 15).

This view is reinforced by 'Political Judgement' (in *SR*). There Berlin argues that successful decision making in politics is not a matter of adherence to a set of abstract rules derived from a putative 'political science'. Rather, 'what matters is to understand a particular situation in its full uniqueness, the particular men and events and dangers, the particular hopes and fears which are actively at work in a particular place at a particular time: in Paris in 1791, in Petrograd in 1917' (*SR*, 44–5). The most successful statesmen, leaders like Bismarck and the Emperor Augustus, are those with a capacity to 'seize' a situation by integrating or synthesizing disparate and changing data into a coherent pattern. This they do by a process closer to intuition than to the application of theoretical knowledge. 'To seize a situation in this sense one needs to *see*, to be given a kind of direct, almost sensuous contact with the relevant data' (*SR*, 46). What these passages suggest is, first, that choices among competing incommensurable values need not be a matter merely of arbitrarily plumping for one option rather than another. Rather, such choices can be well or badly made, more or less successful. More specifically, good choices in these fields always involve close attention to the particulars of the case.

More specifically still, Berlin sometimes refers to resolving such cases rationally by following 'the general pattern of life in which we believe' (*L*, 47) or 'the forms of life of the society to which one belongs' (*CTH*, 18; *PSM*, 15). That is, the particulars of a case of value conflict always include certain background commitments, whether those of the individuals concerned or those of the society to which they belong. Such background commitments, like those of the judge or the official or the loving son, may help us to resolve value conflicts rationally. Of course, what our background commitments are will often be uncertain, and one set of commitments will sometimes conflict with others. One may think here of Sartre's example of the man torn between joining the Resistance and staying home to look after his mother.[12] This is just to say that the resolution of moral conflict will frequently be messy, consisting 'in some logically untidy, flexible and even ambiguous compromise' (*L*, 92). In the absence of valid monist decision procedures, we should not expect things to be otherwise. But to admit that the reasoned justification of these choices may be messy is not to say that it is impossible.

The idea that reasoned moral decision making is possible without ranking or commensuration departs from the standard modern wisdom offered by the utilitarians and Kant, but is scarcely unique or original to Berlin. Although he does not make the connection, the classic statement of this view is Aristotle's account of *phronēsis*, or practical reasoning.[13] On this view human morality is too complex to be reduced to the kind of monist rules dominant in the modern age. Rather, the only rigid standard for moral decision making is that one should imitate the *phronēmos*, the person of practical wisdom. The *phronēmos* decides what ought to be done in a given situation, how exactly the competing considerations should be balanced, through accumulation of experience in dealing with comparable situations. Experience enables the *phronēmos* to develop a certain skill in practical reasoning, refined against a background of other virtues or dispositions of character which together contribute to a good life overall. Later I shall develop this parallel between Aristotle's ethics and rational choice under value pluralism by arguing that to cope well with choices among incommensurables is to exercise a specific set of skills or virtues. These virtues will provide further guidance to pluralist practical reasoning.

Clearly, a pluralist view of moral choice invites many questions about how to resolve particular hard cases, but that is to be expected of any realistic moral theory. Moreover, Berlin need not resolve all such cases, or even many of them, in order to make his political point, that pluralism has an affinity with liberalism. Even if he had to say that on the pluralist view many concrete ethical problems must be seen as irresolvable dilemmas, he could still insist that pluralists in any case have reason to accept a liberal political framework within which these issues can be contained. But then the question is: why should the framework be liberal? Liberal democracy gives special weight to goods such as toleration, personal autonomy and human rights. Why should that particular constellation of goods be preferred to an alternative set, such as the equality, solidarity and social justice championed by socialists, or the stability, prudence and tradition stressed by conservatives? Indeed, it is the values of conservatism rather than liberalism that seem to be reflected by Berlin's appeal to 'the general patterns of life in which we believe'. In short, how can Berlin's liberalism be justified in the face of his pluralism?

From pluralism to liberalism?

Berlin does believe that liberalism can be reconciled with pluralism, and he sometimes goes further, suggesting that pluralism provides liberalism with positive support. Once more he is neither clear nor consistent, and his texts require careful sifting.

Even something as basic as Berlin's commitment to liberalism is remarkably inexplicit, although present in the background none the less. There are actually very few places in his entire corpus where he expressly declares a distinctively liberal allegiance. His notion of universal values, as I have shown, falls well short of any specifically liberal requirements. Usually he speaks in much more general terms of the conditions for 'a minimally decent society', or of 'normal activity', or of 'civilisation' in contrast with 'barbarism' (*Conv.*, 114; *POI*, 158; *CTH*, 205). Yet a more distinctively liberal sensibility does surface from time to time, in particular in the context of his opposition to Soviet communism. Thus in 'Two Concepts of Liberty', for example, he writes approvingly of the 'frontiers of freedom', or the minimal degree of negative liberty necessary for any genuinely desirable human existence (*L*, 52–3, 171–4, 211). Liberal ideals are presented here not merely as the artefacts of particular cultures but as valid universally. Berlin confirms this commitment to universality in an interview in which he affirms his belief in human rights, although he denies that these can be rationally grounded (*Conv.*, 114). Similarly, despite his preference for negative liberty, he also expresses his appreciation of individualist forms of positive liberty, as understood and advocated by Kant and the romantics (*L*, 39). Although he tends not to associate personal autonomy with the liberal tradition explicitly, those liberals who do so can point to the substance of his endorsement nevertheless.

Supposing that Berlin is a liberal universalist, what does he see as the relation between liberalism and value pluralism? Here, too, the signals are mixed. It is clear enough that he thinks that liberalism and pluralism are compatible, but his reasons for holding this view, in the face of the problems which pluralism raises, are less than obvious. In one widely read piece he writes as if the claim that pluralism and liberalism are in conflict depends on the false assumption that choice under pluralism is always non-rational.[14] It is true that if pluralism did rule out rational choices among competing incommensurable goods, then there could be no reasoned defence of liberalism, or indeed of any other general political position. It is also true that pluralism does not in fact rule out rational choice among incommensurables, since (as Berlin argues) this is possible in at least some concrete situations. But how does that enable Berlin to justify liberalism as a universal project? To justify liberalism universally, it is not enough to say that pluralism permits liberal choices in some cases but not others. Berlin could make the broader claim that the general pursuit of liberal ideals is justified within the broader context of 'the general patterns of life in which we believe', but this would still fall well short of a defence of liberal universalism. It would amount to no more than the justification of liberal institutions where there is already a liberal culture. Liberals, on this understanding of pluralism, would have no arguments to offer to those who are not liberals already.[15]

The possibility of contextual argument under pluralism opens up the possibility of arguments for liberal solutions if the context happens to support these, but not otherwise. So far, liberal universalism and pluralism seem to be at odds. Might Berlin overcome this problem by arguing that a case for liberal universalism is actually implicit in the idea of value pluralism itself? Might it be that liberalism is not merely compatible with pluralism but entailed by it? Here again, Berlin says now one thing, now another. In some places he denies any necessary connection between pluralism and liberalism (*Conv.*, 44). But elsewhere he asserts that pluralism does indeed imply liberalism, as when he refers to 'pluralism, with the measure of negative liberty it entails' (*L*, 216), and when he writes that 'if pluralism is a valid view . . . then toleration and liberal consequences follow' (*POI*, 13).

I shall take it that Berlin does indeed believe, at least in some passages, that pluralism implies liberalism. At any rate, this is his more interesting claim. How does he argue for this? First, we should clear away certain inadequate arguments along these lines which have been attributed to Berlin but which are not his. One such argument is that if pluralism is true, then no particular choice of goods is less rational than any other, and people ought therefore to be given the freedom to make such choices for themselves. Something like this argument is attributed to Berlin by Michael Sandel, who points out its obvious flaw: on this view a liberal commitment to freedom of choice itself represents only one choice, no less but also no more rational than any other, so that a non-liberal system which denied freedom of choice would be equally justified.[16] In effect, this argument reduces pluralism to relativism. However, as I argued earlier, that is not Berlin's view. Under Berlinian pluralism it is not true that all choices are equally valid without restriction. Berlin's insistence that pluralists honour universal values is one reason why that is so, although admittedly this is a weak requirement as he formulates it. Later I shall suggest that pluralism implies other principles that place further restrictions on what counts as a valid choice.

Another attempt to argue from pluralism to liberalism is the claim that Berlin's notion of universal values implies a set of 'minimal human rights', and consequently a 'minimal liberalism'.[17] On this view the 'common moral horizon' includes rights to be free from starvation, arbitrary killing and slavery, and these basic entitlements indicate an embryonic account of human rights. But Berlin does not recognize any such rights as required by the common horizon. As shown earlier, nothing is required by the common horizon except that conduct count as recognizably human. Even the narrower notion of the 'central core' is not substantial enough to support a case for the rights mentioned. No such rights, or even their ethical substance (e.g. prohibitions on slavery), have actually been accepted by all human societies. The appeal to universal values may be a first step on the road from pluralism to liberalism, but the attempt to ground liberalism in universal values alone is unlikely to succeed and is not contemplated by Berlin.

Rather, Berlin proposes two main arguments from pluralism to liberalism, the first of which turns on the idea and value of choice. If pluralism is true, 'the necessity of choosing between absolute claims is then an inescapable characteristic of the human condition. This gives its value to freedom' (*L*, 214). The value-pluralist outlook emphasizes moral plurality and conflict. On this view, choice moves to centre-stage in moral experience unavoidably. If we must choose, Berlin argues, we must value freedom of choice, hence by implication a liberal order based on negative liberty. This argument, at least in the form in which Berlin presents it, is clearly flawed.[18] It is essentially an instance of the naturalistic fallacy, since it passes directly from the fact that choice is unavoidable to the value of freedom of choice. But the mere fact that choice is unavoidable does not make it (or the freedom with which to make it) valuable. Berlin himself observes that many choices among incommensurables are painful, even tragic. Why, then, should we value such choices or the freedom with which to make them? A better solution might be to avoid these choices as far as possible, and one way of doing so may be deliberately to reduce our negative liberty. The necessity of moral choice, alone, is compatible with authoritarian as well as with liberal politics.

Perhaps Berlin intends to argue for the value of choice less directly. He may mean that moral choice is valuable not simply because it is unavoidable, but because it is an expression of a uniquely human dignity. This is the Kantian argument that a capacity for moral choice is distinctive of human beings, and therefore to be respected as a symbol of our special moral status. Thus Berlin writes that our concept of humanity is inseparable from our thinking of human beings 'as capable of pursuing ends for their own sakes by deliberate acts of choice' (*L*, 337). But again, this line of argument comes up against the familiar problem of the naturalistic fallacy. Why does the fact that moral choice is distinctive of humanity make it valuable? Other human capacities are also distinctive, but are either not valuable or morally neutral – for example, 'having sexual intercourse without regard to season; or despoiling the environment and upsetting the balance of nature; or killing things for fun'.[19] In addition, the Kantian case for the value of choice is not distinctively pluralist. Berlin is supposed to be showing how a case for liberalism is entailed by value pluralism. But value pluralism adds nothing to the Kantian argument, which refers to moral choice generally, not choice among incommensurables. This Kantian detour does not show why the fact of pluralism should make us support the liberal commitment to choice.

Berlin's second line of argument from pluralism to liberalism is less explicit but more compelling. The basic claim is that pluralism implies the impossibility of political perfection; hence it implies the need for a form of politics which accommodates and manages the imperfectibility of human life rather than a politics which strives impossibly to transcend it.

> For if they had assurance that in some perfect state, realisable by men on earth, no ends pursued by them would ever be in conflict, the necessity and agony of choice would disappear, and with it the central importance of the freedom to choose. Any method of bringing this final state nearer would then seem fully justified, no matter how much freedom were sacrificed to forward its advance. (*L*, 214)

If perfectibility were possible, then by definition anything would justify its realization. But if pluralism is true, there can be no moral and political perfection, in the sense either of the compatibility or the commensurability of values. Under pluralism there can be no final conception of the good life that will fully realize all human values and excellences; to emphasize one good will always be to neglect others. Nor, if pluralism is true, will it be possible to arrive at a single rule, or simple set of rules, to resolve all moral conflicts. Different general rules will appear equally reasonable from the perspective of different conceptions of the good or general value rankings. Consequently, no conceivable human society will wholly satisfy all of its members. (Indeed, no individual life will wholly satisfy the person living it, assuming that he or she is aware of alternative valuable options.) There will inevitably be disagreements, tensions and conflicts concerning fundamental moral questions: which goods and excellences should be emphasized at the expense of which others, and what are the best rules for resolving conflicts? Human diversity will defeat any attempt to reach social and political perfection. This is the meaning of Berlin's favourite quotation from Kant, which he repeats many times: 'Out of the crooked timber of humanity no straight thing was ever made' (*CTH*, 19, 48; *L*, 92, 216, 238; *POI*, 181; *PSM*, 16; *SR*, 192).

The political implications of this are twofold. On the one hand, this inevitable imperfectibility rules out as utopian those political theories that project the possibility of a wholly satisfying political society. The list of views included here contains some prominent historical opponents of liberalism, in particular classical anarchism and Marxism. On the other hand, pluralist imperfectibility brings with it a positive recommendation: only those forms of politics are plausible which acknowledge and accommodate the effects of imperfection, in particular dissatisfaction, alienation and significant social conflict. Prominent among political forms that meet this description is liberalism, the historical mission of which, going back to Locke's seventeenth-century case for toleration, has always been to manage social conflict rather than eliminate it.[20] For liberals, the task of the state, or of political institutions more generally, is not to perfect the life of the individual or to harmonize relations among social classes or groups. Rather, it is to underwrite the necessary (but not sufficient) preconditions for individual and group striving, and to manage social conflict so as to prevent it from becoming damaging to those same preconditions. In short, pluralism recommends liberalism by way of anti-utopianism.

This second argument is persuasive as far as it goes, and it goes a considerable distance. But the argument is incomplete, because although liberalism answers to pluralist anti-utopianism, so too do other political forms. Conservatism, in particular, seems also to meet the pluralist bill as Berlin describes it. Like liberals, conservatives stress the imperfectibility of the human condition and the need to contain and channel the resulting discontents and conflicts. But, unlike liberals, they recommend as a framework for this palliative work not negative liberty or personal autonomy but adherence to local tradition. It is no accident that one of the chief alternatives to the liberal reading of value pluralism has been broadly conservative in character, as I shall show when I discuss Gray's views in the next chapter.[21]

I conclude that although Berlin intends (in at least some passages) to justify liberalism on value-pluralist grounds, the arguments he advances are, as he states them, not wholly convincing. The argument from choice is logically flawed. The anti-utopianism line, while eliminating some opponents and stressing the realistic face of liberalism, does not single out the liberal position as uniquely the best political expression of pluralism. However, this does not mean that a pluralist case for liberalism cannot be sustained by better arguments than Berlin's. Indeed, it does not follow that Berlin's own arguments should be abandoned completely, since they might be resuscitated and improved. I pursue these possibilities in the next chapter.

Summary

Berlin's concept of value pluralism is central to his thought, emerging out of his critique of moral monism. Monism is the perennial philosophy of the Western world, but also the bedrock on which the totalitarian structures of the twentieth century have been constructed. Moreover, monism is false, since it does not do justice to the deep plurality of moral experience, as shown by the everyday occurrence of dilemma, disagreement and rational regret for lost value even when we have acted rightly. While monism makes possible the justification of authoritarian political systems, the political implications of pluralism, Berlin believes, are broadly liberal. The arguments he offers for this political conclusion, at least in the form in which he presents them, suffer from serious weaknesses or limitations. To improve on them, we shall have to go beyond what Berlin himself says.

7

After Berlin

Berlin's account of pluralism and its implications continues to have a vigorous afterlife, although this has taken time to gather momentum. Throughout the 1960s and 1970s, while 'Two Concepts of Liberty' was minutely examined for its bearing on the idea of freedom, the pluralist theme was hardly noticed. Since the 1980s, however, Berlin's concept of pluralism has become the focus of a lively debate. This was initiated by the appearance of the collections edited by Henry Hardy, confirmed by Berlin's focus on pluralism in 'The Pursuit of the Ideal' (1988), and further stimulated by the work of John Gray in particular.[1] Several issues have been raised, but the main division of opinion is between broadly liberal and non-liberal schools, the former defending or trying to improve on Berlin's links between pluralism and liberal principles, the latter rejecting those links and aligning pluralism with various political alternatives, in particular conservatism and pragmatism.[2]

In this chapter I trace some of the principal moves in this critical literature. I begin by considering the case advanced by Gray, who is the most prominent spokesman for the non-liberal camp. I argue that Gray's case not only departs from Berlin's intentions, but also mistakes the logic of Berlinian pluralism. My rejection of Gray's view leads into a positive case for liberalism on pluralist grounds. By reflecting on the nature of pluralism itself I arrive at principles which identify liberalism as the best political system from a pluralist point of view. Having responded to the anti-liberal challenge, I then consider a split within the liberal camp, between the view that pluralism points to a form of liberalism based on toleration, including toleration of illiberal ways of life within the liberal state, and an opposing view that liberal pluralism should emphasize personal autonomy, thereby supporting a state which promotes liberal forms of life in preference to others. Here I side with the latter alternative. The pluralist case I outline goes beyond the arguments explicitly offered by Berlin, but it revives and extends some of those arguments and remains in keeping with the general spirit of his outlook.

Gray's agonistic interpretation

For Gray, Berlin's basic concept of value pluralism is correct, but it possesses an 'enormous subversive force' that Berlin himself does not fully appreciate.[3] Pluralism not only fails to support liberalism, Gray argues; it positively undermines most forms of liberal political thought. On this view, the message of pluralism is that liberalism is an 'agonistic' form of politics, that is, that liberal values are always in competition with others on an equal footing rather than always superior. They are only locally valid, not universally. Gray concedes that his reading takes 'a step for which there is no clear authority in Berlin's writings, and which he might well be reluctant to follow'.[4] But he insists that the underlying logic of Berlin's pluralism points away from liberal universalism rather than towards it.

Berlin never responded publicly to Gray's interpretation, but it is indeed certain that he would be reluctant to accept it. For Gray, the best possible world under pluralism is one in which there is a wide variety of ways of life and political regimes, some liberal, some not.[5] There is nothing in this vision that would exclude from the range of legitimate variety a regime like that of the Soviet Union or even Nazi Germany. Gray claims that his view does exclude these extremes, defining as 'illegitimate' those political systems that subject their people to 'universal evils' such as torture, persecution, humiliation, genocide, poverty and ill health.[6] But he immediately adds that these universal evils imply no 'minimal morality' for human beings, since different societies may have very different interpretations of what counts as an instance of any such evil, and may rank or trade off evils in very different ways when they conflict. Moreover, 'there is nothing unreasonable in putting the claims of one's way of life over those of universal values'.[7] It seems that a sincere Nazi may reasonably fight on, inflicting universal evils on

others, in order to preserve the Nazi way of life. Further, even if
Gray's position did somehow exclude the Nazis from the legitimate
range of societies under pluralism, it explicitly does not exclude
those illiberal regimes (the Ottoman and Hapsburg Empires,
Castro's Cuba) that disvalue negative liberty and personal
autonomy in less spectacular ways.[8]

Berlin strongly approved of cultural diversity, but he would not
be happy with these political conclusions. He would agree with
Gray that liberals cannot rely on the notion of universal values alone
to make their case, since genuine universals are far too generic to
indicate liberalism as their sole or uniquely best political expression.
Indeed, Berlin goes further, since he states quite explicitly that the
human moral horizon is compatible with Nazism (*POI*, 12–13;
Conv., 38) – an admission which Gray tries, unconvincingly, to draw
back from. Berlin's alternative notion of the 'central core' of human
values would not go much further, for reasons discussed in the last
chapter. Nevertheless, Berlin insists that pluralism implies liberalism. His case, as outlined in the previous chapter, appeals not
just to value universality but to other features and implications of
pluralism: the value of choice and the inevitability of social and
political imperfection.

The weaknesses and limitations of that case, as Berlin presents
it, have already been examined. To these difficulties Gray adds
further claims of his own about the nature of Berlinian pluralism,
to the effect that pluralism does not support liberalism but rather
undermines it. In place of liberalism he proposes various alternatives as more fittingly pluralist. The first, especially prominent
in his earlier work on pluralism, can be labelled his 'subjectivist'
view, since it appeals to those passages in which Berlin appears
to say that choices among incommensurables must be non-rational.
As Gray puts it, pluralism imposes on us 'radical' rather than
rational choices among incommensurables: 'choice without criteria,
grounds, or principles'.[9] Therefore, the choice of liberal values
in preference to the alternatives must also be fundamentally non-
rational. Liberalism is not justifiable by universal reason, but is at
best a historically contingent set of preferences or traditions. We
need not linger over this argument, since it rests on the irrationalist interpretation of choice under pluralism, which, as seen earlier,
does not do justice to our actual moral experience, and which Berlin
rightly repudiates. Decisive rational choice among incommensurables does seem possible in at least some concrete cases.

Gray soon came to accept this objection to the subjectivist reading, and abandoned it in favour of a contextualist approach: 'our

histories and circumstances, our needs and goals, may give good reasons for different choices'.[10] This is similar to Berlin's appeal to 'the general pattern of life in which we believe' (*L*, 47). But, unlike Berlin, Gray turns contextualism into another line of pluralist argument against liberalism. He argues in effect that if under pluralism a reasoned ranking of values is possible in context, it is possible *only* in context. The traditional project of liberalism is not contextual but universal: the classic justifications of liberalism (Lockean natural rights, Benthamite utilitarianism, Millian self-development, Rawlsian neutrality) privilege liberal goals not merely for particular societies but for all societies. Liberal universalism is therefore at odds with value pluralism and must be rejected. At most, pluralism is compatible with an 'agonistic' liberalism which self-consciously claims no more than local authority.[11] Pluralism points away from universalism of any kind and towards the authority of local tradition. Only cultural tradition can provide us with the context we need for the reasoned resolution of conflicts among incommensurable goods.

Gray's traditionalist contextualism can be challenged on three grounds. First, is it true that under pluralism we can choose among conflicting basic values *only* for reasons generated by context? Might it not be possible to find principles for reasoned choice within the concept of pluralism itself? This possibility is broached by Berlin in his arguments from choice and anti-utopianism, and I return to it in the next section. Secondly, supposing that pluralism commits us to reasoning in context, why must context be identified with tradition? Gray believes that there is reason to privilege liberal values only within the context of a pre-existing liberal tradition: in effect, liberalism is justified only where it already exists. But that view rests on a very narrow understanding of 'context', which may be interpreted more broadly to include not only pre-existing culture but also wider social, economic or civilizational circumstances. Given some such broader interpretation of the relevant context, we may arrive at a much broader defence of liberalism. For example, Joseph Raz argues that the liberal ideal of personal autonomy is appropriate, unavoidable even, not only for currently liberal societies but for all societies under 'the conditions of the industrial age and its aftermath with their fast changing technologies and free movement of labour'.[12] These are conditions such that no good life can be enjoyed without the capacity to adapt oneself to rapidly altering circumstances. Whatever the precise merits of Raz's argument, he opens up the possibility of a much broader contextual case for liberalism than that allowed by Gray.[13]

A third problem with Gray's traditionalism is that it neglects the possibility of conflicts within and among traditions. Reference to local tradition is supposed by Gray to resolve conflicts among incommensurables. But what happens when the relevant tradition is itself divided over these issues, or when there are deep disagreements as to what the tradition requires? Indeed, if pluralism is true, these are likely to be widespread problems, since value incommensurability tends naturally to generate reasonable disagreement over moral questions, in particular over questions of how one ought to live in general. (I return to the subject of reasonable disagreement about conceptions of the good life in the next section.) Further, even if a given tradition was univocal on how to resolve a particular conflict of incommensurables, what should pluralists do when they are confronted by multiple traditions sanctioning conflicting resolutions?

This problem of divided or multiple traditions has now been conceded by Gray, who in his most recent work has moved away from traditionalism towards a new position. Where traditions collide, he suggests, such conflicts can be 'settled by achieving a modus vivendi' among the parties, in which they 'find interests and values which they have in common and reach compromises regarding those in which they diverge'.[14] This points to an approach to politics very different from the culture-based conservatism of Gray's 'middle' period. Rather than loyalty to tradition, *modus vivendi* indicates a loose kind of pragmatism, an *ad hoc* response unguided by any consistent principles other than a general preference for accommodation over conflict. Again, however, Gray presents his view as a critique of the traditional claims of liberalism: 'liberal institutions are merely one variety of *modus vivendi*, not always the most legitimate'.[15] According to Gray, the only limits to legitimate *modi vivendi* are set by an ultra-thin notion of 'minimal standards of decency and legitimacy', explicitly consistent with non-liberal solutions.[16]

The notion of *modus vivendi* might seem to be the ideal political expression of value pluralism, since it looks so open-ended. But a moment's reflection is enough to reveal the problems with it from a pluralist point of view. The Munich Agreement of 1938 would count as a legitimate *modus vivendi* according to Gray's definition, but a settlement that won a temporary peace by delivering the Czechs into the hands of the Nazis is surely a poor expression of value pluralism. It is unclear whether Gray intends his *modus vivendi* to be a balance of power based on self-interest or a moral settlement based on a principled commitment to peaceful coexistence. But in either case is Gray not reverting to what he condemns as monism in the liberal theories he rejects? His *modus vivendi* is no different from liberalism in giving general priority to certain values over others – in the case of *modus vivendi* it is either peace or self-interest that is overriding. Further, if Gray is commending *modus vivendi* as a universal rule, then he is in effect advancing his favoured values as universally overriding, the very position he attributes to the liberals and rejects in the name of pluralism.

Gray might deny that he is asserting *modus vivendi* as a universal rule. In one passage he presents it as 'a contingent good' that is 'worth pursuing only insofar as it advances human interests', which may change.[17] But if the application of *modus vivendi* is really contingent on changing human interests, then we are left to ask when it applies and when it does not. In those cases where it does not apply, what then? Are we referred back to traditionalism, or even subjectivism? On these questions Gray gives no guidance. In fact he usually speaks of *modus vivendi* in terms suggesting not contingency but permanence. 'All ways of life have some interests in common', and these common interests 'give us reason to pursue coexistence'.[18] But what the common interests are, Gray does not say beyond noting that they are 'many and varied'. This conflicts with his insistence (probably correct) earlier in the same book that genuinely universal goods are few and highly generic.[19] Further, even if he identified a set of interests genuinely common to all human beings, he would still have to explain how these 'give us reason to pursue coexistence'. Finally, supposing that there are common interests which give us reason to pursue coexistence, there are also likely to be other common interests which give us reason to abandon coexistence in at least some significant number of cases. Gray himself admits that 'it is frequently those interests that divide us'.[20]

So we are back to the question of why a pluralist outlook should be tied more especially to the good of peace (or self-interest) rather than to other goods. Certainly pluralists will sometimes, even often, have good reason to prefer peace to the alternatives, but not always. The Munich Agreement is a case in point. This is not to deny that pluralism sometimes implies an important role for compromise, especially in cases where reason indicates no single solution or where moral agreement is impossible. But even in those cases compromise is not invariably justified from a pluralist point of view, and where it is, justified pluralist compromise should be guided by principles of the kind I shall come to shortly.[21]

Gray's various attempts to align Berlinian pluralism with non-liberal approaches to politics are all deeply unsatisfactory. His early subjectivism fails to allow for the possibility of reasoned choice among conflicting incommensurables in context. The conservative contextualism of his middle period is too narrow and rigid, since it ignores contexts wider than cultural traditions and neglects conflicts among and within such traditions. Finally, his notion of *modus vivendi* is vague and undeveloped, and its general privileging of either peace or self-interest makes it hard to distinguish from the monism that he sees as a fatal flaw in liberalism.

A pluralist case for liberalism

At this point Gray might reply that although his constructive account of pluralist politics may need clarification or amendment, at least his main critical point holds: if value pluralism is true, then liberal universalism, including Berlin's, is untenable because no moral universalism is tenable. Could liberals resist Gray on this point and argue beyond contextualism? They might do so by challenging Gray's argument at its first step and resisting the claim that under pluralism context is the *only* source of reasons for ranking goods. Another source could be the concept of value pluralism itself. By reflecting on the components of the pluralist idea, we might arrive at principles of not merely particular but universal application. Such principles might be derived from the components of pluralism analysed in the last chapter. Indeed, this is essentially what Berlin is trying to do in his arguments from choice and anti-utopianism, which appeal to the pluralist notions of value plurality, conflict and incommensurability. I have concluded that the particular arguments offered by Berlin are not wholly successful as they stand. Still, it may be that better arguments can be constructed using the same basic strategy. Here are four possibilities.

1. Universal values

It might be argued, for example, that the first component of value pluralism, the universality of at least some values, suggests a principle of respect for a minimal universal morality. It might then be added that liberalism satisfies that moral minimum, while other political forms do not. We have already seen why this argument, although it may be a first step along the road from pluralism to liberalism, does not get us very far. It is fair to claim that liberalism is at least compatible with Berlin's notion of a minimal universal morality because of the liberal commitment to human rights. But Berlin's conceptions of the 'human horizon' and 'central core' of universals are so thin that they fall far short of singling out a distinctively liberal order as their only or best political expression. Not only liberalism but many other political views, some extremely illiberal, are consistent with Berlin's universal goods.[22]

Could Berlin respond by making his account of moral universality 'thicker' or more demanding, so that it excluded non-liberal societies? A model for this move might be provided by the 'human capabilities' approach of Martha Nussbaum and Amartya Sen, according to which a good life for a human being requires the possession of real capacities to exercise certain essential 'human functions', the list of these being fairly detailed and extensive.[23] It could then be argued that such capacities are best realized under a liberal form of politics. The general difficulty with this strategy is the obvious tension between identifying goods at a sufficient level of specificity to single out liberalism as a necessary political context and, on the other hand, ensuring that the goods are described in sufficiently general terms to count as genuinely universal, in the sense of essential or desirable for any good life.[24] While such an approach should not be ruled out prematurely, it is probably best to remain somewhat sceptical of it. Again, the appeal to universals is best regarded as a first step on the road from pluralism to liberalism, but no more than that.

2. Incommensurability

Respect for universal values is only the first element of the pluralist idea; another is incommensurability. Gray argues that this tells against liberalism. If some values are incommensurable, he argues, then so too are the 'forms of life' in which they are instantiated.[25] If incommensurability prevents reasoned universal ranking, then that applies as much among ways of life as among values. And since liberalism is the political expression of a particular form of life (emphasizing negative liberty, personal autonomy, etc.), it follows that there can be no good reason to uphold liberalism as universally superior to alternative political views based on alternative conceptions of the good. But I have already shown that the claim that cultures or ways of life are wholly incommensurable is mistaken. On the pluralist view, ways of life cannot be wholly incommensurable, because at least some values are universal. All forms of life must overlap to that extent. Incommensurability does not undermine liberalism in the way that Gray supposes.

Moreover, incommensurability provides liberalism with some positive support. In the previous chapter I noted Berlin's argument that a key implication of value incommensurability is the imperfectibility of human lives in general and of political life in particular. To acknowledge the reality of value incommensurability is to rule out views like classical Marxism and anarchism as utopian, and to commend more realistic positions which accept and accommodate imperfection and conflict. Liberalism falls within this latter class of realistic positions. But I also noted that liberalism is not the only political form consistent with the anti-utopianism that follows from value incommensurability. Conservatism is another candidate, and Gray's *modus vivendi* is perhaps a third. If liberalism is to be picked out as uniquely fitted to the pluralist outlook, its supporters need a stronger principle.

3. Diversity

Could Berlinian pluralism provide more determinate support for liberalism by way of a principle of 'diversity'? Liberal pluralists could argue as follows. Value pluralism suggests that, subject to qualification, it is better that a society embrace more values rather than fewer. As Bernard Williams writes, 'if there are many and competing genuine values, then the greater the extent to which a society tends to be single-valued, the more genuine values it neglects or suppresses. More, to this extent, must mean better.'[26] When it comes to determining the best political vehicle for this diversity of goods, liberalism surely has a strong claim. Its traditional emphasis on individual liberty, toleration and personal autonomy clears social spaces within which individuals and groups can pursue a wide range of different purposes.

How exactly does pluralism imply the desirability of more, rather than fewer, goods within a single society? This implication seems to be denied by Gray when he defends the possibility of a society that acknowledges the truth of value pluralism but consistently chooses for itself a relatively narrow, illiberal or authoritarian culture.[27] Such a society can recognize the value of other goods and ways of life, but simply opt to preserve its own insular and monolithic traditions. Liberal pluralists can reply that such a society is not truly pluralist in outlook, because it does not take seriously the value diversity that pluralism stands for. If pluralism is true, then there are many intrinsic goods, that is, goods that are valuable for their own sake. ('Valuable' here means contributing to human well-being objectively, not just valued *de facto* by particular persons or societies.[28]) Each of these goods has, prima facie, an independent claim on our respect: we should take them all seriously. To take a good seriously in this sense is not necessarily to promote it in every case, since pluralists recognize, following Berlin, that not all goods can be realized simultaneously: to emphasize one may be to neglect or downplay another. Precisely which goods can be pursued in combination with which others will depend on the circumstances.[29] Further, in some cases it may be hard to judge with any precision which of two rival packages of goods is more expressive of diversity. Nevertheless, subject to these qualifications, pluralism commits us to allowing or encouraging the pursuit of as many genuine goods as the circumstances allow. It follows that pluralism commits us to the promotion of as many forms of life as possible – subject to a similar qualification as to the compatibility of the forms of life at issue, and to a further important limitation I shall come to in a moment. To accept value pluralism is to have good reason to take seriously and promote a diversity of goods and ways of life.

Supposing that pluralism implies an ethic of diversity along these lines, liberal pluralists argue that this is best satisfied politically by the toleration and individual liberty characteristic of liberalism. Again, Gray opposes this claim. He agrees that pluralism implies diversity, but interprets this as a commitment to a diversity not so much of particular goods as of whole ways of life. Since different ways of life give rise to different political systems, pluralist diversity therefore endorses a diversity of political regimes. Liberalism is one of these, but once more possesses no privileged status. For pluralists, Gray claims, the best world is not one in which liberal principles triumph universally, but rather one containing many different political forms, some liberal and some not.[30]

There are two main problems with Gray's position here. First, he assumes that to value a diversity of forms of life is to value a diversity of political regimes. But some political regimes are more hospitable than others to diverse ways of life. This is true both externally, in their treatment of other states, and internally, in their treatment of different ways of life within their own territory. On the whole it is liberal polities, or polities with substantial liberal components, that have the best records when it comes to tolerating and promoting multiple ways of life both at home and abroad. This is not to say that liberal polities have been limitlessly tolerant in these respects, merely that they have done better, on balance, than non-liberal regimes. Therefore it is unlikely that pluralist diversity would be advanced by replacing liberal regimes with non-liberal ones. Non-liberal regimes would, it is true, add something to human diversity, but they would take away a good deal more.

The second problem with Gray's view is that he assumes that the diversity to which pluralists are committed is principally a diversity of cultures or ways of life. The problem with this assumption was identified in the previous chapter, namely that it blurs the boundary between pluralism and cultural relativism. On a distinctively pluralist view, it is particular goods, like liberty and equality, that are incommensurable, not whole cultures. Whole cultures, indeed, cannot be entirely incommensurable on a pluralist view, because on such a view there are at least some values, however thinly described, that are universal or cross-cultural, and that therefore represent points of overlap among cultures.

What these points show is that the ideal of diversity implicit in pluralism refers, primarily, not to political regimes or forms of life, as assumed by Gray, but to goods or values. Rather than valuing and promoting a diversity of regimes or cultures without regard to their content, value pluralists should value and promote a diversity of regimes and cultures that are themselves internally diverse, that is, that exhibit internally a diversity of goods and (secondarily) ways of life. Once more, liberalism has a strong claim to being acknowledged as the political form most accommodating of this kind of diversity, for the reasons given above: its distinctive freedoms enable individuals and groups to pursue disparate goods within the same polity.

Again, that is not to claim that a liberal polity is limitlessly accommodating or wholly neutral among conceptions of the good life. In this connection Gray objects 'that liberal societies tend to drive out non-liberal forms of life, to ghettoize or marginalize them, or to trivialize them'.[31] Indeed, liberal pluralists should concede that even the most liberal of orders is based implicitly on a general value ranking which privileges individual liberty and toleration, and in so doing places limits on other goods. However, some such ranking is unavoidable in any political system, as are the costs of such a ranking in terms of alternative values forgone or downplayed. The liberal ranking arguably leaves more room for a variety of goods and conceptions of the good to be pursued than does any known alternative. Certainly liberalism appears superior on this score to

Gray's preferred device of *modus vivendi*, assuming the *modus vivendi* is not itself liberal in form. Peace can sometimes be bought only at the price of reduced liberties, and consequently a diminished range of human goods. The Munich Agreement, for example, represented a net reduction in the ends open to the Czechs. Contrary to Gray, the kind of diversity commended by pluralism is better served by liberal univeralism, such as that of Berlin, than by Gray's ill-defined *modus vivendi*.

4. Reasonable disagreement

To the argument from diversity may be added a further, closely related, consideration which also tends in a liberal direction. This is that value pluralism strongly implies the reasonableness of much disagreement about the nature of the good life, and that liberalism is the best vehicle we have for the containment of that kind of reasonable disagreement.

Conceptions of the good may be thought of as schemes for ranking basic human goods across a generality of cases. Christians, for example, emphasize humility and love for one's neighbour as especially important values for all human beings in all or most circumstances. The ethics of classical paganism, which live on to some extent in the military and sporting spheres, celebrate personal strength and self-assertion in the same general terms.[32] If at least some basic values are incommensurable, then many such general rankings will be prima facie reasonable, and many will be equally reasonable. This is not to say that pluralism endorses all conceptions of the good, since some do better than others when judged by the pluralist standards of respect for universals, moral and political realism, and diversity of goods. But within those limits there will be much legitimate variation. Consequently, many disagreements concerning the merits of rival conceptions of the good will also be reasonable. Where disagreements are reasonable in this sense, they are likely to be permanent. A realistic and prudent form of politics will therefore accept and accommodate reasonable disagreement rather than trying to overcome it. Liberalism, its defenders may fairly claim, is just such a realistic and prudent political form.

This branch of the liberal-pluralist case overlaps the influential position of John Rawls in *Political Liberalism* (1993), where he argues precisely that liberalism can be justified as the best political container for reasonable disagreement concerning the good life.

However, the pluralist and Rawlsian views are not on all fours.[33] Rawls maintains that liberalism should be a strictly 'political' settlement, avoiding appeal to any 'comprehensive moral doctrine', or controversial account of moral truth. Berlinian pluralism, on the other hand, may seem to be just such a comprehensive view, since it involves disputed claims about the true character of moral values. This contrast has led the Rawlsian theorist Charles Larmore to criticize the liberal-pluralist case as resting on a theory of morality which is too controversial to serve the goal of liberal neutrality.[34] For Larmore, pluralism cannot be the basis for a liberalism that aspires to be neutral among competing conceptions of the good, because pluralism is itself a controversial conception of the good.

Berlinian liberals might reply as follows.[35] First, it may be questioned whether Berlinian pluralism counts as a comprehensive moral doctrine in Rawls's terms. Pluralism itself is a meta-thesis about the statues of values, not a substantive moral view about what actions are right or which lives are good. Secondly, even if pluralism does count as a comprehensive moral doctrine, it is not 'controversial' in the same sense as those conceptions of the good which most concern Rawls, especially religious conceptions. So far as pluralism has ethical implications, they do not point to any narrowly exclusive way of life; on the contrary, they imply the legitimacy, reasonableness and value of many ways of life. Thirdly, pluralism is in any case no more controversial a basis for liberalism than Rawls's theory. For one thing, Rawls's view controversially requires people to restrict their comprehensive beliefs to the private realm in order to maintain the putative neutrality of the state.[36] But that requirement is itself not neutral among conceptions of the good, since it already assumes a liberal disposition to live and let live. Furthermore, it is at least arguable that the bedrock Rawlsian assumption, of the fact of reasonable disagreement among conceptions of the good, itself presupposes a pluralist account of morality. The reasonableness, and therefore permanence, of the moral disagreement that concerns Rawls depends, in his view, on certain 'burdens of judgement', or obstacles to agreement when it comes to distinctively moral questions. Some of the most significant of these look very much like the claims of Berlinian pluralism: for example, the observation that 'often there are different kinds of normative considerations of different force on both sides of an issue and it is difficult to make an overall assessment'.[37]

Note that this argument from reasonable disagreement (to some extent also the argument from diversity) is in essence a restatement and extension of Berlin's anti-utopian view. Berlin had linked pluralism with moral and political imperfectibility, which I argued was consistent with liberalism without singling it out as superior to other non-utopian forms, like conservatism. The argument from reasonable disagreement in effect takes the next step by bringing out more explicitly the theme of indefeasible conflict that was only implicit in Berlin's account. It is that theme of reasonable, therefore permanent, moral conflict that recommends liberalism against conservatism. Whereas the conservative response to the conflicts generated by value pluralism is to appeal to the authority of local tradition or a unitary conception of the good, liberalism acknowledges the further point that under pluralism there will be widespread reasonable disagreement about the worth of particular traditions, because there will be widespread reasonable disagreement about the merits of rival conceptions of the good. Of course, liberal pluralists must also argue that this reasonable disagreement does not extend to the conception of the good underlying liberalism itself. But this they can do on the ground stated earlier: that all political societies must base their institutions on some general ranking of goods, and that the liberal configuration, although not without costs, has a strong claim to being more capacious than the alternatives.

I conclude that there are good reasons for Berlinian pluralists to be liberals. The pluralist principle of respect for universal values starts us on the road to liberalism by demonstrating that under pluralism political regimes and ways of life are not immune to external criticism, but can be critically evaluated for good reason. The principle that we should recognize the implications of value incommensurability takes us a stage further. If significant human goods are incommensurable, then moral and political perfectibility must be ruled out as utopian, and with it certain traditional ideological opponents of liberalism: notably classical Marxism and anarchism. Moreover, liberalism is identified as belonging among those political forms that possess a realistic appreciation of the inevitability of moral loss and social conflict. More importantly still, the pluralist commitment to the promotion of value diversity and to respect for reasonable disagreement singles out liberalism as having a strong claim to being the best expression of value-pluralist politics, since liberalism is capable of accommodating a wide diversity of values and ways of life.

Reformation or Enlightenment?

I have laid out a pluralist case for liberalism, one that goes beyond Berlin's actual arguments but which builds upon them and remains within the spirit of his general position. Supposing that this case is accepted so far, the next question is: what kind of liberalism will this be? This is, of course, a very large issue, and I shall address only one major dimension of it here. (I shall say a little more in the next chapter.) As framed by William Galston, this is the debate between 'Reformation' and 'Enlightenment' forms of liberalism.[38] Reformation liberalism is based on toleration, and sees the liberal state as a political container for many different conceptions of the good, including some non-liberal or illiberal ones. 'Enlightenment' liberalism takes personal autonomy as its guiding ideal, and supports a state willing actively to promote characteristically liberal conceptions of the good. The key practical point at issue between the two views is the appropriate liberal attitude to non-liberal minority groups within the liberal state, the Reformation view being more hands-off and the Enlightenment view more interventionist.

In this debate Galston takes the Reformation side, and in his recent work he tries to provide this position with a grounding in Berlinian pluralism. The strongest of Galston's arguments along these lines is a version of the argument from diversity.[39] From the pluralist point of view we should value and promote a diversity of goods, hence a diversity of conceptions of the good, and for this goal the best political vehicle is a tolerance-based liberalism. By contrast, the autonomy-based liberalism of Kant and Mill is too sectarian, expressing one particular understanding of the human good to the exclusion of other legitimate beliefs.[40] Rather, the liberal state should provide 'maximum feasible accommodation' of all ways of life within the state.[41] The state should respect the 'expressive liberty' of all its citizens, or their right to lead 'their lives as they see fit, within a broad range of legitimate variation, in accordance with their own understanding of what gives life meaning and value'.[42] If that understanding is an expressly illiberal one, like that of a fundamentalist religion, the expressive liberty of the group's members should still be respected.[43]

Whether Berlin would agree with Galston is doubtful. In his more Herderian moods Berlin is inclined to regard whole ways of life as incommensurable with one another, and thus intrinsically valuable each on its own terms. This strand of Berlin's thought would seem

to favour Galston's Reformation view, with its emphasis on toleration of group practices even where these are illiberal. On the other
hand, uncritical acceptance of illiberal cultural practices, such as
patriarchy and censorship, seem to be at odds with Berlin's concern
for the negative liberty of the individual.[44] Moreover, I have argued
that the claim that whole cultures are incommensurable is not
Berlin's best view, since it does not fit with his acceptance of a
'horizon' or 'core' of universal values and with his notion of empathetic understanding. Rather, the logic of Berlin's position allows,
even requires, that ways of life be open to critical comparison and
evaluation, whether favourable or not.

The standards against which cultures can be evaluated under
pluralism include, as shown in the previous section, value diversity.
This suggests the basic problem with Galston's position from a pluralist point of view, namely that pluralist diversity does not justify
a Reformation-style toleration of groups regardless of their content.
Galston does not go as far as Gray in identifying the incommensurability of values with the incommensurability of political regimes,
but he tends similarly to equate diversity of goods with diversity
of cultures. The problem with this, as I argued in the case of Gray,
is that value diversity is not necessarily promoted by cultural diversity if the cultures concerned are internally monolithic or uniform.
Pluralist diversity translates into cultural diversity only to the
extent that cultures themselves promote a diversity of goods. When
Galston recommends liberalism as a container for a diversity of conceptions of the good, in effect he endorses the point I made earlier
against Gray: that if value diversity is to be promoted, then it should
be promoted not only among political regimes but within them
too.[45] The best world from the point of view of pluralist diversity is
a world of liberal states, because these are internally diverse and
therefore more accommodating than are non-liberal states of different ways of life. But if that is so, then the Enlightenment liberal
can invite Galston to take his own reasoning a step further. If value
diversity should be promoted within political regimes, then it
should be promoted within ways of life or conceptions of the good
too. The best world will be one consisting of political regimes that
accommodate many ways of life, but these must themselves be
internally diverse.

Not only does pluralist diversity not support blanket Reformation toleration of groups, it implies a case for Enlightenment promotion of personal autonomy. Pluralist diversity applies within
groups as well as among them. For a group's way of life to be

internally diverse it must enable its members to be personally autonomous. That is because an internally diverse way of life must be one that allows its members to interpret its general values for themselves in different ways, following paths they have chosen for their own reasons. The mere right to exit the group is obviously not enough to promote the group's internal diversity, since it allows divergence to be managed by exclusion rather than accommodation.[46] Nor is a more general commitment to negative liberty alone enough for internal diversity. As Berlin concedes, negative liberty is consistent with 'choices' being empty and valueless, as in cases where I lack the necessary material resources. Even the material 'conditions of liberty' in Berlin's sense are not enough, since one can possess resources without having any idea of how to use them in ways other than the conventional. This is not to say that a right of exit, negative liberty more generally, and the material conditions of liberty are unimportant; indeed, they are essential to an internally diverse way of life. But a further necessary condition is personal autonomy. For people to be able to pursue genuinely divergent goals rather than familiar ones, they must be able to stand back from their society's or their group's customs and conventions and subject these to critical scrutiny. That is, an internally diverse way of life involves the capacity to make one's own choices in a strong sense, and that is the definition of personal autonomy.[47]

Galston's concern for pluralist diversity should lead, then, not to the toleration of multiple ways of life without regard to their content, but to the promotion of those ways of life which value personal autonomy. The better expression of pluralism is not Reformation but Enlightenment liberalism. That conclusion is confirmed by another line of thought, which can be seen as a revival and development of Berlin's argument from choice.[48] Recall Berlin's failed attempt to pass directly from the necessity of choice under pluralism to the valuing of choice under liberalism. That argument can be restated to avoid the naturalistic fallacy, as follows. Pluralism imposes hard choices on us. To cope well with those choices, we need to develop certain dispositions of character, or virtues. Those virtues overlap the character traits distinctively promoted by liberal forms of politics, in particular the exercise of personal autonomy. In short, liberalism promotes the virtues required for coping successfully with the exigencies of choosing among conflicting incommensurables. The argument avoids the naturalistic fallacy, because it passes not from necessity to value but from necessity to necessity.

If pluralism is true, we cannot avoid hard choices, and if we are to cope well with these hard choices, we need to be autonomous.

I should admit straight away that this argument depends on a significant assumption. Liberal virtues are necessary to cope well with choices under pluralism if to 'cope well' with such choices means to choose for a good reason. It is only if we are first committed to rational choice under pluralism that we need the virtues requisite to practical reasoning. But why should we be committed to reason here? Why not say that from a pluralist point of view rational choice is itself merely one value among others, and that one may equally cope with pluralist choice by plumping arbitrarily? A reply is suggested by Nussbaum, who argues that practical reasoning is 'architectonic' among the basic human functions she identifies, in the sense that it 'organise[s] and arrange[s] all of the others, giving them in the process a characteristically human shape'.[49] Similarly, under pluralism, practical reason is needed to organize choices among incommensurable goods. In the absence of practical reasoning our choices would be arbitrary, incoherent and perhaps self-defeating. Unless we give some thought to how the ends we endorse fit together, we are in danger of creating lives that, as John Kekes puts it, 'are too scattered . . . In such lives there are many values, but between their favorable evaluation and realization come the distractions of other values whose realization also recedes for the same reason.'[50] Lives like these are undesirable from a pluralist point of view because they fail to do justice to, or take seriously, the goods they purport to value. This notion of taking goods seriously was introduced earlier in connection with diversity, and I shall return to it in a moment.

My argument is that rational choice under pluralism requires the exercise of certain liberal virtues. I shall now consider the steps in this argument in a little more detail. First, pluralism imposes hard choices upon us. We saw earlier that this is true in two senses: such choices involve absolute loss, and they must be made without reliance on any simple monist rule like utilitarianism. Secondly, to cope well with those hard choices (i.e. to choose for a good reason), we need to develop certain dispositions of character, or virtues. This claim recalls the link made in the last chapter with Aristotelian practical reasoning. Aristotle's person of practical wisdom is able to see what she ought to do in a given situation because she has developed, through experience of cognate situations, a skill in practical judgement. That skill or virtue is supported by other virtues, according to Aristotle, in particular courage, justice and temperance. Similarly, a person confronted by a hard choice among incommensurables will be assisted in choosing well if he informs his reflections with certain attitudes of mind which may likewise be called virtues.

What, then, are the pluralist virtues? Once more I suggest we can answer this question by reflection on the nature of pluralism itself. In this way I propose four candidates. The first is generosity or open-mindedness, which is closely connected to the idea of taking plural values seriously. To be a pluralist is, in part, to acknowledge that many goods and ways of life are objectively valuable. Consequently, acknowledging the truth of pluralism commits one to respecting the full range of legitimate goods and good lives, that is, to endorsing those goods and lives prima facie. This does not mean that pluralists must endorse all such goods and lives equally in every particular case, since clearly there is insufficient 'social space' to do this within the life of an individual or even a society.[51] But pluralists should affirm all such goods and lives as possessing real value, even if they must sometimes choose against them in concrete instances. This is what I mean by the pluralist injunction to take goods seriously. If a good is genuine, then we must promote it where we can, and where we cannot, we must choose against it with regret. The implication is that we should approach pluralist choices with a certain attitude, namely one of respect for the full range of human goods and lives, including those we cannot accommodate within our own decisions. This amounts to a high degree of open-mindedness when dealing with the values and cultures of others. As Michael Walzer puts it, 'you have to look at the world in a receptive and generous way to see a pluralism of Berlin's sort'.[52]

For the same reason, pluralists should approach their choices with what Berlin calls a 'sense of reality', a feeling for the real costs of moral and political decisions, conditioned in particular by the implications of incommensurability.[53] This is the second pluralist virtue: call it 'realism'. A third virtue can be labelled 'attentiveness'. Pluralists' rejection of neat abstract rules, and insistence on the particularity of moral solutions, should make them attentive to the relevant details of the choice situation, including the claims and circumstances of those people affected by the choice.[54] A fourth virtue is 'flexibility'. In the absence of decisive monist rules, pluralists need to be flexible in tailoring their judgement closely to the situation to which they attend.

These pluralist virtues are also characteristically liberal virtues. Generosity towards the range of human goods and lives is a recognizable trait of liberalism at its best.[55] One sees it, for example, in Mill's valuing of individuality and social diversity.[56] Realism in the face of unavoidable costs and conflicts is a theme which, I have already argued following Berlin, separates liberals from their more utopian opponents, including classical Marxists and anarchists. Attentiveness is represented by the core liberal concern for the fate of individual human beings, as captured, for example, by Kant's doctrine of respect for persons.

Above all, pluralist flexibility overlaps the liberal commitment to personal autonomy. Of the several links between pluralist practical reasoning and liberalism, this is the most significant, since personal autonomy is the most distinctive of liberal virtues, at any rate on the Enlightenment view. To judge flexibly in the light of value pluralism is to judge for one's own reasons in a strong sense, that is, autonomously. In part this is because conflicts among incommensurable goods cannot be decided for good reason merely by the mechanical application of a standard monist rule. If utilitarianism, for example, represents only one possible ranking of incommensurables, then utilitarian calculation can be no more than one consideration among others in pluralist judgement. The rational pluralist cannot rely on utilitarianism or any other ready-made monist procedure to resolve deep moral conflicts, but must go behind such perspectives to weigh the values they embody for herself.

Nor can pluralists answer such questions merely by appealing to the authority of local tradition. Traditionalism is especially unhelpful in modern societies characterized by widespread disagreement about conceptions of the good. But on the pluralist view the problem is not merely an aspect of modernity; it is rooted in the moral experience of humanity. For pluralists, reasonable disagreement concerning the good life is a permanent possibility in all human societies because of the deep structure of human values. Traditional and other conceptions of the good life represent, as I suggested above, generalized rankings of incommensurable values. Although I have argued that pluralists should not accept that all such conceptions are automatically on a moral par, nevertheless the wide range of genuine human goods implies a wide range of legitimate permutations of those goods, that is, of reasonable rankings. Concerning these, there is consequently room for people to disagree on reasonable grounds. Pluralists cannot resolve the deepest value conflicts simply by citing a local or personal conception of the good, because under pluralism these are subject to reasonable disagreement.

Reasonable disagreement about the good is experienced both *among* cultural groups or belief systems and also within them. Moreover, individuals can experience the centrifugal pull of incommensurable goods not only interpersonally, but also within themselves. Berlin's own inner conflicts, surely among the deepest sources of his pluralism, are a case in point. Here too there is a link between pluralism and personal autonomy. For where the nature of the good life is subject to reasonable disagreement, conceptions of the good cannot be permanent bases for decision, but must be subject to revision themselves. That kind of decision is possible only through the exercise of personal autonomy.

In short, value pluralism imposes on us choices that are demanding to a degree such that they can be made well only by autonomous agents. If pluralism is true, then the best lives, those informed by critical choices among the available options, will be characterized by personal autonomy. This is not at all to say that heteronomous lives are without value. Such lives may exhibit many other goods that should be taken seriously from a pluralist point of view, and must be valued accordingly. Indeed, such lives may well be better than autonomous lives in certain respects. But, if my argument is correct, lives such as these cannot be among the best possible overall, since they lack the key capacity for good decision making in the face of inevitable value conflict.

If that is true, then pluralism implies a case not only for liberalism, but specifically for Enlightenment liberalism, under which the promotion of personal autonomy is a legitimate goal of public policy. This conclusion follows, given the plausible claim that the conditions for personal autonomy, both cultural and economic, are unlikely to be sustained, at least for many people, in the absence of some significant degree of deliberate state intervention. I say more to support this claim in the final chapter.

Note that although this sequence revives Berlin's argument from choice, it also transforms that argument significantly. Whereas Berlin had linked pluralist choice with liberty in its negative form (freedom of choice), my reformulation endorses personal autonomy, which belongs to the positive category. This supports the view canvassed in chapter 4, that Berlin's 'Two Concepts of Liberty' should be more alive to the central place of positive freedom, in the form of personal autonomy, in the liberal outlook. Again, the reassertion of liberal pluralism builds on Berlin's views, but also goes beyond them.

My pro-Enlightenment conclusion may seem surprising bearing in mind Berlin's pluralist starting point. The basic claim of value pluralism is that within the human repertoire there are many distinctly legitimate goods, and that none of these is always overriding. Does Enlightenment liberalism not collide with pluralism by according a universal privilege to a single good, namely, personal autonomy? Enlightenment liberals could reply that they do not demand that autonomy be privileged in every context. The pluralist-Enlightenment view does not deny the possibility of cases, in both private and public life, where personal autonomy appropriately yields to rival considerations such as urgency or security or the demands of personal relationships. The point is that these and other moral decisions are unavoidably made within a political framework informed by some general ranking of values. Berlinian pluralists can do no more than insist that this ranking should as far as possible answer to fundamental pluralist concerns. Among these are concerns for value diversity and reasonable disagreement, which argue for a politics capable of accommodating many goods and ways of life. Thus far, pluralism might seem to suggest a 'liberalism of toleration'. But these same pluralist principles of diversity and reasonable disagreement require that the ways of life in question be themselves internally diverse. Ways of life are internally diverse when they allow their members to follow different paths of their own choosing, and that involves acknowledging personal autonomy as a significant value. This line is reinforced by the further pluralist insight that personal autonomy is required for coping with the exigency of choices among incommensurables. In the end, pluralism points beyond toleration to the stronger, Enlightenment form of liberalism. Within such a framework there will be a great diversity of goods, among which personal autonomy will be prominent but not always overriding. There will also be a great diversity of ways of life, but they will have in common a respect for personal autonomy.

Summary

Berlin's liberal reading of the political implications of pluralism has been strongly challenged in recent years, in particular by the influential anti-liberal interpretations offered by Gray. But these are vulnerable to several lines of reply, and the replies suggest ways of reviving and extending the pluralist case for liberal universalism consistent with Berlin's intentions. As to what kind of liberalism this will be, there is divergence between a Reformation view which emphasizes negative liberty and toleration and an Enlightenment view which stresses the value of personal autonomy. I have argued that, despite superficial parallels between aspects of Berlin's position and the Reformation view, it is the Enlightenment version that fits better with the logic of his pluralist commitments. These arguments travel a good distance beyond Berlin's explicit statements, but they draw on the clues he has left us.

8

Berlin's Achievement

In this final chapter I assess Berlin's place within the liberal tradition, and his significance as a moral and political thinker overall. I begin by arguing that he stands for a distinctively 'realist' form of liberalism, the ambitions of which have been tempered by the failure, indeed incoherence, of Enlightenment utopianism and by the experience of twentieth-century totalitarianism. This raises the question, however, of whether Berlin's message is purely negative in character, a warning to liberals and others to abandon utopian hopes, or whether he has any positive programme to offer beyond the warning. Here I examine Berlin's position as it relates to two fields of public policy: social justice and cultural rights. In the case of social justice I argue that Berlin says less than he ought to, but that his pluralism could provide the basis for a defence of the welfare redistribution he in fact favours. When it comes to the political status of cultures, Berlin tends to support states in which political recognition is afforded only to a single national culture, but his own deeper principles suggest a position closer to a form of multiculturalism within liberal limits. Finally, I address the question of how Berlin's thought should be evaluated all things considered, answering that he will continue, deservedly, to be influential. The weaknesses in his thought are counterbalanced by the depth of his analysis of totalitarianism, the originality of his formulation of value pluralism and its implications, and the vitality of his unique empathetic method of inquiry.

Berlin's realism

What kind of liberal is Isaiah Berlin? I have already given some answers to this question. Despite his sympathy with historicist thinking, Berlin's liberal convictions are fundamentally universalist rather than 'agonistic' (to use John Gray's term), or only locally valid. He urges the validity of human rights, including the securing of a minimal area of negative liberty for the individual, as a condition for any truly satisfactory human life (*L*, 52–3, 171–4, 211; *Conv.*, 114). Moreover, I have argued that Berlin's liberal universalism is consistent with his value pluralism, and even required by it. Pluralism is not relativism; it implies a set of principles which cut across cultural boundaries and which justify liberal institutions in cross-cultural terms. I have also argued that in the debate between Reformation and Enlightenment liberals, although Berlin's declared preference for negative liberty seems to draw him towards the former camp, the logic of his deepest commitments, including his commitment to pluralism, actually points towards the latter, autonomy-based version. On the issue of classical or *laissez-faire* versus social or welfare state liberalism, Berlin's attraction to negative liberty does not commit him to the politics of the minimal state. On the contrary, he explicitly states his allegiance to redistribution in the name of both freedom and justice. I shall return to this aspect of Berlin in the next section.

Another possible division among liberal thinkers is between optimists and pessimists. All liberals believe that human beings are at least in some degree susceptible to reasoned argument and education, and that by these means human affairs can be improved. But some liberals are distinctly more hopeful than others about the extent to which, and the speed with which, this goal might be reached or approached. For some, liberalism is the inheritor of an Enlightenment project that envisages, as Gray puts it, 'universal convergence on a cosmopolitan and rationalist civilization'.[1] The historical champions of this view include some of the French Encyclopedists and their successors, the most spectacular examples being Condorcet and William Godwin.[2] In the contemporary world, the most prominent representative of this more ambitious liberalism is probably Francis Fukuyama.[3] By contrast, the less optimistic kind of liberal sees the tradition not as a triumphant parade but as a holding action, in which a thin but more or less distinct political line is maintained between desirable and undesirable forms of human life. This strand of liberal thought extends from Locke's defence of toleration and natural rights against religious bigotry and political absolutism, to the 'liberalism of fear' formulated by Judith Shklar.[4]

Looked at in these terms, Berlin clearly belongs more on the side of the pessimists, or realists. Anti-utopianism is a constant in his work, as illustrated by his frequent references to the limits placed on perfectibilist ambitions by 'the crooked timber of humanity'. For Berlin this is an insight that applies as much to the ambitions of liberals as to the hopes of Marxists. I have frequently mentioned Berlin's injunction to beware of all abstract ideals and projections, and to maintain a check on the real human costs of policies. This emerges strongly, for example, in his discussions of the Russian thinkers of the nineteenth century, especially in his defence of Herzen's 'sense of reality' and Turgenev's unglamorous gradualism in the face of the revolutionary enthusiasms of the next generation of young radicals. Similarly, in 'Political Ideas in the Twentieth Century' Berlin enters a plea for a tempering of the 'Messianic ardour' of the age, going so far as to quote 'the wicked Talleyrand's "Surtout, Messieurs, point de zèle"' (*L*, 92).[5] In these cases it is usually the social engineering of socialists and social democrats that Berlin has in mind when he calls for moderation, but he makes the same point in relation to liberal policies too. As he argues in 'Two Concepts of Liberty', even the demand for negative liberty can be overstated and turned into a destructive obsession, as by the nineteenth-century worshippers of *laissez-faire* (*L*, 37–8). The sense of reality should qualify liberalism too.

Another occasion for the realist theme is Berlin's essay on J. S. Mill. Like the essay on Turgenev, this is one of the most revealing on the nature of Berlin's liberalism in general. In John Gray's interpretation, Berlin's liberalism is presented as 'starkly' different from Mill's.[6] Gray sees Mill as very much a spokesman for the Enlightenment project, a thinker for whom every moral question has a correct answer given by a ready formula – the kind of monist and utopian view which Berlin's value pluralism opposes. But Berlin's view of Mill is actually more nuanced, indeed displaying a strong ambivalence which is highly instructive concerning the tensions in Berlin's own outlook.[7]

Berlin begins by rejecting the stock picture of Mill as a high-minded prig, a 'Victorian schoolmaster' (*L*, 247). Mill's *Autobiography*, Berlin argues, gives us another picture: that of a generous, warm-hearted thinker who as a young man rebelled against the scientistic and coldly rational utilitarianism of his father, James Mill, and Jeremy Bentham. J. S. Mill sought to humanize Benthamite utilitarianism by reconciling it with the attention to character and the inner life of the emotions that he found in the romantic philosophers and poets. Above all, Berlin asserts, Mill's guiding values are 'diversity, versatility, fullness of life'; his hatreds are 'narrowness, uniformity, the crippling effect of persecution, the crushing of individuals by the weight of authority or of custom or of public opinion' (*L*, 221). He is, as a consequence, 'the greatest champion' of toleration, of the individual and of minorities and dissenters, the enemy of 'the grey, conformist congregation that worships the wicked principle that "it is the absolute social right of every individual that every other individual shall act in every respect exactly as he ought"' (*L*, 218, 224, 244). The parallels with Berlin himself are immediately obvious.

Berlin has reservations, however. Mill's championing of individual liberty is magnificent, but his arguments are weak and unconvincing. In part this is because Mill has not wholly emancipated himself from his father's Benthamism. For example, Mill tries to preserve the utilitarian doctrine that 'happiness' is the sole end of human morality, while at the same time acknowledging that human wants and satisfactions are diverse. The result, Berlin argues, is an unconvincing compromise, its inadequacy revealed when Mill confesses that utility is 'much too complex and indefinite an end to be sought except through the medium of various secondary ends' (*L*, 226). The 'secondary' ends, Berlin argues, are in fact 'the many diverse (and, perhaps, not always compatible) ends which men in fact pursue for their own sake' (*L*, 226). Inside the monism imposed by Mill's utilitarian education there is a suppressed sense of pluralism struggling to get out.

The utilitarian shell is also responsible, Berlin believes, for Mill's failure as a prophet. The 'outdated psychology' of rational hedonism – according to which human beings are assumed always to want the most efficient means to 'happiness', understood as pleasure – prevents him from grasping, as Marx, Freud and others were to do, 'the strength of irrational and unconscious factors in human behaviour' (*L*, 219, 227–8). Behind the narrow psychology lies, once again, the scientism of the Enlightenment, the belief that human conduct can be reduced to a set of laws. This was the dream shared by Bentham and James Mill, the latter described by Berlin as 'the last of the great *raisonneurs* of the eighteenth century' (*L*, 219). The dream was first systematized in its utilitarian form by Helvétius, one of Berlin's 'six enemies of human liberty'. In the hands of Mill, utilitarianism is not so much dangerous as myopic. Its underlying scientistic faith, still flourishing in Mill's day, was destined to be shattered in the twentieth century, which saw the rise of extreme nationalism and of the secular religion of world communism. Berlin's liberalism does depart from Mill's to this extent: while Mill remains confident of the potential of reason alone to bring about moral and political improvement, Berlin's is a vision chastened by totalitarianism and world war. Liberalism, for Berlin, no longer rides a wave of progress; it holds the line between civilization and barbarism.

Yet Berlin does not see Mill as a simple optimist. Although Mill is no prophet, he sees clearly the deficiencies of his own society: stifling conformity, a lack of education among the mass of the population, economic exploitation and sexual discrimination. Against this backdrop the promise of the coming age of democracy is ambiguous. It is to mitigate the worst effects of a misguided democracy that Mill formulates the great principle of the essay *On Liberty*: that individual liberty should be restricted only in order to prevent people harming others. This is, after all, a defensive line in keeping more with the liberalism of fear than that of perfectibility. Improvement along rational lines is possible, Mill believes, but it can only be gradual, not revolutionary. Moreover, Berlin detects traces in Mill, as already mentioned, of an embryonic value pluralism, and so of a sense that there can be no 'final answer' to moral and political questions, even in principle.

Between Mill's realistic, diversity-loving side and his scientistic utilitarian inheritance, Berlin finds a powerful and unresolved tension. Like Tolstoy, Mill strains to uphold a monist system which his deeper instincts and experience deny, and which his intellectual honesty leads him continually to qualify and subvert. Mill, like Tolstoy, is a fox in hedgehog's clothing. At another level the conflict in Mill is between the Enlightenment and Counter-Enlightenment components of his thought, the former supplied by Bentham and his father, the latter by Coleridge and the romantics (*L*, 219, 248). But the clash between Enlightenment and Counter-Enlightenment, and between monism and pluralism, is present not only in Mill but in Berlin too, and indeed in the liberal tradition and modern thought more generally. Berlin, too, feels the pull of the Enlightenment ideals of individual liberty and objective inquiry in one direction, and of the Counter-Enlightenment's unchosen identifications and 'inside view' in the other. Moreover, we are all now, he reminds us, 'children of both worlds' (*RR*, 141).

The message for liberalism is that while the freedom and rational improvement advocated by Mill are indeed desirable and possible to a degree, liberal expectations should be moderate. We live in a world which is neither wholly governed (or governable) by reason, nor morally harmonious or unitary, even in potential. This is not to say that we should abandon reason: Berlin is still 'a liberal rationalist' (*Conv.*, 70). But we should admit that the force of reason has its limits. Irrational and unconscious drives may frustrate the best of arguments, and even if our ideals were realized they would come into frequent conflict. In such a world a liberal order is the best we can hope for, and this must be realistic. It must give maximum play to a diversity of goods and ways of life, while accepting and managing the friction and frustration that diversity brings. Moral and political perfection is not merely hard to achieve but conceptually incoherent, and that is as true of liberal visions of perfection as of any other.

Social justice

Berlin alerts liberals to the danger of their own species of utopianism, urging realism and moderation. But does he contribute anything of value to the liberal tradition beyond this? The following criticism is offered by Christopher Hitchens:

> Berlin supplied many admonitions that were strictly in the negative, most of them warning liberals against the hazard and the fallacy of monism. But who can remember anything he suggested about what liberalism, or liberals, might actually accomplish? Rawls, Dworkin and Galbraith have all laid out avenues of political meliorism. Berlin's design omits these spacious features.[8]

Is it true that Berlin lacks a positive political programme, and if so, does it matter? I suggest that this claim is true to a significant degree, and that it does matter. Berlin's comparative neglect of public policy questions is a real weakness in his position overall. But I also suggest that what Berlin does tell us is rich in policy-guiding implications. Those implications are not drawn out by Berlin himself, but principles and arguments capable of guiding the policy of liberal states can and should be derived from his position none the less. I shall discuss this contention in relation to two important fields of policy: social justice and the political status of cultures.

On the subject of social justice I showed in chapter 4 that although Berlin's preference for negative as against positive liberty has led some readers to see him as a defender of classical or *laissez-faire* liberalism, this is a mistake. He does insist on a rather narrow distinction between negative liberty and the conditions for (or value of) its exercise. On this view a person could, strictly speaking, be negatively free even if poverty prevents her from using that freedom and so diminishes its value for her. This kind of position has been used by *laissez-faire* writers, such as Hayek and Nozick, to argue against the legitimacy of state relief of poverty.[9] But I also argued that although Berlin accepts the narrowly negative view of liberty here, he does not, and need not, accept the *laissez-faire* policy argument so often built upon it. For Berlin, liberals may reasonably believe that the conditions of liberty are as important as liberty itself, and they may hold that the state should act positively to secure them. Thus 'the case for social legislation or planning, for the Welfare State and socialism, can be constructed with as much validity from consideration of the claims of negative liberty as from those of its positive brother' (*L*, 38–9). Alternatively, the goal of welfare state intervention could be conceived neither as liberty nor its preconditions, but as the separate good of 'equality or fairness or justice', yielding the same recommendation for government action (*L*, 172).

Berlin is indeed quite explicit in his rejection of *laissez-faire* and his support for 'social' or 'egalitarian' liberalism, the liberalism of welfare redistribution. To this end he compares the *laissez-faire* obsession with negative liberty – 'the bloodstained story of economic individualism and unrestrained capitalist competition' – with other tyrannical expressions of moral monism, and declares that 'the case for intervention by the State and other effective agencies, to secure conditions for both positive, and at least a degree of negative, liberty for individuals, is overwhelmingly strong' (*L*, 38). He frequently voices support for Roosevelt's New Deal, which he describes as a 'great liberal enterprise', and 'certainly the most constructive compromise between individual liberty and economic security which our own time has witnessed' (*L*, 84). Ignatieff reports that Berlin voted for Attlee's Labour Government in 1945 (although he transferred his vote to the Liberals in 1950), and describes him as 'in convictions . . . a liberal social democrat' (*Life*, 196, 197).

Beyond these general expressions of allegiance to social justice, however, Berlin never develops this side of his thought. Apart from his brief comments about the conditions for negative liberty, he offers no defence of the welfare state. Nor does he show much interest in the defences offered by others. For example, he seems to have paid little attention to the ground-breaking work of John Rawls, whose *A Theory of Justice* (1971) has for many years set the agenda not only for the discussion of distributive justice, but also for the defence of liberalism more generally. In an interview published in 1998, Berlin expressed respect for Rawls but also scepticism about Rawls's method of deriving principles of justice from a hypothetical 'original position' of impartiality (*Sal.*, 30). Justice, Berlin observes, is only one 'ultimate value' among others, which also have their claims; moreover, Rawls pays insufficient attention to the influence of 'irrational impulses' (*Sal.*, 30). Similarly, Berlin never engaged in public with the influential work of Ronald Dworkin, even though Dworkin was an Oxford colleague and personal friend who contributed to three Berlin *Festschriften*. As for the earlier social liberals, Berlin says that he 'was not deeply impressed' by either T. H. Green or L. T. Hobhouse (*Sal.*, 20). Green features in 'Two Concepts' chiefly as a 'well-meaning' liberal whose positive conception of liberty unwittingly supplies grist to the mills of despotism (*L*, 41–2n.).

Why this comparative neglect of liberal theories of social justice? Berlin's justifications are not persuasive. One is that he finds hostile critics more exciting intellectually than allies. 'You see, it's the enemy who interests me, brilliant opponents who so to speak put their swords, their rapiers into one and find the weak spot' (*Sal.*, 20). Again, 'I am interested in the views of the opposition because I think that understanding it can sharpen one's own vision . . . I am more interested in critical attacks which lead to knowledge than simply in repeating and defending the commonplaces of and about the Enlightenment' (*Conv.*, 70). The brilliant opponent can test one's beliefs as the ally cannot. But then, why is Berlin not interested in the brilliant enemies of the welfare state, for example his contemporary Hayek?[10]

His answer might be that in his day the welfare state looked secure and the views of thinkers like Hayek had little influence. In the Introduction to *Four Essays on Liberty* (1969), he writes, 'I had supposed that enough had been said by almost every serious modern writer concerned with this subject about the fate of personal liberty during the reign of unfettered economic individualism,' and concludes that 'liberal ultra-individualism could scarcely be said to be a rising force at present' (*L*, 38, 39). But although this explains his priorities in the 1950s and 1960s, it does not account for his public silence on issues of justice in the 1970s when the welfare state came under serious and sustained attack. It is true that by this time Berlin had retired from most of his academic duties, but he remained a public figure and was still writing. Moreover, there is evidence that right up to his death in 1997 he was privately dismayed by the effects in Britain of Margaret Thatcher's free market revolution.[11]

More important still, Berlin's own principles, in particular his value pluralism, point to the need for closer attention to the defence of the welfare state than he actually provides. The force of some objections to the social liberal or social-democratic state is acknowledged by Berlin himself. Having voted for Labour in 1945, he came to detest Attlee's Government as promoting a morally narrow, levelling uniformity, painting 'a miserable grey on grey' (*Life*, 197). In 1949 in 'Political Ideas in the Twentieth Century' he worries that the same technocratic approach that has turned the Soviet Union into a nightmare is active on a lesser scale in the Western welfare state too. The technocracy of both worlds rests on the assumption that only the means of public policy are in question, because the ends are already settled. A deeper assumption still is the monist faith that those ends are ultimately reconcilable in a single system. Berlin suggests that there is a tendency among social democrats, almost as much as among Communists, to suppose that all goods can be realized together, that moral conflicts can be flattened out, hard choices avoided.

The same theme of the hard choices involved in schemes of social justice is central to 'Two Concepts'. T. H. Green is described there as 'exceptionally enlightened', 'mild and humane', a 'genuine liberal' who rightly denounced 'the monstrous assumption' that working people in an unregulated labour market were '(in any sense that mattered to them) free agents in negotiating with employers' (*L*, 41n., 53, 180n., 196). But Green's attempt to capture all his social goals within a single redefined notion of freedom is misguided. His positive conception of liberty, in which to be truly free is necessarily 'to make the best of ourselves', contains 'the fatal ambiguity' that confuses liberty with morally right action (*L*, 41–2n.). In general, seekers after social justice who are also lovers of liberty are tempted to run these two together as if they are identical or one necessarily leads to the other (*L*, 172–3). Hence Berlin's plea that liberty must be kept distinct from that which it is not. If liberty is to be traded off for the sake of justice, as sometimes it should be, we should be clear that that is what is happening, and not try to suppose that more justice necessarily means more liberty. We must not try to hide from ourselves the reality of hard choices.

Now, if the welfare state inevitably involves us in hard choices among fundamental values like liberty and justice, then that raises the question of which choices are justified. Given Berlin's view of the plurality and incommensurability of such values, why should we accept the particular solutions or trade-offs or compromises that are characteristic of the welfare state? Why agree, for example, to trade off the liberty of taxpayers in return for greater equality for welfare recipients? For free-market thinkers like Hayek and Nozick, no such trade-off is legitimate. Why are these thinkers wrong, if they are? Given the challenge to moral justification that issues from his own notion of pluralism, Berlin cannot simply take the welfare state for granted, as he tends to do.

Berlin does not justify his welfare state commitments in the face of pluralism, but that does not mean he could not. He could do so by arguing along the lines sketched in the last chapter. There I suggested that reflection on the nature of Berlinian pluralism yields principles which, even if they cannot resolve every hard choice among incommensurables, at least point to a liberal political framework for such choices. Further, I argued that the kind of liberalism in play here is likely to take a strong 'Enlightenment' form in which the state is entitled to promote personal autonomy as a necessary component of the best ways of life under pluralism. My proposal now is that the same pluralist line of argument can be marshalled to construct a Berlinian case for welfare redistribution.

The case goes roughly as follows.[12] In a *laissez-faire* society, a society which rejects redistribution, the market will be dominant not only as a mechanism of distribution and governance but also culturally, that is, as a source and arbiter of values. The values of the market – individual choice, freedom of contract, self-reliance, efficiency – will become the central values of the society. From the point of view of Berlinian pluralism this will have serious costs, since the dominance of market values will exclude or sideline other goods. Of course, no society can realize all human values equally; some will inevitably be emphasized at the expense of others. But compared to the situation under redistribution, the range of goods emphasized by *laissez-faire* is likely to be unduly narrow.

The relative narrowness of *laissez-faire* can be argued on each of the liberal-pluralist principles discussed in the last chapter: universality, realism, diversity, reasonable disagreement and personal autonomy. First, the goods excluded or marginalized by *laissez-faire* will arguably include some very basic values that pluralists would regard as universal, such as the need for adequate food, housing and medical care, even the enjoyment of satisfying personal and social relations other than those created by contract.

Secondly, in a market culture the temptation is to regard all goods as commodities, commensurated by money, and to see trade-offs as neatly resolvable by cost–benefit analysis. But this way of seeing things and of making decisions violates the pluralist insistence on the incommensurability of goods. It does so because to acknowledge incommensurability is to accept a commitment to realism concerning the absolute and sometimes tragic nature of the losses that result from value conflict. That reality is papered over by cost–benefit calculations, which give the illusion of seamless net gain, but do so only by commensurating the incommensurable.[13]

Thirdly, the culture of the market may collide with the pluralist commitment to promoting a diversity of values. True, the market is clearly a force for diversity through its championing of individual choice. But while *laissez-faire* generates more diversity than a command economy, it should again be compared with a more balanced system. Choice is an especially important value for pluralists, but there are other significant goods which the market is likely to push to the margins and which would have to be restored by state intervention. These include, most specifically, 'public goods', or facilities and services not well provided by market mechanisms, but also more general ideals such as equality in its various senses, and social solidarity or the related sense of 'belonging' stressed by Berlin. On this point liberal pluralists should be prepared to learn from the insights of the socialist, communitarian and republican traditions of political thought.

Fourthly, whole ways of life which emphasize non-market goods and virtues will find themselves under pressure from *laissez-faire*. The result will be a decline in opportunities to express reasonable disagreement concerning the good life. Finally, the culture of *laissez-faire* will be an unreliable environment for the personal autonomy required for pluralist choice. The exercise of personal autonomy requires economic resources. Even the acquisition of autonomy presupposes the resources necessary to provide an education. Since the rewards of the market, left to itself, are so unevenly distributed, a *laissez-faire* society is likely to be one in which only some people, not all, are genuinely autonomous or in a position to benefit from their autonomy.

In short, a society which rejects redistribution and relies on the market alone to distribute its goods will be objectionable from a pluralist point of view. The basic problem is that such a society will be lopsided, emphasizing the goods and virtues of the market at the expense of all others. Consequently, the more desirable society is one that restores a balance between market and non-market goods, and such a society will be broadly redistributive rather than *laissez-faire*. A further question is precisely what form pluralist redistribution should take, whether the traditional New Deal or welfare state assumed by Berlin, or a 'new social democracy' modified along 'Third Way' or other lines; but that is an issue I leave open.[14]

The claims of culture

Another policy area of great contemporary concern is that of the legitimate claims of 'cultures' as opposed to individual persons or states. How far should cultures be respected and preserved? In particular, to what extent should liberal democracies tolerate or otherwise accommodate within the polity cultural minorities whose practices and values are illiberal, for example those based on fundamentalist religions? By contrast with his comparative silence on matters of social justice, Berlin has a good deal to say about culture, as will be apparent already. The problem here is that of extracting from his various comments a coherent and persuasive position. I shall argue that Berlin's actual remarks on culture tend on the whole to favour monocultural nation-states as an ideal, but that the underlying logic of his comments suggests a policy of multiculturalism, or state support for cultural minorities, within liberal limits.

In general, Berlin believes that human cultures are valuable and that cultural diversity is desirable. He gives two main reasons. First, he sometimes says that cultures are incommensurable, so that each stakes a set of moral claims that cannot be compared with those of other cultures ranked against them. This is the view he claims to find in Vico and Herder, but I have argued that it is not his best view. It amounts to cultural relativism, and so conflicts with his commitment to human rights and liberalism, and it is incompatible with his notion of moral universals and cross-cultural empathetic understanding. On the whole, despite those interpretations that have seized on the relativist aspect of Berlin, he should not be read as endorsing the claims of cultures uncritically.[15]

Berlin's second main account of the value of culture is that membership of a flourishing culture answers to the human need for belonging. This goes back to his personal identification with the Jewish experience of diaspora and with Zionism. A sense of belonging, of feeling at home in your surroundings among people who understand you, is for Berlin a basic good for all human beings. This way of valuing cultures looks much more likely than the notion of cultural incommensurability to be reconcilable with a liberal outlook. If cultures were incommensurable, then each must be judged only on its own terms, which may be illiberal. But if cultures are valuable only so far as they promote human belonging, then that may provide grounds not only for affirming the worth of some cultures but also for criticizing those aggressive cultures that are destructive of others, hence destructive of other forms of belonging conceived as a universal good.

However, there are still problems. First, even if belonging is a universal good, on Berlin's pluralist view it is only one such good among others. What happens when belonging comes into conflict with, for example, individual liberty? Are we then faced with a choice between being either liberals or partisans of culture, but not both? This is a variant of the question raised in chapter 5, as yet unanswered, concerning the apparent conflict between the component values of liberal nationalism: again liberty and belonging. I shall return to this shortly. A second problem is that belonging may be insecure if it is *merely* cultural, that is, if one's culture is not protected politically, whether by a state or by some other institution dedicated to preserving cultural autonomy within a state. Does Berlin's support for culture imply support for the politicization of culture, in the form either of nationalism or multiculturalism?

Berlin's response to this second problem is ambivalent, especially in his discussions of nationalism. There is no doubt that he sees national identity as one of the most important forms of cultural identification, if not the most important. But should nations also be states? Recall that Berlin writes approvingly of what he calls Herder's 'cultural nationalism', or support for the preservation of national identity in a non-political way, in contrast with 'political nationalism' and its demand for statehood (*TCE*, 179–83; *TCN*, 19). He seems to be attracted to Herder's idea that the state is a dead hand on culture, both the culture it is meant to protect and that of other states, towards which it tends to behave aggressively. Yet Berlin also insists that the 'full-blown' political nationalism of the nineteenth and twentieth centuries should be accepted as a continuing reality which liberals should not expect to transcend. More than this, he sometimes hints that some moderate forms of political nationalism are positively desirable, even from a liberal point of view. In 'Two Concepts', for example, he expresses sympathy with those who pass from the notion of individual autonomy to the ideal of collective self-determination, even though these ideas should be kept conceptually distinct both from one another and from negative liberty (*L*, 208–12). This pro-nationalist line has been taken up by recent theorists like Ignatieff, Tamir and David Miller, who argue that the political expression of national identity is a necessary condition for a stable and workable liberal democracy.[16]

On the whole, despite his approval of Herder, Berlin probably believes that in the real world national cultures have to be protected politically. The Herderian vision of multiple nations simply co-existing peacefully without such protection is in all likelihood no more than an ideal for Berlin, rather than a realistic goal of policy. National cultures generally need their own states to secure them. When it comes to the claims of cultural minorities within nation-states, however, Berlin is much less inclined to concede a case for political status. Questioned about the multicultural movement in American academia, he replies with distaste:

> Yes, I know. Black studies, Puerto Rican studies, and the rest. I suppose this too is a bent-twig revolt of minorities which feel at a disadvantage in the context of American polyethnicity. But I believe that the common culture which all societies deeply need can only be disrupted by more than a moderate degree of self-assertion on the part of ethnic or other minorities conscious of a common identity. (*TCN*, 21)

The limitation of 'a moderate degree of self-assertion' seems intended to rule out much of what is now included under the heading of multiculturalism: public recognition of, and support for, cultural minorities, through policies ranging from legal exemptions through affirmative action measures in their various forms, to devices of political representation and self-government.

Berlin holds the same view even with regard to those cultural minorities with whom he could be expected to have most sympathy, namely Jewish minorities.

> There are still to be met among us the pathetic descendants of the old Bundists and Yiddishists, the modern advocates of '*galut* nationalism', which is based on the notion of modern nations as a motley

amalgam of highly diverse and quasi-autonomous communities, in which Yiddish-speaking Jewish groups, living lives full of picturesque native colour, with folk-song and ancient crafts, and quaint traditional customs, would form a rich, if exotic, ingredient. (*POI*, 180)

For Berlin, 'these sorry absurdities' offer 'a totally unreal vision of what modern societies were or could be' (*POI*, 80). This is not to say that people cannot or should not live as Jews within a non-Jewish nation-state; on the contrary, Berlin argues strongly for the legitimacy of that option. But Jewishness should not, he believes, be asserted as a separate political identification within the state's public sphere. Berlin's model for the treatment of cultural minorities is neither assimilation nor multiculturalism (except in a weak sense). Rather, it is an intermediate position which could be called 'integration', where members of the group maintain their distinct identity within the family and voluntary associations, while accepting the same public rights and duties as other citizens.[17]

Supposing that this is Berlin's position, is it justified? In effect, he distinguishes between 'national' cultures, which he says are rightly protected by a state, and minority cultures within states, to which he extends no such protection. There are two problems with this. First, what if a minority culture is also national? This possibility is prominent in the thought of the liberal multiculturalist Will Kymlicka, who defines as 'national' cultural groups which were formerly self-governing and territorially concentrated, which have been incorporated into a larger state, but which want to maintain their identity as a distinct society.[18] Typical examples include indigenous peoples. As Kymlicka observes, 'many Western democracies are multinational' in the sense that they contain more than one national group of this kind.[19] Should Berlin not extend political status at least to these national minorities? Secondly, do Berlin's basic principles not require that he go further still? His stronger reason for valuing cultures is that they answer to the human need for belonging. If so, then that will be true not only of national cultures, whether these be majorities or minorities, but also of others. Immigrant cultures, too, provide their members with a sense of belonging. If the good of cultural belonging deserves political protection in the case of national cultures, why not also in the case of immigrant cultures? Such protection need not take the form of the self-determination that is arguably appropriate only to national groups, but could be provided by the other forms of special accommodation listed earlier.

In short, Berlin's commitment to national belonging seems to push him closer to multiculturalism than he explicitly admits. However, a Berlinian multiculturalism will be qualified by two countervailing values. The first is social unity. One of the dimensions of Berlin's realism, as discussed earlier, is his belief that the actual practice of liberal politics is not guaranteed by reason alone, but requires favourable social conditions. Liberalism is unlikely to flourish in a society riven by serious internal conflict to the point of chronic instability – the fate of the Weimar Republic is perhaps an example. Consequently, a successful liberalism will be one characterized by relatively high levels of trust and co-operation, and for that purpose the general acceptance within the society of a common cultural identity is instrumentally valuable, indeed essential. Hence Berlin's dislike of the more aggressive forms of multiculturalism, the tendency of which is to divide societies in ways that undermine the cultural basis necessary for free institutions.

The second qualification to Berlinian multiculturalism follows from his commitment to individual liberty. On the one hand, the good of belonging should draw Berlin towards endorsing the state's active intervention in the preservation of all viable cultures within its jurisdiction. This tends to separate Berlin's view from those forms of liberalism which accept a policy of 'benign neglect' of minority cultures.[20] On the other hand, the good of individual liberty counts against the state's uncritical endorsement of cultures and practices which diminish the freedom of individuals. In this respect Berlin's view must be distinguished from the position of those multiculturalists who would preserve any and all cultures with little qualification, and who regard liberal principles as themselves culturally relative.[21]

What balance should Berlinians strike between belonging and liberty? My suggestion is that liberty will take priority where there is a conflict. My reason once again appeals to the case presented in the last chapter in favour of liberalism in its Enlightenment form. There I argued that Berlinian pluralism implies the desirability of cultural diversity, but only so far as the cultures concerned themselves promote a diversity of goods. This internal diversity of cultures in turn requires that their members possess a capacity for exercising personal autonomy. It is thus liberty in the form of personal autonomy that must be weighed against belonging in the scales of cultural policy. In those scales autonomy will weigh more heavily where there is a conflict, since it is autonomy that stands at the heart of the kind of liberal politics that best satisfies the insights of pluralism. In particular, this will be a form of politics which maximally accommodates the full range of human goods, and which equips people to make good choices among those goods when they conflict. A system which gives priority to belonging over liberty will not pass this test, since it will tend to favour settled local traditions regardless of the extent to which these value diversity or personal autonomy.

Note that this argument also resolves the apparent tension within the concept of liberal nationalism, introduced in chapter 5. There I reported the objection that if individual liberty and group belonging are incommensurables in Berlin's terms, then their combination within liberal nationalism is incoherent and that position is an oxymoron. The weakness of this criticism should now be evident: it assumes that merely to identify contending values as incommensurables is to show that there can be no rational resolution when they conflict. As I have argued in previous chapters, the better view is that rational choices among competing incommensurables may be possible in context. Moreover, the concept of pluralism itself implies certain general principles that have political implications, as in the argument I have just sketched. Berlin's position can thus be regarded as a form of liberal nationalism, in which the value of liberty is ranked ahead of that of belonging, for good reason, where there is a conflict.

To sum up, Berlin's deepest commitments suggest a position that is closer to multiculturalism than he allows, although this is a multiculturalism qualified by a concern for social unity, and a multiculturalism within liberal limits. More specifically, it is, I suggest, a multiculturalism similar to that of Kymlicka.[22] According to this view, the liberal state has the right and the duty to act to preserve cultures, especially national cultures, on the ground that membership of a flourishing culture is part of the well-being of all citizens. But that policy is balanced by the need for social cohesion, and is subject to the promotion of personal autonomy in all cases. Cultural preservation and national identity are important, but they come second to the fundamental liberal-pluralist concern for the liberty of the individual. Again, the argument has travelled some distance beyond Berlin's actual words, but not, I believe, beyond the general contours of his liberal-pluralist outlook.[23]

Judging Berlin

How does Berlin rate as a thinker overall? This is a difficult question, especially on Berlin's own pluralist terms, since on those terms it involves comparisons and rankings among incommensurables. How can we weigh Berlin's originality against Rawls's argumentative rigour, or his realism against the influence of Marx? Put like this, the problem is like that of ranking great artists, which Berlin declares to be irresolvable (*PSM*, 8, 567). I have argued that, on Berlin's own better view, to identify a value conflict as a conflict of incommensurables is not necessarily to abandon hope of a reasoned resolution. Such a resolution can appeal either to context or to the implications of pluralism itself. Pluralism itself, I have argued, indicates the superiority of a liberal political framework over the known alternatives. On the ground of pluralism, therefore, we could say that Berlin, as a liberal, is on the right track.

Even within the context of the liberal tradition, however, the question of Berlin's overall ranking remains hard to answer. I have already laid out some of his strengths and weaknesses within the liberal frame: the greater realism of his position compared with that of 'utopian' liberals like Condorcet, balanced by his lack of attention to the policy implications of his view compared with other social liberals like Rawls and Kymlicka. Nevertheless, a thorough response to this question would still require many comparisons across distinct and perhaps incommensurable dimensions of value, and even then might not be possible. I therefore propose an unpluralistic short-cut, which is to reduce all these questions, for the sake of argument, to one: is it likely that Berlin will continue to be read? Even this question is very large, and any answer will be speculative. But I suggest that the answer is yes, for reasons that address his achievement in three main areas: his account of the conceptual roots of totalitarianism, his highlighting of value pluralism and its implications, and his characteristic approach to the history of ideas.

First, Berlin must be counted as one of the most significant analysts of twentieth-century totalitarianism. The tracing of the intellectual origins and the moral psychology of totalitarian thinking is the undertaking I have presented as Berlin's master project. In this he tackles the greatest challenge to moral and political understanding of his time, and his response is subtle, profound and highly distinctive. For Berlin, the totalitarian regimes may have emerged in part from accidents of historical circumstances, from economic factors and from the personalities of leaders, but most importantly their origins lie in ideas. Ideas are powerful; they make or destroy the lives of millions of actual human beings. Ideas are also highly malleable: they can be forged into the principles of a free society or distorted into an ideology of oppression.

The ideas that Berlin finds underlying totalitarian regimes are not simple or one-dimensional but complex and layered, like the multiple levels of an archaeological excavation. At the surface or most recent level is the betrayal of freedom by eighteenth- and nineteenth-century intellectuals. This is not an outright rejection of individual liberty. On the contrary, liberty is often elevated in this period to a supreme position among goods. Once there, however, it is twisted into new forms that in the end amount to the very opposite of its genuine meaning. What is the 'genuine' meaning of liberty? On this question, as on so many others, Berlin is ambiguous, although fruitfully so. Sometimes he seems to insist that negative non-interference alone is the 'normal' or root meaning of liberty, yet at other times he allows that the most basic insight common to positive conceptions of liberty, the value of controlling one's own life, is equally, or incommensurably, a fundamental human good. I have argued that the true originality and importance of the seminal 'Two Concepts of Liberty' lies not in Berlin's formulation of the negative–positive distinction itself, which had been drawn by others, but rather (in part) in his critique of the positive idea, which he links with authoritarianism, with conceptual confusion, and with deeper tendencies in Western thought. I also argued that in his concern to make those links, and to identify liberalism with the negative idea, Berlin tends to underestimate the extent to which one version of positive liberty, namely personal autonomy, is also central to the liberal tradition. Still, Berlin's position remains, on the whole, resilient after four decades of criticism, and it continues to be debated. What is certain is that Berlin opened up critical discussion of the concept of freedom in much the same way that Rawls later opened up discussion of social justice and the foundations of liberalism. For this reason alone, G. A. Cohen is right to link Berlin and Rawls as 'the most celebrated twentieth century Anglophone political philosophers'.[24]

The concept of liberty is only the beginning of Berlin's archaeology of totalitarianism. The betrayal of freedom rests on a deeper layer of thought: that of the eighteenth-century Enlightenment and Counter-Enlightenment. In their extreme forms, one makes scientific reason into a fetish, the other rejects it altogether. Each is the principal source of its own corresponding form of totalitarianism. The Counter-Enlightenment rejection of reason and universality lays the groundwork for fascism. But Enlightenment faith in reason and universality itself becomes dangerous when trumpeted as the basis for a utopia: the scientistic stream of the Enlightenment is the chief foundation of Marxism and Soviet communism. These are only the principal lines of Berlin's account; the details are more nuanced. But it is Berlin's capacity for painting intellectual history with such bold strokes that gives his work much of its characteristic shape and power.

Finally, scientism rests on moral monism: the belief that all moral questions have a single answer, and that all the answers fit together systematically. Monism is the ur-faith not just of nineteenth-century utopianism and eighteenth-century rationalism, but of the dominant strand, the *philosophia perennis*, of Western thought as a whole. The search for the conceptual foundations of fascism and communism ends in the unearthing of a deep assumption which few would have noticed and fewer still would have questioned. On its face, the monist assumption seems harmless, even beneficial, since the same assumption underpins the progress we have made in understanding the natural world. Indeed, even in the moral world the monist assumption may be beneficial in the hands of some thinkers, like Locke, Kant and Mill. The problem is that monism can also be pressed into service by those with less benign intentions and visions.

Berlin's alternative to moral monism is value pluralism, and this provides the second reason why he will continue to be read. His idea is that human values are in reality irreducibly multiple, often incompatible and sometimes incommensurable, and that conflicts among such values frequently generate hard choices not resolvable by any simple abstract rule. This is one of his most distinctive contributions, and perhaps his most far-reaching. The notion of pluralism is intimated, on Berlin's own account, by several earlier Western thinkers, including most notably Vico, Herder and the romantics, and goes back at least as far as Machiavelli.[25] Among Berlin's more immediate predecessors, Max Weber approaches Berlin's view in some respects, and broadly similar outlooks can be found in Berlin's contemporaries Michael Oakeshott and Stuart Hampshire.[26] But Berlin is the first writer to formulate the idea explicitly as the centre-piece of a sustained political philosophy. The notion of pluralism runs through his political thought almost from the beginning, at first sensed rather than articulated, but made increasingly explicit as he went on. Berlin never analyses the concept carefully, and some of his treatments of it are vague and inconsistent. But his position is highly original, powerfully intuited, and copiously illustrated from his reading in the history of ideas.

The precise implications of Berlinian pluralism remain in dispute. Berlin saw the idea as a weapon against authoritarian modes of thought based on monism. Some critics have claimed that pluralism also possesses, as Berlin did not seem to appreciate, the power to challenge and disturb liberal positions such as his own. I have argued that although Berlin has a case to answer here, that case tends to trade on relativist and irrationalist interpretations of pluralism which Berlin did not intend and which should be rejected. Pluralism is compatible with reasoned choice among incommensurables in context. Moreover, pluralism itself implies a set of principles which recommend a liberal political framework. These arguments suggest that Berlinian pluralism is not just a source of anti-monist warnings or admonitions to exercise moderation, but that it possesses considerable potential in helping us to think constructively about politics and public policy. In the previous two sections I sketched ways in which this might be done in the fields of distributive justice and cultural claims.

The third reason why Berlin's work is likely to survive is the extraordinary urgency and vividness of his discussions of ideas and the thinkers who generated them. This aspect of Berlin has two components. The first is his method of imaginative empathy, modelled on the *fantasia* of Vico and the *Einfühlung* of Herder, in which he 'enters into' the mind he wishes to understand, whether the mind of an individual or that of a whole society. He speaks to us with the voice of that mind, leaving us to respond as we see fit. The brilliance with which Berlin achieves this effect is attested by many readers. Brian Barry, for example, otherwise a stern critic, identifies Berlin's 'greatest strength' as 'his ability to convey, and make real, the fact that every text – however abstract its subject matter – was produced by a human being with his . . . own passions, prejudices, *idées fixes* and blind spots'.[27] The other component of Berlin's method is his insistence that the ideas he discusses matter not merely for their own sake, or from the viewpoint of a purely antiquarian interest, but because they are immediately and intensely relevant to us now, having made us who we are, for good or ill.

This approach to ideas employs a unique combination of philosophy and history. Its roots lie in Berlin's formative years in 1930s Oxford, where he witnessed the struggle between the logical positivists and the Hegelians. Berlin was broad-minded enough to see the strengths and weaknesses of each: the robust empiricism of the logical positivists, limited by their abstract, disembodied reasoning; the speculative excesses of the Hegelians, mitigated by their sense of historical specificity. Berlin tried to combine the best of both worlds. He declared himself an empiricist, but defined 'philosophy' as precisely what the logical positivists left out: those 'queer questions' that can be settled neither by observation nor by deduction. This is the realm of assumptions, paradigms or, as Berlin puts it, the 'category-spectacles' through which we make sense of the world. To understand concepts and categories such as these, he argues, the God's-eye methods of the natural sciences are inadequate because merely 'external'. The basic categories of human understanding are informed by human purposes, and can be grasped only by adopting the 'inside view', that is, by trying to see with the eyes of those whose categories they are. Hence the centrality of *Einfühlung*. Further, each such view is situated concretely in time and place, and since time and place vary, so too do the concepts and categories they produce. For Berlin, to do philosophy, properly understood, is necessarily to study history.

But philosophy and history are also sufficiently distinct undertakings to make the task of combining them problematic. Philosophical questions – what is truth, justice, freedom? – tend towards the universal, abstract and eternal, pulling apart from historical inquiries into concrete events and circumstances. A case in point is Berlin's critique of positive liberty in 'Two Concepts', where he shifts uneasily between the historical claim that positive conceptions of liberty have in fact been used for authoritarian ends in the past and the philosophical claim that there is something authoritarian about the positive conception as such. How far is Berlin's marriage of the philosophical and historical sensibilities a successful one? One thinks here of Berlin's own comments on similar projects of reconciliation pursued by his predecessors: Tolstoy's attempt to interweave a universal philosophy of history with the particularities of the novel, Mill's ambition of uniting Bentham's utilitarianism with Coleridge's romanticism. Berlin's judgement that these enterprises are ultimately failures suggests that there are questions to be asked about the coherence of his own programme.

Berlin's method has been criticized for this very reason. From the philosophical side he has been accused, with some justice, of lack of rigour in analysis and argument, and of vagueness in definitions and distinctions. It is true that Berlin's claims are often left unproved and untested. Indeed, it is sometimes unclear just what claim is being made, since it can be less than obvious in whose voice Berlin is speaking at any one time, whether his own or that of the historical figure he is discussing. His own position is typically hinted at through his treatment of others, rather than stated expressly. In those cases where a critical claim is definitely being asserted, Berlin is inclined to back up the assertion not with a logical demonstration but with loose associations of the 'slippery slope' kind, such as those connecting positive liberty and moral monism with authoritarian politics in 'Two Concepts'.

Historians, on the other hand, have sometimes seen Berlin's broad-brush approach to the history of ideas as showing too little regard for details, qualifications and precise contexts. Indeed, Berlin's whole conception of the history of ideas as tracing the development of categories and concepts through different historical periods looks dubious to some theorists. The 'Cambridge contextualist' school, most prominently represented by Quentin Skinner, questions whether concepts like 'liberty' can properly be understood as 'developing' historically at all. For Skinner, 'there are no perennial problems in philosophy', only particular questions and answers intelligible within the historical context in which they arise.[28] On this view, Berlin's narrative, in which Rousseau's conception of liberty flows into that of Fichte, Hegel and Marx, is not only questionable empirically, but incoherent.

To his philosophical critics Berlin would reply that what is most important to him is not coherence of argument but power of overall vision. What counts in the great thinkers is their 'central vision of life, of what it was and what it should be' (*FIB*, 3). Their detailed arguments are

> but the outworks of the inner citadel – weapons against assault, objections to objections, rebuttals of rebuttals, an attempt to forestall and refute actual and possible criticisms of their views and their theories; and we shall never understand what it is they really want to say unless we penetrate beyond this barrage of defensive weapons to the central coherent single vision within, which as often as not is not elaborate and complex, but simple, harmonious and easily perceptible as a single whole. (*FIB*, 3)

In Berlin's own case the central vision, liberal pluralism, is not so simple and harmonious, but the larger point holds. It is confirmed by his friend Avishai Margalit: 'Berlin did not like what the Oxford philosopher Price used to call argybargy philosophers. You should state your position, and it should be compelling. If it is not, no argument will help. So he was not troubled by problems of coherence.'[29] Once again the force of the overall view is more valuable to Berlin than philosophical argy-bargy.

To his historian critics Berlin might reply that his goal is not the accurate recording of details of the past for its own sake, but the use of the past to illuminate the present. 'The importance of accurate historical knowledge', he writes, has often been underestimated by students of ideas and should be accorded its proper place, 'but it is not everything . . . the importance of past philosophers in the end resides in the fact that the issues which they raised are live issues still (or again)' (*TCE*, 8). For this purpose broad patterns of development are more pertinent than specialized facts narrowly contextualized.

> Quentin Skinner rightly says that you can only fully understand ideas if you understand the political circumstances in which they were produced . . . But the essence of the ideas themselves does not emerge from Quentin Skinner's historical accounts. If he were right we would not be able to understand Plato or Aristotle. We don't know what Athens looked or felt like. . . . Yet the ideas themselves have lasted. They have moved and excited people for more than two thousand years. If Skinner's requirements are not met how can this be? It can't be that the adequate understanding of ideas depends solely upon an adequate understanding of context. (*Sal.*, 22)

Berlin's point is reinforced by the Vico scholar Leon Pompa, who writes that what is especially valuable in Berlin's approach to Vico is his linking of that thinker with others 'more through . . . similarity of insight than by any direct historical association. In so doing, he brought to light facets of [Vico's thought] which would have remained unacknowledged were it considered solely in terms of its strictly historical context and connections.'[30]

The contextualist critique of Berlin's historiography is ironic to a degree, since Berlin himself sometimes says, especially in his treatment of Vico and Herder, that historical periods are incommensurable with one another. But this view is corrected by his subsequent insistence on the possibility of transhistorical understanding by way of a common human horizon. The human horizon enables us to enter into past worlds imaginatively, and to compare their beliefs and aspirations with our own. This is how Berlin succeeds not only in elucidating the thinkers he studies but also in bringing them to life.

These replies will not allay all objections, but Berlin's own pluralist outlook implies that they should not be expected to. Philosophers can still reasonably complain about Berlin's lack of rigour. How do we know that a position is 'compelling' unless we test it thoroughly? Historians can still question his interpretative accuracy. Unless we are careful about context, how can we be sure that the ideas we attribute to past thinkers are not merely our own projections? Berlin would not, or should not, claim that his method is without costs. But if his pluralism is correct, he can rightly remind us that there can be no method without costs. Philosophical rigour, historical accuracy and vividness of presentation are distinct and incommensurable considerations. This does not mean that, in trying to strike a balance among them, anything goes; but it does suggest that in all likelihood more than one way of striking that balance will be reasonable. The balance struck by Berlin is not the only one possible, but its value is attested by the continuing power of his work to engage, fascinate and provoke his many readers.

Notes

Chapter 1   Hedgehog and Fox

1 Ignatieff, 'On Isaiah Berlin', 10. Something of Berlin's range can be seen in *PSM*, which contains 'The Pursuit of the Ideal' (also in *CTH*), where Berlin surveys the general lines of his own thought. 'My Intellectual Path' (*POI*; *First and Last*) and 'Epilogue: The Three Strands in My Life' (*PI*) are also useful guides to Berlin's overall position and development. The first volume of his letters has now been published: *Flourishing*, in the USA entitled *Letters 1928–1946*. Important interviews include *Conv.* and *Sal.* The secondary literature on Berlin is growing rapidly, and includes to date three book-length critical studies: Kocis, *A Critical Appraisal of Sir Isaiah Berlin's Political Philosophy*; Galipeau, *Isaiah Berlin's Liberalism*; and J. Gray, *Isaiah Berlin*. Ignatieff's biography, *Life*, is excellent. Significant collections of articles on Berlin include Ryan, ed., *The Idea of Freedom*; E. and A. Margalit, eds, *Isaiah Berlin: A Celebration*; Dworkin, Lilla and Silvers, eds, *The Legacy of Isaiah Berlin*; Mali and Wokler, eds, *Isaiah Berlin's Counter-Enlightenment*. Recent surveys include Harris, 'Isaiah Berlin: *Two Concepts of Liberty*'; idem, 'Berlin and His Critics'; Lessnoff, *Political Philosophers of the Twentieth Century*, ch. 8; Kenny, 'Isaiah Berlin's Contribution to Modern Political Theory'; D. Kelly, 'The Political Thought of Isaiah Berlin'; Ryan, 'Isaiah Berlin: Political Theory and Liberal Culture'; Cracraft, 'A Berlin for Historians'. For a comprehensive bibliography of writing by and about Berlin, see *The Isaiah Berlin Virtual Library*, the website maintained by Berlin's editor and literary trustee, Henry Hardy.
2 Berlin, 'Political Ideas in the Romantic Age'.
3 Crick, 'Most Intellectual of Academics'.
4 P. Gray, 'The Foxy Philosopher'.
5 Ryan, 'Wise Man', 29.
6 Wokler, 'A Modern Candide', 8.

7 Hitchens, 'Moderation or Death'.
8 Podhoretz, 'A Dissent on Isaiah Berlin'.
9 For the criticism from the left, see Hitchens, 'Moderation or Death', 9–10; for the criticism from the right, see Podhoretz, 'A Dissent on Isaiah Berlin'.
10 See especially 'Jewish Slavery and Emancipation' (*POI*); and 'Benjamin Disraeli, Karl Marx and the Search for Identity' (*AC*).

Chapter 2 Three Strands

1 Ryan, 'Isaiah Berlin', 345–6.
2 See also Berlin, 'J. L. Austin and the Early Beginnings of Oxford Philosophy' (*PI*) and 'My Intellectual Path' (*POI*; *First and Last*) for his view of this period.
3 Ayer, *Language, Truth and Logic*.
4 See e.g. Strauss, 'Relativism'; Sandel, 'Introduction'; Anderson, 'The Pluralism of Isaiah Berlin'; Kateb, 'Can Cultures be Judged?'; Sandall, 'The Book of Isaiah'. I pursue the question of Berlin's alleged relativism in ch. 5.
5 For this reason page references to *KM* will be to the 1st edn.
6 G. A. Cohen, 'Isaiah's Marx, and Mine', 121–2.
7 Ibid., 122–3.
8 A. Kelly, *Toward Another Shore*, 1–2.
9 Tolstoy's thought is also examined, to similar effect, in 'Tolstoy and Enlightenment' (1960), in *RT*.
10 Berlin's Zionism is discussed by Galipeau, *Isaiah Berlin's Liberalism*, ch. 7; and by Avishai Margalit, Richard Wollheim and Michael Walzer in Dworkin, Lilla and Silvers, eds, *Legacy of Isaiah Berlin*, part III.
11 On the Jewish quest for belonging within alien cultures, see also 'Benjamin Disraeli, Karl Marx and the Search for Identity'. On rejection of assimilation, see 'The Life and Opinions of Moses Hess'. Both are in *AC*.
12 See *Life*, 185, for the likely origins of this image in a Jewish joke. Berlin later came to regret his use of the hunchback metaphor, with its suggestion that to be Jewish was to be deformed, and he refused to allow the republication of the essay in his lifetime.
13 Koestler, 'Interview'; also *idem*, 'Judah at the Crossroads', where he replies to Berlin.
14 See, similarly, Charles Taylor on the 'dialogical' nature of identity: 'The Politics of Recognition', 32.
15 See e.g. 'Nationalism: Past Neglect and Present Power', in *AC*, 339–41. Berlin's view of nationalism is discussed in ch. 5 below.
16 Raz, *The Morality of Freedom*; *idem*, 'Multiculturalism: A Liberal Perspective'; Kymlicka, *Liberalism, Community and Culture*; *idem*, *Multicultural Citizenship*.

17 Eliot, *After Strange Gods*, 20. The debate between Berlin and Eliot is discussed by Ignatieff in *Life*, 185–8.
18 Barry, 'Isaiah, Israel and Tribal Realism', 8.
19 Berlin, 'Israel and the Palestinians'.

Chapter 3 The Betrayal of Freedom

1 This aspect of Berlin's intellectual development is emphasized by D. Kelly, 'Political Thought of Isaiah Berlin', and Cherniss, 'The Road to Liberty'.
2 Hayek, *The Road to Serfdom*; Popper, *The Open Society and its Enemies*; Talmon, *The Origins of Totalitarian Democracy*. Berlin says that he was influenced by Popper but not by Hayek, and that he came to his thesis about freedom independently of Talmon (*Sal.*, 23).
3 The article appears in *SM* as 'The Artificial Dialectic: Generalissimo Stalin and the Art of Government'. Its background is described by Hardy in his Preface (*SM*, pp. xxvi–xxxii). For other explicitly Cold War pieces by Berlin, see the remaining essays in *SM*.
4 'Democracy, Communism and the Individual', 4.
5 Ibid., 5.
6 Ibid.
7 Kekes, 'Cruelty and Liberalism'.
8 Carr, *What is History?*, 40. For other critical discussions of 'Historical Inevitability', see Geyl, 'Historical Inevitability'; E. Nagel, 'Determinism in History'.
9 See, similarly, 'The Sense of Reality' (in *SR*).
10 'Political Ideas in the Romantic Age'. For references to the 'torso', see the Editor's Preface by Henry Hardy.
11 See Lilla, 'Inside the Clockwork'.

Chapter 4 Two Concepts of Liberty

1 The genesis, delivery and afterlife of Berlin's lecture is described by Ignatieff (*Life*, ch. 15), and the revision of the piece for its inclusion in *Four Essays on Liberty* by Hardy, 'The Editor's Tale' (*L*, pp. ix–xxiv).
2 T. Gray, *Freedom*, 8.
3 This is Berlin's definition of negative liberty at its broadest. 'Two Concepts' contains several different, and inconsistent, formulations: Miller, 'Introduction' to Miller, ed., *Liberty*, 13. The scope and implications of negative liberty on Berlin's view is a question I return to later.
4 See also *FIB*, 5. Berlin presumably means normal for modernity, since he also argues that the clear-headed demand for negative liberty – as opposed to self-mastery or collective sovereignty – is peculiar to the modern age (*L*, 33–4).

5 See e.g. MacCallum, 'Negative and Positive Freedom', 102; T. Gray, *Freedom*, 171; Swift, *Political Philosophy*, 54.

6 Macpherson, 'Berlin's Division of Liberty', 95–6, 104–9; T. Gray, *Freedom*, 9–10; Hunt, 'Freedom and its Conditions'; Swift, *Political Philosophy*, 55–68.

7 See e.g. Green, 'Liberal Legislation and Freedom of Contract'.

8 A point conceded by Swift, *Political Philosophy*, 64.

9 See e.g. Patterson, *Freedom*, 3; T. Gray, *Freedom*, 10; Coole, 'Constructing and Deconstructing Liberty', 90; Knowles, *Political Philosophy*, 81.

10 Woolcock, *Power, Impartiality and Justice*, 59–60.

11 *Con.* T. Gray, *Freedom*, 8.

12 Berlin focuses on the confusion between freedom and knowledge in 'From Hope and Fear Set Free' (*L*, 252–79).

13 See the discussions of the limits of negative liberty and the validity of freedom as non-domination later in the chapter.

14 Further references are given by Harris, 'Berlin and His Critics' (*L*, 349–66).

15 MacCallum, 'Negative and Positive Freedom', 102.

16 Ibid., 106.

17 J. Gray, 'On Negative and Positive Liberty', 326; Baldwin, 'MacCallum and the Two Concepts of Freedom'; Skinner, 'A Third Concept of Liberty', 237.

18 MacCallum, 'Negative and Positive Freedom', 108–10.

19 J. Gray, 'On Negative and Positive Liberty', 325.

20 Feinberg, *Social Philosophy*, 16; T. Gray, *Freedom*, 11.

21 J. Gray, *Isaiah Berlin*, 43.

22 Wittgenstein, *Philosophical Investigations*, §§ 65–7.

23 For a different line of attack on the negative–positive distinction, see Megone, 'One Concept of Liberty', where it is argued that only the negative conception is valid. Megone's view is discussed by T. Gray, *Freedom*, 132.

24 Taylor, 'What's Wrong with Negative Liberty'.

25 For a recent treatment of the issue of measurement, see Carter, *A Measure of Freedom*.

26 Macpherson, 'Berlin's Division of Liberty', 97–104; T. Gray, *Freedom*, 9; Hunt, 'Freedom and its Conditions', 294–8; Swift, *Political Philosophy*, 56.

27 Spencer, *The Man Versus the State*; Hayek, *The Road to Serfdom*; idem, *The Constitution of Liberty*; Nozick, *Anarchy, State, and Utopia*.

28 Miller, 'Constraints on Freedom'.

29 M. Cohen, 'Berlin and the Liberal Tradition'; Crowder, 'Negative and Positive Liberty'; Christman, 'Liberalism and Individual Positive Freedom'; Bellamy, 'T. H. Green, J. S. Mill and Isaiah Berlin on the Nature of Liberty and Liberalism'; West, 'Spinoza on Positive Freedom'.

30 Crowder, *Classical Anarchism*.

31   The distinction between liberalism based on toleration or diversity and liberalism based on personal autonomy is laid out by Galston, who argues for the 'diversity' interpretation (*Liberal Pluralism*, ch. 2). For accounts advocating autonomy-based liberalism, see Raz, *Morality of Freedom*; Kymlicka, *Multicultural Citizenship*, ch. 8. I return to this debate in ch. 7.

32   Mill, *On Liberty*, ch. 3.

33   Taylor, 'What's Wrong with Negative Liberty', 146.

34   See Raz, *Morality of Freedom*, part V; Taylor, 'What is Human Agency?'; Benn, *A Theory of Freedom*; Macedo, *Liberal Virtues*, ch. 6.

35   Raz, *Morality of Freedom*, ch. 14.

36   See also Crowder, *Liberalism and Value Pluralism*, 198–211.

37   Skinner, *Liberty before Liberalism*, 36–41; idem, 'A Third Concept of Liberty', 247–55; Pettit, *Republicanism*, 21–7.

38   Pettit, *Republicanism*, 21.

39   Ibid., 19, 21, 41.

40   Skinner, 'The Idea of Negative Liberty', 194; idem, *Liberty before Liberalism*, 113.

41   Skinner, 'A Third Concept of Liberty', 255–6, 262.

42   Ibid., 256.

43   Pettit, *Republicanism*, 85.

44   This leaves open the possibility that non-domination is better seen not as distinct from negative liberty, as on Pettit's view, but as a species of negative liberty, emphasizing freedom from dependence rather than coercion, which seems to be closer to Skinner's position.

45   The conclusion that Berlin's position and that of the republicans are complementary rather than opposed is also reached, for different reasons from those given here, by Woolcock, *Power, Impartiality and Justice*, 47; Wall, 'Freedom, Interference and Domination'.

46   Farganis, 'Liberty: Two Perspectives on the Women's Movement'.

47   Hirschmann, 'Toward a Feminist Theory of Freedom', 51. It should be clear from my earlier exposition that this claimed alignment of positive liberty with community and care is true only for the more collectivist versions of positive liberty, not for the more individualist.

48   Coole, 'Constructing and Deconstructing Liberty', 84–5.

49   Ibid., 87.

50   Ibid., 90–1.

51   Ibid., 93.

52   Postmodernism is compared with Berlinian pluralism by McKinney, 'Towards a Postmodern Ethic', which emphasizes overlap, and by Crowder and Griffiths, 'Postmodernism, Value Pluralism and International Relations', where contrast is stressed. The line between pluralism and ethical relativism in Berlin's work was touched on in ch. 2, and is further discussed in chs 5 and 6.

53   Hunt, 'A Note on Woolcock's Defence of Berlin', 469; Etzioni, 'Thickening the Soup'.

54 Dworkin, 'Two Concepts of Liberty'; Porter, *Rethinking Unionism*; Siame, ' "Two Concepts of Liberty" through African Eyes'.

Chapter 5   The Enlightenment and its Critics

1 Berlin's account of the originality and content of Vico's theory of knowledge has been disputed. See e.g. Aarsleff, 'Vico and Berlin', and Zagorin, 'Vico's Theory of Knowledge' (both with subsequent exchanges with Berlin). Another important interpretation is that of Lilla, who takes issue with Berlin's picture of Vico as a forerunner of modern pluralism. Stressing the theological component of Vico's thought, Lilla sees him as 'a far more profound critic of the modern age than has previously been supposed', one whose goal is not 'a more humane tempering of Enlightenment doctrines' but a reassertion, although in 'the new language of modern science', of the order and authority found in premodern societies (*G. B. Vico*, 6).

2 Gay, 'Intimations of Partiality', 3.

3 Hook, 'Isaiah Berlin's Enlightenment', 64. Berlin was probably well aware of this distinction: see *TCE*, vii.

4 Lilla, 'Wolves and Lambs', *passim*. Berlin's approach in this respect is defended by Ignatieff, 'Understanding Fascism?'

5 Berlin therefore distinguishes between the Counter-Enlightenment and romanticism as distinct phases in the attack on the Enlightenment. However, his comments in this connection are somewhat ambiguous. We have seen that he believes that the late eighteenth century constituted a watershed in European thought amounting to 'the deepest and most lasting of all changes in the life of the West' (*RR*, p. xiii). In this passage, in a set of notes introducing his lectures on *The Roots of Romanticism*, he describes this change as occurring 'before what is properly called the romantic movement' (*RR*, p. xii). Yet in the main body of the lectures he makes the same claim for romanticism itself (*RR*, 1). Presumably he has in mind a process of change which began with the Counter-Enlightenment thinkers and continued with romanticism proper, a movement very much under their influence. Romanticism can be seen on this view as a branch of the Counter-Enlightenment, and the Counter-Enlightenment thinkers as precursors of romanticism.

6 Berlin's claim that 'the heart of romanticism' is the doctrine of the invention of reality by the untrammelled will is another point at which his history of ideas has been questioned: Gay, 'Intimations of Partiality', 4. Berlin himself declares that attempting to define 'romanticism' is a 'trap' he does not intend to fall into (*RR*, 1). In context he probably means his remarks about the heart of romanticism to apply only to the German stream of the movement. Even so, a recent commentator has judged that Berlin's view should be accepted only with 'severe qualification': Richards, *The Romantic Conception of Life*, 6n. On

the account given by the German romantics, the relation between the self and nature is not merely one of creator to creation but a complex symbiosis. Further, while Berlin's reading of romanticism emphasizes the pluralist theme of multiple and irreconcilable ideals, the romantics typically 'strove to unify, at least as an ideal goal, what they found separate and fragmented' (ibid., 202).

7 A phrase Berlin attributes usually to Schiller, once to Diderot. Henry Hardy has been unable to find it in either author, though he notes that Schiller does express 'the view of nationalism it encapsulates' (*RR* 161n.). The metaphor of a bent twig being re-straightened actually occurs in Plekhanov, *Essays in the History of Materialism* (which is listed in the *KM* bibliography), vii – a point I owe to Joshua Cherniss. However, Plekhanov's meaning is different from Berlin's. Hardy has suggested to me that Berlin probably attached Plekhanov's phrase to the view of nationalism he found in Schiller, thereafter misattributing 'the bent twig' usually to Schiller (plausibly but wrongly), but on one occasion to Diderot (unaccountably).

8 See 'Joseph de Maistre and the Origins of Fascism', in *CTH*.

9 'Irrationalism also depends on the cult of action for action's sake. Action being beautiful in itself, it must be taken before, or without, any previous reflection. Thinking is a form of emasculation' (Eco, 'Ur-Fascism', 80). See also Mussolini, 'The Doctrine of Fascism', 329; Griffin, 'General Introduction', 6.

10 Ignatieff, *Blood and Belonging*, 4–5.

11 Ibid., 10.

12 Tamir, *Liberal Nationalism*, 6.

13 See also Miller, *On Nationality*. Note, too, that Berlin's passage from 'Two Concepts of Liberty' in which he links belonging with understanding (*L*, 203) is quoted by another liberal nationalist: Ignatieff, *Blood and Belonging*, 10.

14 Berlin is singled out for questioning by Cocks, *Passion and Paradox*, ch. 4. For criticism of liberal nationalism in general, see Levinson, 'Is Liberal Nationalism an Oxymoron?'; Vincent, 'Liberal Nationalism: An Irresponsible Compound?'

15 For Berlin's account of Machiavelli as anticipating a value-pluralist position, see 'The Originality of Machiavelli', in *AC* and *PSM*.

16 Momigliano, 'On the Pioneer Trail'.

17 For criticisms of Berlin along these lines see Strauss, 'Relativism'; Sandel, 'Introduction'; Anderson, 'The Pluralism of Isaiah Berlin'; Kateb, 'Can Cultures be Judged?'; Sandall, 'The Book of Isaiah'. A partial defence of Berlin is offered by Lukes, *Liberals and Cannibals*, chs 6–8.

18 Two other universalist elements in Herder receive similar treatment. At one point Berlin asks directly, 'Is there, then, no progress? Are all cultures equally valuable?', and replies, 'This is not Herder's view' (*TCE*, 215). The reason given is that 'there is *Fortgang*', Herder's

concept of cultural 'advance' (*TCE*, 215). But this soon turns out to mean not universal or cross-cultural progress (as in Turgot or Condorcet or Voltaire), but the idea that 'each society, each culture, develops in its own way' (*TCE*, 216). *Fortgang* provides no more of a basis for cross-cultural criticism than does *Humanität*. Secondly, Berlin also mentions Herder's appeal to the 'natural'. This is a submerged theme in much of Herder's thought, but it surfaces in his opposition to the state as a corrupt form of human relationship, by contrast with the 'natural relations' of family, friends and shared culture (*TCE*, 182, 186, 189, 231). On this basis Herder would surely condemn Nazi Germany, for example, as unnatural, the perversion rather than proper development of a culture. But Berlin rightly sees the problem with this argument, namely its assumption that 'everything that is natural is valuable', and vice versa (*TCE*, 197). To assert that a practice or an institution is good simply because 'natural' is to explain nothing. 'In this respect Herder is a true child of the Enlightenment at its most naïve', concludes Berlin (*TCE*, 197).

19 Anderson, 'The Pluralism of Isaiah Berlin', 245; Galipeau, *Isaiah Berlin's Liberalism*, 63; Kateb, 'Can Cultures be Judged?', 1030; Lessnoff, *Political Philosophers of the Twentieth Century*, 220.

20 In ch. 6 I question the extent to which such judgements can appeal to universal values alone. In ch. 7 I propose a further set of normative standards derived from the idea of pluralism itself.

Chapter 6 Pluralism and Liberalism

1 It might be tempting to suggest Rawls's 'lexical ordering' of liberty over equality as an example here (*A Theory of Justice*, 42–3). But this is not enough to make Rawls a monist in any straightforward sense, since he does not argue for this ranking in all circumstances, but only within the particular context of his 'special conception' of justice (ibid., 62–3, 151–2) and of the public political culture of a 'constitutional democracy' (*idem*, *Political Liberalism*, 13–14).

2 It is arguable, though, that this third type of monism is strictly a subtype of the first two, since it may be that any such procedural rule depends on an assumed common currency or ranking. The categorical imperative, for example, arguably depends on accepting a certain kind of consistency as an overriding end in moral conduct. I leave this question open.

3 See e.g. the manifesto of the Italian proto-Fascist futurists: Futurist Party, 'The Futurist Vision of the New Italy', 29–31.

4 This is not to say that Herder's view (if Berlin's account of it is correct) is without its own difficulties in this respect, as I argued in ch. 5. So far as his 'cultural pluralism' shades into cultural relativism, with the effect that all cultures are morally equal and impervious to external criticism, that view, too, may bring comfort to a Fascist regime. But I

also argued that 'cultural pluralism' in this sense, involving the incommensurability of cultures, is not the best interpretation of the basic notion of value pluralism. I return to this in chs 7 and 8.

5 On the case for the truth of value pluralism, see Nussbaum, *The Fragility of Goodness*, ch. 10; *idem*, *Love's Knowledge*, ch. 2; Raz, *Morality of Freedom*, chs 13–14; Stocker, *Plural and Conflicting Values*; Lukes, 'Making Sense of Moral Conflict'; T. Nagel, 'The Fragmentation of Value'; Kekes, *The Morality of Pluralism*; MacKenzie, 'Berlin's Defence of Value-Pluralism'; Crowder, *Liberalism and Value Pluralism*, 64–73. Those sceptical of value pluralism include J. Griffin, *Well-Being*, ch. 5; *idem*, 'Mixing Values'; Hurka, 'Monism, Pluralism and Rational Regret'; R. Dworkin, 'Do Liberal Values Conflict?' (with a reply by Bernard Williams, 'Liberalism and Loss'). For other discussions of pluralism, see the articles collected in G. Dworkin, ed., 'Symposium on Pluralism and Ethical Theory', and in Chang, ed., *Incommensurability, Incomparability, and Practical Reason*.

6 Also 'Reply to Ronald H. McKinney', 559.

7 J. Gray, *Isaiah Berlin*, 43–4. See also Wolf, 'Two Levels of Pluralism'.

8 See the typology of value conflict laid out by Richardson, *Practical Reasoning about Final Ends*, ch. 7, *passim*.

9 Berlin, 'The End of the Ideal of a Perfect Society'.

10 Berlin and Williams, 'Pluralism and Liberalism: A Reply'.

11 Godwin, *Enquiry Concerning Political Justice*, 169–70.

12 Sartre, *Existentialism and Humanism*, 35–6.

13 In 'Political Judgement' Berlin explicitly refers to the process he is describing as 'practical reasoning', although without mentioning Aristotle (*SR*, 47). Berlin usually associates Aristotle with the monist outlook, as illustrated, for example, by Aristotle's doctrine 'of the contemplative life as the highest that a man can lead' (*L*, 295). For other descriptions of Aristotle as a monist, see *POI*, 6, 65; *PSM*, 313; *RR*, 27, 138; *TCE*, 59, 145. Yet Aristotle is also categorized by Berlin as a pluralist 'fox' rather than a monist 'hedgehog' (*RT*, 23). For an account of Aristotle's practical reasoning as acknowledging the incommensurability of values by contrast with Plato's unitary view of the good, see Nussbaum, *Fragility of Goodness*, ch. 10; *idem*, *Love's Knowledge*, ch. 2. Nussbaum's pluralist reading of Aristotle is disputed by Larmore, *The Morals of Modernity*, ch. 6.

14 Berlin and Williams, 'Pluralism and Liberalism: A Reply'.

15 This objection has been directed against the contextualist defence of liberalism offered by Rawls in *Political Liberalism*: see Scheffler, 'The Appeal of Political Liberalism'. Broader contextualist justifications of liberalism can be found in Constant, 'The Liberty of the Ancients', and Raz, *Morality of Freedom*, part V. For a liberal-pluralist assessment of these arguments, see Crowder, *Liberalism and Value Pluralism*, 112–15.

16 Sandel, 'Introduction', 8.

17 Riley, 'Crooked Timber and Liberal Culture'; *idem*, 'Interpreting Berlin's Liberalism'; *idem*, 'Defending Cultural Pluralism: Within Liberal Limits'.

18 Crowder, *Liberalism and Value Pluralism*, 81–2; Galston, *Liberal Pluralism*, 53.

19 Williams, *Morality*, 73.

20 Locke, *A Letter Concerning Toleration*; *idem*, *Two Treatises of Government*.

21 See also Kekes, *Morality of Pluralism*; *idem*, *Against Liberalism*; *idem*, *A Case for Conservatism*.

Chapter 7   After Berlin

1 Gray, *Liberalisms*; *idem*, *Post-Liberalism*; *idem*, *Isaiah Berlin*; *idem*, *Enlightenment's Wake*; *idem*, 'Where Pluralists and Liberals Part Company'; *idem*, *Two Faces of Liberalism*.

2 Defined in these terms, the liberal-pluralist school includes Hausheer, 'Berlin and the Emergence of Liberal Pluralism'; Crowder, 'Communication'; *idem*, 'From Value Pluralism to Liberalism'; *idem*, *Liberalism and Value Pluralism*; *idem*, 'Two Value-Pluralist Arguments for Liberalism'; Dzur, 'Value Pluralism versus Political Liberalism?'; Blokland, 'Berlin on Pluralism and Liberalism'; Lukes, 'Making Sense of Moral Conflict'; *idem*, *Liberals and Cannibals*, chs 6–8; Galston, 'Value Pluralism and Liberal Political Theory'; *idem*, *Liberal Pluralism*; Riley, 'Crooked Timber and Liberal Culture'; *idem*, 'Interpreting Berlin's Liberalism'; *idem*, 'Defending Cultural Pluralism'. Apart from Gray, the chief exponent of explicitly anti-liberal pluralism is the conservative thinker John Kekes, in his books *Morality of Pluralism*, *Against Liberalism*, *A Case for Conservatism*. In addition, some writers have argued that liberalism should be defended, but not on the basis of value pluralism: E. Mack, 'Isaiah Berlin and the Quest for Liberal Pluralism'; Crowder, 'Pluralism and Liberalism' (an argument now superseded by the later publications listed above); Larmore, *Morals of Modernity*, ch. 6; Newey, 'Value-Pluralism in Contemporary Liberalism'; Gaus, *Contemporary Theories of Liberalism*, ch. 2. For related discussions, see A. Mack, ed., 'Liberty and Pluralism'.

3 J. Gray, *Isaiah Berlin*, 1. For critical discussions of Gray, see Lomasky, 'Liberal Obituary?'; Katznelson, 'A Properly Defended Liberalism'; Legutko, 'On Postmodern Liberal Conservatism'; Colls, 'Ethics Man'; Crowder, 'John Gray's Pluralist Critique of Liberalism'; *idem*, *Liberalism and Value Pluralism*, chs 5 and 6; Weinstock, 'The Graying of Berlin'; Galston, *Liberal Pluralism*, ch. 5; Talisse, 'Two-Faced Liberalism'.

4 J. Gray, *Isaiah Serlin*, 2.

5 Ibid., 152.

6 J. Gray, *Two Faces of Liberalism*, 66, 107.

7 Ibid., 67.

8 Ibid., 109.

9 J. Gray, *Isaiah Berlin*, 61; see also 8, 9, 61; *idem, Enlightenment's Wake*, 69–70.
10 J. Gray, *Isaiah Berlin*, 154–5; *idem, Two Faces of Liberalism*, 36.
11 Gray, *Isaiah Berlin*, 1, 6; *idem, Enlightenment's Wake*, ch. 6, *passim*.
12 Raz, *Morality of Freedom*, 369.
13 Another contextual case of similar breadth to Raz's is presented by Benjamin Constant, who argues in 'The Liberty of the Ancients Compared with that of the Moderns' that the liberal notion of freedom as non-interference with the individual is appropriate to modern commercial civilization.
14 J. Gray, 'Where Pluralists and Liberals Part Company', 99; see also *idem, Two Faces of Liberalism*, 5–6.
15 J. Gray, 'Where Pluralists and Liberals Part Company', 101; see also *idem*, 'Pluralism and Toleration in Contemporary Political Philosophy', 332.
16 J. Gray, *Two Faces of Liberalism*, 109.
17 Ibid., 135.
18 Ibid., 136.
19 Ibid., 109.
20 Ibid., 136.
21 On compromise under pluralism, see Bellamy, *Liberalism and Pluralism*; Crowder, *Liberalism and Value Pluralism*, 246–55.
22 J. Gray, *Two Faces of Liberalism*, 109.
23 Nussbaum, 'Aristotelian Social Democracy'; *idem, Women and Human Development*; Nussbaum and Sen, eds, *The Quality of Life*, part I.
24 Fabre and Miller, 'Justice and Culture', 14.
25 J. Gray, *Isaiah Berlin*, 142–3.
26 Williams, 'Introduction' to *CC*, p. xvii.
27 J. Gray, *Isaiah Berlin*, 151–2.
28 Compare Berlin's usual view, which is that values are whatever is in fact valued: see e.g. *L*, 45, and *Conv.*, 37. I depart from Berlin on this matter, because his account makes all values a function of empirical preference, which (among other problems) commensurates them in a way inconsistent with the fundamental message of value pluralism: see Crowder, *Liberalism and Value Pluralism*, 73–4, n. 1.
29 For an account of pluralist 'diversity' as involving not only multiplicity but also 'coherence' among goods and ways of life, see Crowder, *Liberalism and Value Pluralism*, 138–45.
30 J. Gray, *Isaiah Berlin*, 152.
31 Ibid., 154.
32 For Berlin's account of the clash between Christian and pagan civilizations, see 'The Originality of Machiavelli', in *AC* and *PSM*.
33 For Berlin's comments on Rawls, see ch. 8.
34 Larmore, *Morals of Modernity*, ch. 6.
35 See Crowder, *Liberalism and Value Pluralism*, ch. 7; Galston, *Liberal Pluralism*, ch. 4.

36   Kymlicka, *Multicultural Citizenship*, 162; Mulhall and Swift, *Liberals and Communitarians*, ch. 7.
37   Rawls, *Political Liberalism*, 57.
38   Galston, *Liberal Pluralism*, ch. 2. A similar distinction is drawn, using different terminology, by Kymlicka, *Multicultural Citizenship*, 154.
39   Galston, *Liberal Pluralism*, 59–60.
40   Ibid., 25–6.
41   Ibid., 20.
42   Ibid., 3.
43   Galston hedges his 'expressive liberty' with several qualifications in favour of traditional individual liberties, which are likely to limit the range of illiberal practices to be accommodated: ibid., 29, 50, 102, 106, 126–7. But presumably at least some illiberal activity is permitted, since that is the whole point of distinguishing Reformation from Enlightenment liberalism.
44   It might be replied that the negative liberty of the individual is not impaired by the illiberal practices of a group if the group accords the dissenting individual a right of exit: see Kukathas, *The Liberal Archipelago*, 24–5. In practice, however, the right of exit tends to be one of the liberties most under threat within illiberal groups. For a typology of ways in which exit can be effectively obstructed, see Barry, *Culture and Equality*, 150–4. Further, it is arguable that a right of exit, to be genuinely effective, requires that the person contemplating exit be autonomous, hence that the group respect and promote individual liberty in the form of personal autonomy. See n. 46 below.
45   Galston, *Liberal Pluralism*, 56: 'While the expressivist norm does possess substantial if not unrestricted moral force, it cannot rightly be used to immunize regimes against charges that they repress some of their citizens.'
46   It is, however, arguable that an effective right of exit presupposes personal autonomy, because only an autonomous person is in a position to make a decision that is genuinely his or her own about whether to go or stay. See Galston's concession that real exit rights involve, among other things, education in ways that exclude 'servility' to the wishes of others, including parents (*Liberal Pluralism*, 104–5). This seems indistinguishable from requiring that children should be educated to think for themselves, that is, to be autonomous.
47   Mill, *On Liberty*, ch. 3; Raz, *Morality of Freedom*, part V; Taylor, 'What is Human Agency?'; Benn, *A Theory of Freedom*; Macedo, *Liberal Virtues*, ch. 6.
48   For a fuller version of this argument, see Crowder, *Liberalism and Value Pluralism*, ch. 8.
49   Nussbaum, 'Aristotelian Social Democracy', 226; *idem, Women and Human Development*, 82.
50   Kekes, *Morality of Pluralism*, 97–8.
51   Rawls, *Political Liberalism*, 57.

52   Walzer, 'Are There Limits to Liberalism?', 31.
53   I refer here to the 'sense of reality' as Berlin applies this term to Herzen (*RT*, 111, 207). Compare the rather different way in which Berlin uses the term elsewhere (*SR*, 4; *CC*, 141–2). I suggested a possible link between the two usages in ch. 3.
54   Nussbaum, *Love's Knowledge*, 101.
55   Galston, *Liberal Pluralism*, 61–2.
56   Mill, *On Liberty*, ch. 3; see also Berlin's treatment of Mill in 'John Stuart Mill and the Ends of Life' (*L*, 218–51), discussed in ch. 8.

Chapter 8   Berlin's Achievement

1   J. Gray, *Enlightenment's Wake*, 121.
2   Condorcet, *Sketch for a Historical Picture of the Progress of the Human Mind*; Godwin, *Enquiry Concerning Political Justice*.
3   Fukuyama, *The End of History and the Last Man*.
4   Locke, *A Letter Concerning Toleration*; idem, *Two Treatises of Government*; Shklar, 'The Liberalism of Fear'.
5   'Above all, gentlemen, no zeal whatsoever' (*L*, 92, n. 2).
6   J. Gray, *Isaiah Berlin*, 59.
7   To be fair, Gray does note some of these tensions (ibid., 59–61).
8   Hitchens, 'Moderation or Death', 7.
9   Hayek, *The Constitution of Liberty*; Nozick, *Anarchy, State, and Utopia*.
10   Berlin says that he 'was not influenced by Hayek' (*Sal.*, 23).
11   G. A. Cohen recounts that, shortly before his death, Berlin 'confessed himself unable to see why there had been a turn away, in our time, from the use of the state for progressive purposes, even by a Labour Government. He was entirely hostile to total state control – he thought that the claims of socialist planning were illusory – but he was passionately against Thatcherism: he knew that "free" markets destroy people's lives' (Cohen, 'Freedom and Money', 7, n. 14).
12   For a fuller presentation of this argument, see Crowder, *Liberalism and Value Pluralism*, 226–36.
13   For a similar argument concerning the tendency of the market to erase distinctions among goods, see Walzer, *Spheres of Justice*, ch. 4. Pluralist critiques of cost–benefit analysis are provided by Sen, 'The Discipline of Cost–Benefit Analysis'; Nussbaum, 'The Costs of Tragedy'; Richardson, 'The Stupidity of Cost–Benefit Analysis'.
14   See Giddens, *Third Way*; idem, and *Third Way and its Critics*; Gamble and Wright, eds, *The New Social Democracy*.
15   These considerations also count against the view that Berlin values cultures primarily on 'aesthetic' grounds: Kateb, 'Can Cultures be Judged?'
16   See ch. 5.
17   See Kymlicka, *Multicultural Citizenship*, 10–11, 14–16.
18   Ibid., 10.

19 Ibid., 11.
20 Ibid., 3–4, 49–50.
21 Berlin's position is distinguished from the more extreme forms of multiculturalism by E. Mack, 'The Limits of Diversity'.
22 See Kymlicka, *Multicultural Citizenship; idem, Politics in the Vernacular; idem, Contemporary Political Philosophy*, ch. 8.
23 For another argument that Berlin's principles can, and should, be turned to multicultural ends, see Tamir, 'Whose History? What Ideas?', and *idem*, 'A Strange Alliance'.
24 G. A. Cohen, 'Freedom and Money', 6.
25 See the list of 'Writings about pluralism before/independently of Isaiah Berlin' in Hardy, ed., *The Isaiah Berlin Virtual Library*.
26 Weber, 'Politics as a Vocation', and 'Science as a Vocation', in *From Max Weber*; Oakeshott, *Rationalism in Politics*; Hampshire, *Morality and Conflict; idem, Justice is Conflict*. See also Lamprecht, 'The Need for a Pluralistic Emphasis in Ethics'; *idem*, 'Some Political Implications of Ethical Pluralism'; Brogan, 'Objective Pluralism in the Theory of Value.'
27 Barry, 'Isaiah, Israel and Tribal Realism', 7.
28 Skinner, 'Meaning and Understanding in the History of Ideas', 50.
29 Margalit, in Dworkin, Lilla and Silvers, eds, *The Legacy of Isaiah Berlin*, 189.
30 Pompa, 'Isaiah Berlin 1909–1997', 133.

Bibliography

Works by Berlin

The following is a list of Berlin's principal publications together with some broadcasts, interviews and unpublished papers referred to in the text. For a comprehensive bibliography of writing by and about Berlin, see Henry Hardy, ed., *The Isaiah Berlin Virtual Library* <http://berlin.wolf.ox.ac.uk>

Books

Most of Berlin's books are collections of essays or lectures, the titles of which are listed under the relevant book title. The following list updates and adds to that given by Hardy in *PSM*.

Karl Marx: His Life and Environment (London: Thornton Butterworth; Toronto: Nelson, 1939). Later editions published by Oxford University Press, 1948, 1963, 1978, and by Fontana, 1995, with an introduction by Alan Ryan.

Concepts and Categories: Philosophical Essays, ed. H. Hardy (London: Hogarth, 1978).
  Introduction by Bernard Williams
  The Purpose of Philosophy
  Verification
  Empirical Propositions and Hypothetical Statements
  Logical Translation
  Equality
  The Concept of Scientific History
  Does Political Theory Still Exist?
  'From Hope and Fear Set Free'

Russian Thinkers, ed. H. Hardy and A. Kelly (London: Hogarth, 1978).
Introduction by Aileen Kelly
Russia and 1848
The Hedgehog and the Fox
Herzen and Bakunin on Individual Liberty
A Remarkable Decade [1838–1848]
   I   The Birth of the Russian Intelligentsia
   II   German Romanticism in Petersburg and Moscow
   III Vissarion Belinsky
   IV Alexander Herzen
Russian Populism
Tolstoy and Enlightenment
Fathers and Children: Turgenev and the Liberal Predicament

Against the Current: Essays in the History of Ideas, ed. H. Hardy (London: Hogarth, 1979).
Introduction by Roger Hausheer
The Counter-Enlightenment
The Originality of Machiavelli
The Divorce between the Sciences and the Humanities [Voltaire and Vico]
Vico's Concept of Knowledge
Vico and the Ideal of the Enlightenment
Montesquieu
Hume and the Sources of German Anti-Rationalism [Hume and Hamann]
Herzen and his Memoirs
The Life and Opinions of Moses Hess
Benjamin Disraeli, Karl Marx and the Search for Identity
The 'Naïveté' of Verdi
Georges Sorel
Nationalism: Past Neglect and Present Power

Personal Impressions, ed. H. Hardy, 2nd edn (London: Pimlico, 1998).
Introduction by Noel Annan
Winston Churchill in 1940
President Franklin Delano Roosevelt
Chaim Weizmann
Einstein and Israel
Yitzhak Sadeh
L. B. Namier
Felix Frankfurter at Oxford
Richard Pares
Hubert Henderson at All Souls
J. L. Austin and the Early Beginnings of Oxford Philosophy
John Petrov Plamenatz

212 *Bibliography*

Maurice Bowra
David Cecil
Memories of Virginia Woolf
Edmund Wilson at Oxford
Auberon Herbert
Aldous Huxley
Meetings with Russian Writers in 1945 and 1956
Epilogue: The Three Strands in My Life

The Crooked Timber of Humanity: Chapters in the History of Ideas, ed. H. Hardy
(London: John Murray, 1990).
The Pursuit of the Ideal
The Decline of Utopian Ideas in the West
Giambattista Vico and Cultural History
Alleged Relativism in Eighteenth-Century European Thought
Joseph de Maistre and the Origins of Fascism
European Unity and its Vicissitudes
The Apotheosis of the Romantic Will: The Revolt against the Myth of an
    Ideal World
The Bent Twig: On the Rise of Nationalism

The Sense of Reality: Studies in Ideas and Their History, ed. H. Hardy (London:
Chatto & Windus, 1996).
Introduction by Patrick Gardiner
The Sense of Reality
Political Judgement
Philosophy and Government Repression
Socialism and Socialist Theories
Marxism and the International in the Nineteenth Century
The Romantic Revolution: A Crisis in the History of Modern Thought
Artistic Commitment: A Russian Legacy
Kant as an Unfamiliar Source of Nationalism
Rabindranath Tagore and the Consciousness of Nationality

The Proper Study of Mankind: An Anthology of Essays, ed. H. Hardy and R.
Hausheer (London: Chatto & Windus, 1997).
Foreword by Noel Annan
Introduction by Roger Hausheer
The Pursuit of the Ideal
The Concept of Scientific History
Does Political Theory Still Exist?
'From Hope and Fear Set Free'
Historical Inevitability
Two Concepts of Liberty
The Counter-Enlightenment

The Originality of Machiavelli
The Divorce between the Sciences and the Humanities
Herder and the Enlightenment
The Hedgehog and the Fox
Herzen and his Memoirs
Conversations with Akhmatova and Pasternak
The Apotheosis of the Romantic Will
Nationalism: Past Neglect and Present Power
Winston Churchill in 1940
President Franklin Delano Roosevelt

The First and the Last, introduced by H. Hardy (New York: New York Review Books, 1999).
'The Purpose Justifies the Ways'
My Intellectual Path
Tributes by Noel Annan, Stuart Hampshire, Avishai Margalit, Bernard Williams, Aileen Kelly

The Roots of Romanticism, ed. H. Hardy (London: Chatto & Windus, 1999).
In Search of a Definition
The First Attack on the Enlightenment
The True Fathers of Romanticism
The Restrained Romantics
Unbridled Romanticism
The Lasting Effects

The Power of Ideas, ed. H. Hardy (London: Chatto & Windus, 2000).
My Intellectual Path
The Purpose of Philosophy
One of the Boldest Innovators in the History of Human Thought [Vico]
Russian Intellectual History
The Man Who Became a Myth [Belinsky]
A Revolutionary without Fanaticism [Herzen]
The Role of the Intelligentsia
Liberty
The Philosophy of Karl Marx
The Father of Russian Marxism [Plekhanov]
Realism in Politics
The Origins of Israel
Jewish Slavery and Emancipation
Chaim Weizmann's leadership
The Search for Status
The Essence of European Romanticism
Meinecke and Historicism
General Education

Three Critics of the Enlightenment: Vico, Hamann, Herder, ed. H. Hardy (London: Pimlico, 2000).
　Vico and Herder
　　Introduction
　　The Philosophical Ideas of Giambattista Vico
　　Vico's Theory of Knowledge and its Sources
　　Herder and the Enlightenment
　The Magus of the North: J. G. Hamann and the Origins of Modern Irrationalism

Freedom and its Betrayal: Six Enemies of Human Liberty, ed. H. Hardy (London: Chatto & Windus, 2002).
　Introduction
　Helvétius
　Rousseau
　Fichte
　Hegel
　Saint-Simon
　Maistre

Liberty, incorporating *Four Essays on Liberty* (1969), ed. H. Hardy (Oxford: Oxford University Press, 2002).
　'The Editor's Tale', by Henry Hardy
　Introduction
　Political Ideas in the Twentieth Century
　Historical Inevitability
　Two Concepts of Liberty
　John Stuart Mill and the Ends of Life
　'From Hope and Fear Set Free'
　Liberty
　The Birth of Greek Individualism
　Final Retrospect
　The Purpose Justifies the Ways
　A Letter to George Kennan
　Notes on Prejudice
　'Berlin and His Critics', by Ian Harris
　Concordance to *Four Essays on Liberty*

Flourishing: Letters 1928–1946, ed. H. Hardy (London: Chatto & Windus, 2004). Published in the United States as *Letters 1928–1946*, ed. H. Hardy (New York: Cambridge University Press, 2004).

The Soviet Mind: Russian Culture under Communism, ed. H. Hardy (Washington, DC: Brookings Institution Press, 2004).
　Foreword by Strobe Talbot
　The Arts in Russia under Stalin

A Visit to Leningrad
A Great Russian Writer [Mandel'shtam]
Conversations with Akhmatova and Pasternak
Boris Pasternak
Why the Soviet Union Chooses to Insulate Itself
The Artificial Dialectic: Generalissimo Stalin and the Art of Government
Four Weeks in the Soviet Union
Soviet Russian Culture
The Survival of the Russian Intelligentsia
Glossary of Names by Helen Rappaport

Other publications

'Reply to Ronald H. McKinney, "Towards a Postmodern Ethics: Sir Isaiah Berlin and John Caputo"', *Journal of Value Inquiry* 26 (1992), 557–60.
[with Bernard Williams] 'Pluralism and Liberalism: A Reply', *Political Studies* 42 (1994), 306–9.
'Israel and the Palestinians', 16 October 1997. See *The Isaiah Berlin Virtual Library* under 'Berlin and Israel'.

Broadcast

'The End of the Ideal of a Perfect Society' (1975), transcribed in H. Hardy, ed., *The Isaiah Berlin Virtual Library*.

Interviews

[with] Nathan Gardels, 'Two Concepts of Nationalism: An Interview with Isaiah Berlin', *New York Review of Books*, 21 November 1991.
[with] Ramin Jahanbegloo, *Conversations with Isaiah Berlin* (New York: Charles Scribner's Sons, 1992).
[with] Steven Lukes, 'Isaiah Berlin: In Conversation with Steven Lukes', *Salmagundi* (Saratoga Springs, Fall 1998).

The Isaiah Berlin Papers (unpublished), Bodleian Library, Oxford

'Democracy, Communism and the Individual', notes for a lecture at Mount Holyoke College, 1949.
'Political Ideas in the Romantic Age', ed. H. Hardy. This is in active preparation for publication, and will probably appear in 2005, with introductions by Joshua Cherniss and Robert Wokler.

Other works

Aarsleff, Hans, 'Vico and Berlin', *London Review of Books*, 5–18 November 1981, 6–7 (with a reply by Berlin, 7–8; letters, 3–16 June 1981).

Anderson, Perry, 'The Pluralism of Isaiah Berlin', in *A Zone of Engagement* (London: Verso, 1992), 230–50.

Ayer, A. J., *Language, Truth and Logic* (London: Gollancz, 1936).

Baldwin, Tom, 'MacCallum and the Two Concepts of Freedom', *Ratio* 26 (1984), 125–42.

Barry, Brian, *Culture and Equality* (Cambridge: Polity, 2001).

Barry, Brian, 'Isaiah, Israel and Tribal Realism', *Times Literary Supplement*, 9 November 2001, 7–8.

Bellamy, Richard, 'T. H. Green, J. S. Mill and Isaiah Berlin on the Nature of Liberty and Liberalism', in H. Gross and R. Harrison, eds, *Jurisprudence: Cambridge Essays* (Oxford: Clarendon Press, 1992), 257–85.

Bellamy, Richard, *Liberalism and Pluralism: Towards a Politics of Compromise* (London and New York: Routledge, 1999).

Benn, Stanley I., *A Theory of Freedom* (Cambridge: Cambridge University Press, 1988).

Blokland, Hans, 'Berlin on Pluralism and Liberalism: A Defence', *European Legacy* 4 (1999), 1–23.

Brogan, A. P., 'Objective Pluralism in the Theory of Value', *International Journal of Ethics* 41 (1931), 287–95.

Carr, E. H., *What is History?* [1961], with a new introduction by Richard J. Evans (Basingstoke: Palgrave, 2001).

Carter, Ian, *A Measure of Freedom* (Oxford: Oxford University Press, 1999).

Chang, Ruth, ed., *Incommensurability, Incomparability, and Practical Reason* (Cambridge, Mass.: Harvard University Press, 1997).

Cherniss, Joshua, 'The Road to Liberty: The Development of Isaiah Berlin's Conception of Political Freedom up to "Two Concepts of Liberty"', unpublished M. Stud. thesis, Oxford, 2003. Posted in Hardy, ed., *The Isaiah Berlin Virtual Library*.

Christman, John, 'Liberalism and Individual Positive Freedom', *Ethics* 101 (1991), 343–59.

Cocks, Joan, *Passion and Paradox: Intellectuals Confront the National Question* (Princeton: Princeton University Press, 2002).

Cohen, G. A., 'Isaiah's Marx, and Mine', in E. and A. Margalit, eds, *Isaiah Berlin: A Celebration* (London: Hogarth, 1991), 110–26.

Cohen, G. A., 'Freedom and Money', <http://www.utdt.edu/departmentos/derecho/publicaciones/rtjl/pdf/finalfreedom.PDF> Accessed 26 June 2003.

Cohen, Marshall, 'Berlin and the Liberal Tradition', *Philosophical Quarterly* 10 (1960), 216–27.

Colls, Robert, 'Ethics Man: John Gray's New Moral World', *Political Quarterly* 69 (1998), 59–71.

Condorcet, Marie Jean Antoine Nicolas Caritat, Marquis de, *Sketch for a Historical Picture of the Progress of the Human Mind* [1793], trans. J. Barraclough (London: Weidenfeld & Nicolson, 1955).

Constant, Benjamin, 'The Liberty of the Ancients Compared with that of the Moderns' [1819], in *Political Writings*, ed. B. Fontana (Cambridge: Cambridge University Press, 1988), 307–28.

Coole, Diana, 'Constructing and Deconstructing Liberty: A Feminist and Poststructuralist Analysis', *Political Studies* 41 (1993), 83–95.

Cracraft, James, 'A Berlin for Historians', *History and Theory* 41 (2002), 277–300.

Crick, Bernard, 'Most Intellectual of Academics', *Guardian Weekly*, 16 November 1997, 25.

Crowder, George, 'Negative and Positive Liberty', *Political Science* 40 (1988), 57–73.

Crowder, George, *Classical Anarchism: The Political Thought of Godwin, Proudhon, Bakunin, and Kropotkin* (Oxford: Clarendon Press, 1991).

Crowder, George, 'Pluralism and Liberalism', *Political Studies* 42 (1994), 293–305 (with a reply by Berlin and Bernard Williams at 306–9).

Crowder, George, 'Communication: Isaiah Berlin and Bernard Williams, "Pluralism and Liberalism: A Reply"', *Political Studies* 44 (1996), 649–50.

Crowder, George, 'John Gray's Pluralist Critique of Liberalism', *Journal of Applied Philosophy* 15 (1998), 287–98.

Crowder, George, 'From Value Pluralism to Liberalism', in R. Bellamy and M. Hollis, eds, *Pluralism and Liberal Neutrality* (London: Frank Cass, 1999), 2–17.

Crowder, George, *Liberalism and Value Pluralism* (London and New York: Continuum, 2002).

Crowder, George, 'Two Value-Pluralist Arguments for Liberalism', *Australian Journal of Political Science* 37 (2002), 457–73.

Crowder, George and Martin Griffiths, 'Postmodernism, Value Pluralism and International Relations', in D. S. L. Jarvis, ed., *International Relations and the "Third Debate": Postmodernism and its Critics* (Westport, Conn.: Praeger, 2002), 127–46.

Dworkin, Gerald, ed., 'Symposium on Pluralism and Ethical Theory' issue, *Ethics* 102 (1999), 707–834.

Dworkin, Ronald, 'Two Concepts of Liberty', in E. and A. Margalit, eds, *Isaiah Berlin: A Celebration* (London: Hogarth, 1991), 100–9.

Dworkin, Ronald, 'Do Liberal Values Conflict?', in R. Dworkin, M. Lilla and R. B. Silvers, eds, *The Legacy of Isaiah Berlin* (New York: New York Review Books, 2001), 73–90.

Dworkin, Ronald, Mark Lilla and Robert B. Silvers, eds, *The Legacy of Isaiah Berlin* (New York: New York Review Books, 2001).

Dzur, A. (1998), 'Value Pluralism versus Political Liberalism?', *Social Theory and Practice* 24, 375–92.

Eco, Umberto, 'Ur-Fascism', in *Five Moral Pieces* (London: Vintage, 2002), 65–88.

Eliot, T. S., *After Strange Gods: A Primer of Modern Heresy* (London: Faber and Faber, 1934).

Etzioni, Amitai, 'Thickening the Soup', *Times Literary Supplement*, 7 June 2002, 8.

Fabre, Cécile and David Miller, 'Justice and Culture: Rawls, Sen, Nussbaum and O'Neill', *Political Studies Review* 1 (2003), 4–17.

Farganis, Sondra, 'Liberty: Two Perspectives on the Women's Movement', *Ethics* 88 (1977–8), 62–73.

Feinberg, Joel, *Social Philosophy* (Englewood Cliffs, NJ: Prentice-Hall, 1973).

Fukuyama, Francis, *The End of History and the Last Man* (Harmondsworth: Penguin, 1992).

Futurist Party, 'The Futurist Vision of the New Italy' [1922], in R. Griffin, ed., *Fascism* (Oxford: Oxford University Press, 1995), 29–31.

Galipeau, Claude, *Isaiah Berlin's Liberalism* (Oxford: Clarendon Press, 1994).

Galston, William, 'Value Pluralism and Liberal Political Theory', *American Political Science Review* 93 (1999), 769–78.

Galston, William, *Liberal Pluralism: The Implications of Value Pluralism for Political Theory and Practice* (Cambridge: Cambridge University Press, 2002).

Gamble, Andrew and Tony Wright, eds, *The New Social Democracy* (Oxford: Blackwell, 1999).

Gaus, Gerald F., *Contemporary Theories of Liberalism* (London: Sage, 2003).

Gay, Peter, 'Intimations of Partiality', *Times Literary Supplement*, 11 June 1999, 3–4.

Geyl, Peter, 'Historical Inevitability', in *Debates with Historians* (The Hague: Martinus Nijhoff, 1955), 236–41.

Giddens, Anthony, *The Third Way: The Renewal of Social Democracy* (Cambridge: Polity, 1998).

Giddens, Anthony, *The Third Way and its Critics* (Cambridge: Polity, 2000).

Godwin, William, *Enquiry Concerning Political Justice* [1793], ed. I. Kramnick (Harmondsworth: Penguin, 1976).

Gray, John, 'On Negative and Positive Liberty', in Z. Pelczynski and J. Gray, eds, *Conceptions of Liberty in Political Philosophy* (London: Athlone, 1984), 321–48.

Gray, John, *Liberalisms: Essays in Political Philosophy* (London: Routledge, 1989).

Gray, John, *Post-Liberalism: Studies in Political Thought* (London: Routledge, 1993).

Gray, John, *Isaiah Berlin* (London: HarperCollins, 1995).

Gray, John, *Enlightenment's Wake: Politics and Culture at the Close of the Modern Age* (London: Routledge, 1995).

Gray, John, 'Pluralism and Toleration in Contemporary Political Philosophy', *Political Studies*, 48 (2000), 323–33.

Gray, John, *Two Faces of Liberalism* (Cambridge: Polity, 2000).

Gray, John, 'Where Pluralists and Liberals Part Company', in M. Baghramian and A. Ingram, eds, *Pluralism: The Philosophy and Politics of Diversity* (London and New York: Routledge, 2000), 85–102.

Gray, Paul, 'The Foxy Philosopher', *Time Magazine*, 17 November 1997.

Gray, Tim, *Freedom* (London: Macmillan, 1990).

Green, T. H., 'Liberal Legislation and Freedom of Contract' [1881], in D. Miller, ed., *Liberty* (Oxford: Oxford University Press, 1991), 21–32.

Griffin, James, *Well-Being: Its Meaning, Measurement, and Moral Importance* (Oxford: Clarendon Press, 1988).

Griffin, James, 'Mixing Values', *Proceedings of the Aristotelian Society*, supp. vol. 65 (1991), 101–18.

Griffin, Roger, 'General Introduction', in R. Griffin, ed., *Fascism* (Oxford: Oxford University Press, 1995), 1–12.

Hampshire, Stuart, *Morality and Conflict* (Cambridge, Mass.: Harvard University Press, 1983).

Hampshire, Stuart, *Justice is Conflict* (Princeton: Princeton University Press, 2000).

Hardy, Henry, ed., *The Isaiah Berlin Virtual Library* <http://berlin.wolf.ox.ac.uk>

Harris, Ian, 'Isaiah Berlin: *Two Concepts of Liberty*', in M. Forsyth and M. Keens-Soper, eds, *The Political Classics: Green to Dworkin* (Oxford: Oxford University Press, 1996), 121–42.

Hausheer, Roger, 'Berlin and the Emergence of Liberal Pluralism', in P. Manent et al., *European Liberty* (The Hague: Nijhoff, 1983), 49–81.

Hayek, Friedrich, *The Road to Serfdom* (London: Routledge, 1944).

Hayek, Friedrich, *The Constitution of Liberty* (London: Routledge, 1960).

Hirschmann, Nancy, 'Toward a Feminist Theory of Freedom', *Political Theory* 24 (1996), 46–67.

Hitchens, Christopher, 'Moderation or Death', *London Review of Books*, 26 November 1998, 3–11.

Hook, Sidney, 'Isaiah Berlin's Enlightenment', *Commentary* 69 (1980), 61–4.

Hunt, Ian, 'Freedom and its Conditions', *Australasian Journal of Philosophy* 69 (1991), 288–301.

Hunt, Ian, 'A Note on Woolcock's Defence of Berlin on Positive and Negative Freedom', *Australasian Journal of Philosophy* 73 (1995), 465–71.

Hurka, Thomas, 'Monism, Pluralism, and Rational Regret', *Ethics* 106 (1996), 555–75.

Ignatieff, Michael, 'Understanding Fascism?', in E. and A. Margalit, eds, *Isaiah Berlin: A Celebration* (London: Hogarth, 1991), 135–45.

Ignatieff, Michael, *Blood and Belonging: Journeys into the New Nationalism* (New York: Farrar, Straus and Giroux, 1993).

Ignatieff, Michael, contribution to 'On Isaiah Berlin (1909–1997)', *New York Review of Books*, 18 December 1997, 10.

Ignatieff, Michael, *Isaiah Berlin: A Life* (London: Chatto & Windus, 1998).

Kateb, George, 'Can Cultures be Judged? Two Defenses of Cultural Pluralism in Isaiah Berlin's Work', *Social Research* 66 (1999), 1009–38.

Katznelson, Ira, 'A Properly Defended Liberalism: John Gray on the Filling of Political Life', *Social Research* 61 (1994), 611–30.

Kekes, John, *The Morality of Pluralism* (Princeton: Princeton University Press, 1993).

Kekes, John, 'Cruelty and Liberalism', *Ethics* 106 (1996), 834–44.

Kekes, John, *Against Liberalism* (Ithaca, NY: Cornell University Press, 1997).

Kekes, John, *A Case for Conservatism* (Ithaca, NY: Cornell University Press, 1998).

Kelly, Aileen, *Toward Another Shore* (New Haven and London: Yale University Press, 1998).

Kelly, Duncan, 'The Political Thought of Isaiah Berlin', *British Journal of Politics and International Relations* 4 (2002), 25–48.

Kenny, Michael, 'Isaiah Berlin's Contribution to Modern Political Theory', *Political Studies* 48 (2000), 1026–39.

Knowles, David, *Political Philosophy* (London: Routledge, 2001).

Kocis, Robert, *A Critical Appraisal of Sir Isaiah Berlin's Political Philosophy* (Lewiston, NY: Edwin Mellen Press, 1989).

Koestler, Arthur, 'Interview', *Jewish Chronicle*, 5 May 1950.

Koestler, Arthur, 'Judah at the Crossroads', in *The Trail of the Dinosaur and Other Essays* (London: Collins, 1955), 106–41.

Kukathas, Chandran, *The Liberal Archipelago: A Theory of Diversity and Freedom* (Oxford: Oxford University Press, 2003).

Kymlicka, Will, *Liberalism, Community, and Culture* (Oxford: Clarendon Press, 1989).

Kymlicka, Will, *Multicultural Citizenship* (Oxford: Clarendon Press, 1995).

Kymlicka, Will, *Politics in the Vernacular* (Oxford: Clarendon Press, 2001).

Kymlicka, Will, *Contemporary Political Philosophy*, 2nd edn (Oxford: Clarendon Press, 2002).

Lamprecht, Sterling P., 'The Need for a Pluralistic Emphasis in Ethics', *Journal of Philosophy, Psychology and Scientific Methods* 17 (1920), 561–72.

Lamprecht, Sterling P., 'Some Political Implications of Ethical Pluralism', *Journal of Philosophy* 18 (1921), 225–44.

Larmore, Charles, *The Morals of Modernity* (Cambridge: Cambridge University Press, 1996).

Legutko, Ryszard, 'On Postmodern Liberal Conservatism', *Critical Review* 8 (1994), 1–22.

Lessnoff, Michael, *Political Philosophers of the Twentieth Century* (Oxford: Blackwell, 1999).

Levinson, Sanford, 'Is Liberal Nationalism an Oxymoron? An Essay for Judith Shklar', *Ethics* 105 (1995), 626–45.

Lilla, Mark, *G. B. Vico: The Making of an Anti-Modern* (Cambridge, Mass.: Harvard University Press, 1993).

Lilla, Mark, 'Wolves and Lambs', in R. Dworkin, M. Lilla and R. B. Silvers, eds, *The Legacy of Isaiah Berlin* (New York: New York Review Books, 2001), 31–42.

Lilla, Mark, 'Inside the Clockwork', *New York Review of Books*, 25 April 2002, 43–5.

Locke, John, *Two Treatises of Government* [1689], ed. P. Laslett (Cambridge: Cambridge University Press, 1988).

Locke, John, *A Letter Concerning Toleration: In Focus* [1689], ed. J. Horton and S. Mendus (London and New York: Routledge, 1991).

Lomasky, Loren, 'Liberal Obituary?', *Ethics* 102 (1991), 140–54.

Lukes, Steven, *Marxism and Morality* (Oxford: Clarendon Press, 1985).

Lukes, Steven, 'Making Sense of Moral Conflict', in *Moral Conflict and Politics* (Oxford: Clarendon Press, 1991), 127–42.

Lukes, Steven, *Liberals and Cannibals: The Implications of Diversity* (London: Verso, 2003).

MacCallum, Gerald C., Jr., 'Negative and Positive Freedom', in D. Miller, ed., *Liberty* (Oxford: Oxford University Press, 1991), 100–22.

Macedo, Stephen, *Liberal Virtues: Citizenship, Virtue, and Community in Liberal Constitutionalism* (Oxford: Clarendon Press, 1990).

Mack, Arien, ed., 'Liberty and Pluralism' issue, *Social Research* 66 (1999).

Mack, Eric, 'Isaiah Berlin and the Quest for Liberal Pluralism', *Public Affairs Quarterly* 7 (1993), 215–30.

Mack, Eric, 'The Limits of Diversity: The New Counter-Enlightenment and Berlin's Liberal Pluralism', in H. Dickman, ed., *The Imperilled Academy* (New Brunswick: Transaction Books, 1993), 97–126.

MacKenzie, Iain, 'Berlin's Defence of Value-Pluralism: Clarifications and Criticisms', *Contemporary Politics* 5 (1999), 325–37.

McKinney, Ronald H., 'Towards a Postmodern Ethics: Sir Isaiah Berlin and John Caputo', *Journal of Value Inquiry* 26 (1992), 395–407 (with a reply by Berlin at 557–60).

Macpherson, C. B., 'Berlin's Division of Liberty', in *Democratic Theory: Essays in Retrieval* (Oxford: Clarendon Press, 1973), 95–119.

Mali, Joseph, and Robert Wokler, eds, *Isaiah Berlin's Counter-Enlightenment* (Philadelphia: American Philosophical Society, 2003; transactions of the American Philosophical Society, vol. 93, pt. 3).

Margalit, Edna and Avishai Margalit, eds, *Isaiah Berlin: A Celebration* (London: Hogarth, 1991).

Megone, Christopher, 'One Concept of Liberty', *Political Studies* 35 (1987), 611–22.

Mill, John Stuart, *On Liberty* [1859], ed. G. Himmelfarb (Harmondsworth: Penguin, 1974).

Miller, David, 'Constraints on Freedom', *Ethics* 94 (1983), 66–86.

Miller, David, 'Introduction' to D. Miller, ed., *Liberty* (Oxford: Oxford University Press, 1991), 1–20.

Miller, David, *On Nationality* (Oxford: Clarendon Press, 1995).

Momigliano, Arnaldo, 'On the Pioneer Trail', *New York Review of Books*, 11 November 1976, 33–8.

Mulhall, Stephen and Adam Swift, *Liberals and Communitarians*, 2nd edn (Oxford: Blackwell, 1996).

Mussolini, Benito, 'The Doctrine of Fascism' [1932], in C. Cohen, ed., *Communism, Fascism and Democracy*, 2nd edn (New York: Random House, 1972), 328–39.

Nagel, Ernest, 'Determinism in History' [1959–60], in P. Gardiner, ed., *The Philosophy of History* (Oxford: Oxford University Press, 1974), 187–215.

Nagel, Thomas, 'The Fragmentation of Value', in *Mortal Questions* (Cambridge: Canto, 1991), 128–41.

Newey, Glen, 'Value-Pluralism in Contemporary Liberalism', *Dialogue* 37 (1998), 493–522.

Nozick, Robert, *Anarchy, State, and Utopia* (New York: Basic Books, 1974).

Nussbaum, Martha, *The Fragility of Goodness: Luck and Ethics in Greek Tragedy and Philosophy* (Cambridge: Cambridge University Press, 1986).

Nussbaum, Martha, 'Aristotelian Social Democracy', in R. Douglass, G. Mara and H. S. Richardson, eds, *Liberalism and the Good* (New York: Routledge, 1990), 203–52.

Nussbaum, Martha, *Love's Knowledge: Essays on Philosophy and Literature* (Oxford: Oxford University Press, 1992).

Nussbaum, Martha, 'The Costs of Tragedy: Some Moral Limits of Cost–Benefit Analysis', *Journal of Legal Studies* 29 (2000), 1005–36.

Nussbaum, Martha, *Women and Human Development: The Capabilities Approach*, Cambridge: Cambridge University Press, 2000).

Nussbaum, Martha and Amartya Sen, eds, *The Quality of Life* (Oxford: Clarendon Press, 1993).

Oakeshott, Michael, *Rationalism in Politics* (London: Methuen, 1962).

Orwell, George, *Nineteen Eighty-Four* (London: Secker & Warburg, 1949).

Patterson, Orlando, *Freedom*, vol 1: *Freedom in the Making of Western Culture* (New York: Basic Books, 1991).

Pettit, Philip, *Republicanism* (Oxford: Oxford University Press, 1997).

Plekhanov, Georgy Valentinovich, *Essays in the History of Materialism*, trans. R. Fox (London: John Lane, 1934).

Podhoretz, Norman, 'A Dissent on Isaiah Berlin', *Commentary* 107 (1999), 25–37.

Pompa, Leon, 'Isaiah Berlin 1909–1997', *New Vico Studies* 16 (1998), 129–36.

Popper, Karl, *The Open Society and its Enemies* (London: Routledge & Kegan Paul, 1945).

Porter, Norman, *Rethinking Unionism: An Alternative for Northern Ireland*, new updated edn (Belfast: Blackstaff Press, 1998).

Rawls, John, *A Theory of Justice* (Oxford: Oxford University Press, 1971).

Rawls, John, *Political Liberalism* (New York: Columbia University Press, 1993).

Raz, Joseph, *The Morality of Freedom* (Oxford: Clarendon Press, 1986).

Raz, Joseph, 'Multiculturalism: A Liberal Perspective', in *Ethics in the Public Domain: Essays in the Morality of Law and Politics* (Oxford: Clarendon Press, 1995), 170–91.

Richards, Robert J., *The Romantic Conception of Life* (Chicago: University of Chicago Press, 2002).

Richardson, Henry S., *Practical Reasoning about Final Ends* (Cambridge: Cambridge University Press, 1997).

Richardson, Henry S., 'The Stupidity of Cost–Benefit Analysis', *Journal of Legal Studies* 29 (2000), 971–1003.

Riley, Jonathan, 'Crooked Timber and Liberal Culture', in M. Baghramian and A. Ingram, eds, *Pluralism: The Philosophy and Politics of Diversity* (London and New York: Routledge, 2000), 103–19.

Riley, Jonathan, 'Interpreting Berlin's Liberalism', *American Political Science Review* 95 (2001), 283–95.

Riley, Jonathan, 'Defending Cultural Pluralism: Within Liberal Limits', *Political Theory* 30 (2002), 68–96.

Ryan, Alan, ed., *The Idea of Freedom: Essays in Honour of Isaiah Berlin* (Oxford: Clarendon Press, 1979).

Ryan, Alan, 'Wise Man', *New York Review of Books*, 17 December 1998, 29–37.

Ryan, Alan, 'Isaiah Berlin: Political Theory and Liberal Culture', *Annual Review of Political Science* 2 (1999), 345–62.

Sandall, Roger, 'The Book of Isaiah', in *The Culture Cult: Designer Tribalism and Other Essays* (Westport, Conn.: Westview, 2001), 89–109.

Sandel, Michael, 'Introduction', in M. Sandel, ed., *Liberalism and its Critics* (Oxford: Oxford University Press, 1984), 1–11.

Sartre, Jean-Paul, *Existentialism and Humanism*, trans. P. Mairet (London: Methuen, 1948).

Scheffler, Samuel, 'The Appeal of Political Liberalism', in *Boundaries and Allegiances: Problems of Justice and Responsibility in Liberal Thought* (Oxford: Oxford University Press, 2001), 131–48.

Sen, Amartya, 'The Discipline of Cost–Benefit Analysis', *Journal of Legal Studies* 29 (2000), 931–52.

Shklar, Judith, 'The Liberalism of Fear', in N. Rosenblum, ed., *Liberalism and the Moral Life* (Cambridge, Mass.: Harvard University Press, 1989), 21–38.

Siame, Chisanga N., ' "Two Concepts of Liberty" through African Eyes', *Journal of Political Philosophy* 8 (2000), 53–67.

Skinner, Quentin, 'Meaning and Understanding in the History of Ideas', *History and Theory* 8 (1969), 3–53.

Skinner, Quentin, 'The Idea of Negative Liberty: Philosophical and Historical Perspectives', in R. Rorty, J. Schneewind and Q. Skinner, eds, *Philosophy in History: Essays on the Historiography of Philosophy* (Cambridge: Cambridge University Press, 1984), 193–221.

Skinner, Quentin, *Liberty before Liberalism* (Cambridge: Cambridge University Press, 1998).

Skinner, Quentin, 'A Third Concept of Liberty' (the Isaiah Berlin Lecture), *Proceedings of the British Academy* 117 (2002), 237–68.

Spencer, Herbert, *The Man versus the State* [1884], ed. with an introduction by Donald Macrae (Harmondsworth: Penguin, 1969).

Stocker, Michael, *Plural and Conflicting Values* (Oxford: Clarendon Press, 1990).

Strauss, Leo, 'Relativism' [1961], in *The Rebirth of Classical Political Rationalism: An Introduction to the Thought of Leo Strauss*, selected and introduced by T. Pangle (Chicago: University of Chicago Press, 1989).

Swift, Adam, *Political Philosophy: A Beginners' Guide for Students and Politicians* (Cambridge: Polity, 2001).

Talisse, Robert B., 'Two-Faced Liberalism: John Gray's Pluralist Politics and the Reinstatement of Enlightenment Liberalism', *Critical Review* 14 (2002), 441–58.

Talmon, Jacob, *The Origins of Totalitarian Democracy* (New York: Praeger, 1960).

Tamir, Yael, 'Whose History? What Ideas?', in E. and A. Margalit, eds, *Isaiah Berlin: A Celebration* (London: Hogarth, 1991), 146–59.

Tamir, Yael, *Liberal Nationalism* (Princeton: Princeton University Press, 1993).

Tamir, Yael, 'A Strange Alliance: Isaiah Berlin and the Liberalism of the Fringes', *Ethical Theory and Moral Practice* 1 (1998), 279–89.

Taylor, Charles, 'What is Human Agency?', in *Human Agency and Language: Philosophical Papers*, vol. 1 (Cambridge: Cambridge University Press, 1985), 15–44.

Taylor, Charles, 'What's Wrong with Negative Liberty', in D. Miller, ed., *Liberty* (Oxford: Oxford University Press, 1991), 141–62.

Taylor, Charles, 'The Politics of Recognition', in A. Gutmann, ed., *Multiculturalism: Examining the Politics of Recognition* (Princeton: Princeton University Press, 1994), 25–73.

Vincent, Andrew, 'Liberal Nationalism: An Irresponsible Compound?', *Political Studies* 45 (1997), 275–95.

Wall, Steven, 'Freedom, Interference and Domination', *Political Studies* 49 (2001), 216–30.

Walzer, Michael, *Spheres of Justice: A Defence of Pluralism and Equality* (Oxford: Blackwell, 1983).

Walzer, Michael, 'Are There Limits to Liberalism?', *New York Review of Books*, 19 October 1995 (a review of John Gray, *Berlin*), 28–31.

Weber, Max, *From Max Weber: Essays in Sociology*, ed. H. Gert and C. W. Mills (London: Routledge, 1948).

Weinstock, Daniel, 'The Graying of Berlin', *Critical Review* 11 (1998), 481–501.

West, David, 'Spinoza on Positive Freedom', *Political Studies* 41 (1993), 284–96 (with a reply by Berlin at 297–8).

Williams, Bernard, *Morality: An Introduction to Ethics* (Cambridge: Cambridge University Press, 1976).

Williams, Bernard, 'Introduction', in I. Berlin, *Concepts and Categories*, ed. H. Hardy (London: Hogarth, 1978), pp. xi–xviii.

Williams, Bernard, 'Conflicts of Values', in A. Ryan, ed., *The Idea of Freedom: Essays in Honour of Isaiah Berlin* (Oxford: Clarendon Press, 1979), 221–32.

Williams, Bernard, 'Liberalism and Loss', in R. Dworkin, M. Lilla and R. B. Silvers, eds, *The Legacy of Isaiah Berlin* (New York: New York Review Books, 2001), 91–103.

Wittgenstein, Ludwig, *Philosophical Investigations*, 2nd edn, trans. G. E. M. Anscombe (Oxford: Blackwell, 1968).

Wokler, Robert, 'A Modern Candide', *Times Literary Supplement*, 18 December 1998, 7–8.

Wolf, Susan, 'Two Levels of Pluralism', *Ethics* 102 (1992), 785–98.

Woolcock, Peter, *Power, Impartiality and Justice* (Aldershot: Ashgate, 1998).

Zagorin, Perez, 'Vico's Theory of Knowledge: A Critique', *Philosophical Review* 34 (1984), 15–30 (see also his exchange with Berlin, *Philosophical Review* 35 (1985), 281–96).

Index